THE MESSAGE
OF ISLAM

By Dr. Maqsood Jafri

بِسْمِ اللهِ الرَّحْمٰنِ الرَّحِيْمِ

Published by
Tahrike Tarsile Qur'an
80-08 51st Avenue
Elmhurst, New York 11373

THE MESSAGE
OF ISLAM

By Dr. Maqsood Jafri

Cover Picture
Courtesy: Spaceimages.com - Antennae Galaxies Photo

Published by
Tahrike Tarsile Qur'an
80-08 51st Avenue
Elmhurst, New York 11373
http://www.koranusa.org
E-mail: orders@koranusa.org

First U.S. Edition 2004

Author's Address:
239 Fletcher Avenue
Valley Stream, New York 11580, U.S.A.
E-mail: maqsoodjafri@aol.com

Typing & Typesetting by
Bilqis Esmail - paintingsart@yahoo.com

CONTENTS

INTRODUCTION

Mr. Maqsood Jafri is well-versed inter alia in political philosophy, Islamic history, and comparative religion. He possesses excellent communication skills, has a high command of several languages, and enjoys a superbly developed analytical ability.

He has been engaged in intensive research work on a wide variety of themes in socio-cultural and politico-philosophical spheres, having produced substantial scholarly material in pertinent disciplines, while holding advisory positions in policy matters. He has taught at graduate and post-graduate levels at several academic institutions, has been involved in curricular activities, and has participated in administrative matters.

Mr. Jafri has been attached with many professional, learned, honor, and literary societies, has led many seminars and colloquia, and has attended numerous congresses and conferences around the world. He has been active in community affairs and human rights, has occupied many honorary and voluntary incumbencies, and has been recipient of various awards and prizes of distinction. He is a prolific speaker, having delivered occasional lectures on current issues at many centers of excellence, both at home and abroad.

Mr. Jafri is highly intelligent, diligent, dependable and responsible. He is loyal to his duties, cooperative to his fellow-workers, and helpful to his superiors. He is energetic and enthusiastic in his callings, creative and innovative in his faculties, and decorus and reliable in his character.

In view of the above, I believe, he will prove to be an outstanding candidate for the post he is applying. With this trust, I recommend him to you most warmly and unhesitatingly.

Ibne Hassan
Ph.D., D. Phil, J.S.D.
LL.N.O. New York

PUBLISHER'S NOTE

The Message of Islam written by Maqsood Jafri represents Islam on modern, moderate, rational and universal lines. The author is a well-known rational and modern thinker of the Muslim world. He had been the professor of English literature in Pakistan. He is an eminent speaker and scholar on literature, politics, philosophy, International affairs and religion. He has studied the different religions, isms and ideologies. He believes in Inter-faith dialogue and peaceful co-existence. His book presents Islam as a practical code of life signifying the importance of intellect, liberty, peace, justice, humanity and fraternity. He, like an original thinker discursively discerns and deciphers the rational and practical aspects of religion. He claims that the basic purpose of all prophets' teachings was to guide the human kind towards peaceful and prosperous state and society. The writer is deeply committed to human values and human rights. He categorically rejects extremism and terrorism. This treatise is a philosophical asset for the people interested to know the genesis and tenets of Islam.

Tahrike Tarsile Qur'an, Inc. is publishing its second edition. Its first edition was published in Nov 1996 in Pakistan. We hope it will prove to be a positive contribution in understanding Islam in America and the western world as well.

Aunali Khalfan
Tahrike Tarsile Qur'an, Inc.
Publishers and Distributors of the Holy Quran
80-08 51st Avenue
Elmhurst, New York 11373.
read@koranusa.org

PREFACE

The purpose of writing this treatise is to introduce Islam to the scientific and rational minded persons. The dogmatic and ritualistic approach towards religion has brought bad name to religion and has also harmed the higher cause of peace and humanity. The basic purpose of all divine and revealed religions is the maintenance of universal human values. All battles in the name of religions are open mockery of the divine message and mission. Islam is a misunderstood and misrepresented religion. The very meaning of Islam is peace. Islam is the religion of peace. Peace for whom? Peace for all mankind. It does not encourage class, cult, creed or country differences. It claims to be the religion of love and justice. But unfortunately Islam has been attacked from two fronts. It has been assaulted by double-edged sword. The non-Muslims consider it as a militant and rival religion. They do not even take the trouble to study it. They consider it as a threat to their culture, ideology, life and existence.

A few intellectuals like Thomas Carlyle and Bernard Shaw praised the higher and nobler concepts of Islam. But most of the Westerners like Dante unduly condemned Islam for their personal prejudices. Till today the Westerners are universally criticizing the universal and eternal. The Muslims have also done great injustice to values of Islam. Ninety five percent literature on Islamic is dogmatic, sectarian, metaphysical and sophistic. Priesthood and monarchy have disfigured the real face of Islam. The real and scientific Islam is yet to be explored from the pages of the Qur'an.

Islam promotes egalitarian society. It enhances modern and progressive spirit. It is the religion of life. Unfortunately it has been turned in to the religion of death. Eschatology has become more important than sociology. We do not try to find out the solution of our social problems according to the need of time. The age spirit is the vital factor for the survival of any religion. The Muslim priests have closed all the doors of new and modern research and the reconstruction of religious thought has been abandoned. "Ijtehad" in all fields of life is very essential.

The religious writers are the victim of obscurantism. They are not clear even on the basic issues. They are critical and confused. They criticize other systems but have failed to introduce Islamic scientific system. The religious scholars feel honored on writing traditional voluminous commentaries of the Qur'an to impress their scholarship on others but have totally failed in giving a solution of our political, economic and social problems. Islam provides economic justice and equality to all mankind but all Muslim countries are under the stone wall of feudalism and capitalism. Islam grants political freedom but the Muslim states are under the callous system of monarchy and Militarism. Hence there is a dire need to introduce Islam on rational, human, scientific, and revolutionary lines.

Islam keeps equilibrium between the material and spiritual life. It is consonant with the laws of nature. It condemns superstitions. It is a social code of conduct. Its spiritual side is also for the uplift and betterment of human society. It negates monastic and ascetic approach to life. The stagnant and non-progressive style of the clerics has damaged its concept. The political differences of the Muslims have brought bad name to Islam. They lack tolerance and miss rationality. In my humble way I have tried to discuss the practical and rational aspect of Islam in this treatise. No word is the final word and no man is the last man on any subject. We should reconstruct our religious beliefs in the true democratic, rational and fraternal perspective.

The Qur'an says that the basic aim of the advent of the prophet of Islam is to purify the people and teach them wisdom. Purity of soul and maturity of mind are one of the main ends of Islam. Islam does not believe in aggression, disgression and transgression.

The service of mankind and sincere adoration of God are the cardinal factors of Islamic ideology. The Holy Prophet is the model for mankind till Doomsday.

In a nutshell it can be said that let the Muslims and non-Muslims shedding aside all petty prejudices re-study and reconstruct the universal thoughts of Islam as it is the final message of peace and prosperity for all mankind for all times.

Dr. Maqsood Jafri
Valley Stream
New York 11580

FOREWORD BY DR. SHAHID SHEIKH

Mr. Jafri is an eminent multicultural and multilingual scholar of Islam. His strong passion for research combined with an insatiated yearning for knowledge has led him to an intense intellectual journey to many countries in the Islamic world, Asia and Europe. His conversations with leading international Islamic scholars, frequent lectures, seminars and discussions at international conferences and universities have shaped his values, ideas, visions and convictions. Being a prolific writer endowed with rigorous mental discipline, Mr. Jafri has authored over two dozen books and scores of articles on various aspects of Islam.

In addition, Mr. Jafri frequently lectures on a wide variety of current topics – such as progressive Islam, sectarian violence in the Islamic world, international terrorism and peace, and social justice – in the Islamic world, Asia and Europe. His writings and lectures are highly engaging, full of insights and thought provoking.

Mr. Jafri's latest scholarly work, *The Message of Islam*, is his philosophical treatise outlining his vision of an ideal Islamic state, discusses the modern day realities. With his incisive thought provoking analysis of Islamic history and political philosophy, he lays bare the fundamental problems and flaws in the modern governments in the Islamic world. His vociferous criticism is relentless and deserves serious attention. In addition, this book clearly demonstrates that Mr. Jafri is an original thinker capable of incorporating Islamic history and political philosophy into the modern world.

This well-researched invaluable treatise of Islamic political thought is a major contribution to the existing literature on Islamic political philosophy. Scholars, academics, students and the general public interested in the study of Islamic political philosophy will great benefit from this scholarship.

Dr. Shahid Sheikh, Ed.D.
May 10, 2004

ISLAMIC STATE

An Islamic state is a state that keeps equilibrium between the material and moral needs of all sections of society. Social justice and political liberties are the foundation of the edifice of Islam. In an Islamic state leadership must be in the hands of pure and pious people. A ruler should be an extraordinarily industrious, honest and able man. The authority of divine law must be maintained. The Islamic Government should be tolerant enough to bear the criticism of the public. What is permitted and what is prohibited in Islam must be observed. The government and people must fight against all pernicious and malicious forces which perpetuate the evil designs in the permeation of imperialists and fascists. The basic rights of every man are to be protected and no individual should feel frustration. An Islamic state can be only established if its political system is introduced. Without the implementation of caliphate there can be no cohesion and cooperation between the government and the governed. According to communism the prevailing concept of state represents an interim phase and ultimately it will wither away. Karl Marx bases philosophy of communism on socialism. He says that without economic freedom there can be no political freedom. But it is very ironical to see that communism could not bring political freedom to its followers. It has even not provided economic parity to the people who cherished its delusion. Islam on the other hand believes that political freedom can provide economic freedom. The people who are free to demand their rights and challenge their rulers can only enjoy the fruit of egalitarianism. Communism does not believe in the establishment of any Government. It claims that when the conscience of every man will awake there will be no need of any organized system of government. But practically its claim has proved contrary to its practice. There is no coordination between its theory and practice. For the establishment of an Islamic state the appointment of the caliph in the light of the Qur'anic tenets is very imperative. The correct stance of an Islamic state is only possible if the basic principles of Islamic polity are maintained.

When the Khawarij rebelled against Hazrat Ali they also claimed like the modern Marxists that there was no need of any caliph or government and they could do without any ruler. They further said that the sovereignty belonged to God and every Muslim could act upon the divine injunctions without any external pressure of the government. When Hazrat Ali came to know about their claim he said that the spirit of the claim was good but intention was bad. No Islamic state can be established without the rulership of a man who is the true copy of the character of the Holy Prophet. Islam opposes monarchy and stands for spiritual democracy. Abdul Hassan Ali al Mauwardi maintains that the Muslim caliph should be appointed by the Ummah. He must possess knowledge, sound health, upright character and wisdom. He should be the member of the Qurashites. I personally appreciate the characteristics of a Muslim ruler mentioned by Al-Mauwardi but do not agree with this condition of a Muslim ruler to be the member of Quraish Tribe because Islam discourages every sort of racial discrimination. Al-Ghazali and Taimia have also mentioned the salient features of a Muslim ruler. According to them a caliph should be a pious man and diametrically antagonistic to infidelity but tragically both have failed to give a clear cut picture of an Islamic state craft. The question of the methods of making the Islamic Government still awaits its clear answer in many countries which claim to be Islamic states for so many centuries the Muslims had been miserably exploited by the callous monarchs. Monarchy crushed the spirit of Islam and in the name of Islam the basic rights of the people had been usurped. In the first phase of Muslim history the followers of the holy prophet were the men of sincerity and conviction. An Islamic state produces selfless and guiltless revolutionaries who can never yield to the evil forces. The Holy Prophet did not only bring political change but radically transformed the life of the people in all its walks. Their notion of life was changed and with changed minds they changed the whole of the Arabian peninsula. In a Muslim society the political system is the basic force in the making of society. Though the Holy Prophet had set up a small city state at Medina whose area and population was quite small yet that state was a challenge to the world emperors. Why was it? Only because the Holy Prophet had established a new social order which had broken the back bone of monarchy. Islamic ideals became a living force and changed the direction of negative human psychology. For the perfection of the social mi-

lieu a man with divine wisdom, deep insight and sound character was required and that was found in the person of the Holy
Prophet Muhammad (May Peace Be Upon Him). Islamic state
under the divine leadership of the Holy Prophet teaches us the
lesson that a Muslim leader or ruler must be a man with multifarious noble qualities. Plato terms such a man as a planner of
the worldly affairs. Aristotle names him as the man of civilization. The man equipped with all royal paraphernalia known as
a Monarch is an ideal ruler of the ancient Philosophers. All these
Greek ancient concepts encourage non-representative governments. The human society is constantly marching towards the
ideal of perfection and orderliness. Any ruler who is not disciplined and just can never establish the kingdom of God on the
earth. Leadership must be disciplined because no undisciplined
man can harmonize the society. A lazy man can only add to
lethargy. The whole universe is orderly, systematized and disciplined. In Surah Ar-Rahman the Holy Qur'an has very beautifully pointed out the organized rotation of the Natural objects.
The Nature is systematized then how can it accept anything which
is contrary to ordered system. Similarly the nature of the man
must not be let go out of the track. It must be cured when it is the
victim of spiritual ailment. It needs guidance and proper protection. This is the reason the prophets, the mystics and philosophers had been doing their utmost to cleanse the dirt of vicious
and evil spirits. The inner reformation of every individual ultimately forms a clean community. There must be a balance between the individual and collective ideals and deeds. An Islamic
State needs a natural method of administration. In an Islamic
State there is no concept of Bureaucracy. I have seen the calami-
ties of bureaucratic mentality. The British have left this illegiti-
mate babe in all those parts of the world where they ruled. But
in an Islamic State every man is the servant of the commandments of Allah. The illegal orders of any ruler are not to be complied with Bureaucratic mentality can have no room in an Islamic State. To serve mankind is to serve Allah. But the Bureau-
crats think themselves as the self made rulers and intend to play
with human dignity which is quite un-Islamic. Islam stands for
service and not for rulership.

In an Islamic State every act must have religious sanction.
The matters relate to personal laws include creed, marriage, di-

vorce and inheritance and they are permanent and unchangeable laws. There is some difference in the interpretation of such
laws but no Muslim sect can change them. Similarly the matters
relating to public law such as fiscal, social and criminal laws are
also unchangeable but in the light of 'Ijtehad' the Muslim jurists
can give decisions which fulfil the social demands of the age.
Hence we see that Islamic society is not static. It is a progressive
and a dynamic society. In an Islamic state religious principles
are not like antique dogmas which lag behind and can not keep
peace with the fast flow of social changes. Everything in Islam is
according to the nature of man. Any thing unnatural is un-Islamic. The natural proof of my claim fully swings in the political
arena of human affairs. When the whole world was creeping in
the slush of slavery and monarchy Islam gave the clarion call of
natural consensus in political matters. It laid down certain basic
principles and has kept the door of research and experimentation open for all times and climes. "The starved eats his faith" is
golden principle portraying the truth that in a society akin to
economic injustice has no solid religious foundations. In the same
way we can say, "the slave eats himself." A society producing
people with slavish mentality is as bad as a society producing
slaves. The desire to dominate the menfolk arises when a man
shuns acting like a man. The Islamic concept of Tawhid obliter-
ates all such blemishes which disfigure the fair face of humanity.
Political dictatorship is alien to the message of Islam. It is not
only the political system but educational system also that harms
the Muslim society if it is contrary to the spirit of Islam. Too
much dependence upon Western medias and method is injurious to our existence. Consciously or unconsciously we are de-
Islamizing our society by depending upon Western judicial system. Dependence on west in technology means total annihilation of Muslim Ummah. An Islamic state must work to produce
thinkers, scientists and technicians.

All this can happen if a society is showing the process of modernization with a measure of ambivalence. Ernest Gellner says,
"In our time, a social order is valid under two conditions, (a) If it
is banging about or maintaining an affluent society, (b) If those
in authority are co-cultural with the rest of society."

Elitist societies and regimes end in despondency, failure and
isolation for they do not share the passions and aspirations of

the masses. They arrogantly put out the candle of individual's identity and community's recognition. An Islamic state recognizes the talent and identity of individuals and respects the opinion of the masses. The immoral fluxes and surges of the imperialist world have jeopardized the whole western culture. In order to prepare a contemporary Islamic legal system which can enhance noble and natural proclivities is the urgent need of our time. We will have to reconstruct and reorient some concepts in the light of our current problems. An immediate legal reconstruction must be initiated. Islamic constitutional principles of justice ought to be clearly codified in laying down the foundations of a real Islamic State. The rule of law should be enforced indiscriminately. In Western political systems the head of state is provided many privileges which are repugnant to the very spirit of equality and justice. Where as in Islamic state even the head of state is accountable to the people and law. [The Islamic law distinctly differs from an un-Islamic state on two grounds. Firstly, it ensures basic human rights to every citizen whether Muslim or non-Muslim. The minorities have special rights and the Islamic state does not interfere in their personal and rituals. They are given full protection to live peacefully and amicably. Secondly the state decisions are taken on the principle of equality an rationality rather than on empirical strength.] Quantity can not rule over quality in an Islamic state. This is the reason that Islamic political system does not believe in Monocracy but stands for spiritual democracy in which only the men of wisdom and piety can participate as candidates and as voters.

By introducing a reasonable political system Islam expects that its followers would grant justice to every man breathing over the globe of earth irrespective of color or creed. In our modern era when many Muslim states exist and are not interconnected and lie in the lap of one or the other super power. What should be our role is a question which bothers every serious Muslim thinker. I think every Muslim state should establish Islamic principles in their true spirit and should establish institutions which foster mutual cohesion and solidarity. The citizens of the Muslim states are like the members of one family and should have closer and deeper relations. The present division of the Muslim state into American and Russian blocs is because of their disunity. They claim to be Islamic states but actually either they are imperialists or communists. Iran is the only Islamic state which has openly announced its impartiality and has not sided with any bloc. These two blocs have failed in maintaining liberty and justice in the world. They have inflicted numerous atrocities upon innocent human beings. The Qur'an says, "O believers: be securers of justice, witness for God. Let not detestation for a people move you not to be equitable. Be equitable that is nearer to God fearing." Apart from maintaining justice within an Islamic state it is the religious obligation of an Islamic state it is the religious obligation of an Islamic state to achieve this much power that it can eradicate oppression and repression from all over the world. Jihad is a Pre-requisite of our Islamic state. The basic purpose of Jihad is the intensification of virtue and eradication of evil. It is a means of extension of the message of God to all the corners of the world by wisdom, logic and advice. The Qur'an says, "Call thou to the way of the lord with wisdom and good admonition." Jihad also shows us the way to repel aggression and be advanced in military strength and technical devices. It calls for sacrifice so that injustice and tyranny should be totally finished.

Dr. Ali Shariati in his book "On the Sociology of Islam" writes: "The ideal society of Islam is called the Ummah.

The word Ummah is derived from the root 'amm' which has the sense of path and intention. The Umma is, therefore, a society in which a number of individuals possessing a common faith and goal, come together in harmony with the intention of advancing and moving towards their common goal. While shedding light upon basic functions of an Islamic state Dr. Shariati further writes: "Its social system is based on equity and justice and ownership by the people on the revival of the "System of Abel", the society of human equality and thus also of brotherhood the classless society." Dr. Shariati discards the socialism in Marxian sense. About the Western concept of democracy I would again like to cite from the aforementioned book of this giant of modern Iran. He writes: "The political philosophy and the form of regime of the Ummah is not the democracy of heads, not irresponsible and directionless liberalism which is a play thing of contesting social forces, not putrid aristocracy, not anti popular dictatorship, not a self imposing oligarchy. It consists rather of "Purity of leadership" (not the leader, for that would be fascism), committed and revolutionary leadership, responsible for the movement and growth of society on the basis of its world view and ideology, and for the realization of the divine destiny of man in the plan of creation. This is the true meaning of "Imamate".

I may be excused for quoting such a long paragraph from Dr. Shariati's treatise. I have done it with a purpose and that is that these lines of Dr. Shariati manifest a clear picture of an Islamic State and its basic two objectives, viz: political liberty and social justice. At this point I would like to quote from "Introduction to Islamic Political system", of Ayatullah Baqar-al-Sadr the basic objective of an Islamic regime. He writes, "It is Islamic Government that can enable the man in Muslim World to occupy his rightful place at disruption, backwardness and various other ills from which he is suffering, for its establishment is the only way to unfold the hidden capacities of this man. I vehemently support the thesis of Ayatullah Baqar-al-Sadr and furnish my argument of cultural refinement as an objective of an Islamic Regime. Islam gives us a direction. Our each and every step should be purposeful and towards a destination. The destination of Islam is the creation of cultural society marching towards Allah. Karl Marx through his dialectical and historical materialism proved the concept of private property to be the root cause of all social evils and declared the abolition of private property as panacea of all social evils. Sigmond Freud regarded sexual pleasures to be the motivating and directive force of human activities. Buddha considered seclusion and spiritual rigorous practices as the making factors of human personality. Islam does not intend to suspend our journey and keeps us active and agile by desiring to reach the infinite. This is a continuous journey and aggrandizes us to keep towards eternal struggle for eternity, knowledge, piety and justice. The Qur'an in Surah Al-Ankabut says, "We shall certainly guide those who strive for our cause to our paths". Absolute justice is the desired goal of an Islamic State. The Holy Prophet wrote letters to different emperors admonishing them to maintain justice in their states and stop oppression. When "Ubadah Ibn Samit" toppled down the regime of Khusro it was only with the purpose to liberate the oppressed people of Iran from the fetters of serfdom. Islam does not believe in expansionism. The stalwart impetus of Islamic culture is the spiritual reformation of society whose ultimate objective is complete annihilation of evil forces.

A man believing in the precepts of Islam masters the world. He does not become the slave of the pomp and show. He takes his share according to his needs and leaves the rest for his fellow beings. Anyone avaricious or avid is averse to nobility, decency and humanity. Idol-worship whether in the form of pelf or power is condemned by Islam. A man must live and die for Almighty Allah. An Islamic state must manage its affairs in such a way that no arrogant and greedy person can survive in it. Only God fearing persons can have the opportunities to come up and settle the matters of the Ummah. This spiritual uplift is only possible when the members of an Islamic state act according to the following verses of the Qur'an which instruct them for Jihad. "Believers shall I show you a business that will save you from a painful doom. You should believe in Allah and His Messenger, and should strive for the cause of Allah with your wealth and your lives. That is better for you, if you but knew".

Any state that can not give such psychological training to its people is not functioning according to the Qur'anic precepts. The noble mission of serving God must have priority over all worldly mission. Such noble conceptions aspire man to launch a crusade against all tyrannical and dictatorial forces. Islamic state must wax the virtuous and revolutionary tendencies and wane the evil and selfish designs of its inhabitants. The energies should be utilized for creative and constructive works instead of wasting the potentials in teasing, torturing, exploiting, deceiving and degrading others by conspiracies and jealousies. In an Islamic state talent is given all opportunities to flourish while in imperialist and tyrannical regimes talented people are either imprisoned or strangled. It would not be unjust to say that in Islamic state people live with living conscience and in un-Islamic states conscience dies in human bodies. In an Islamic state the life of a ruler is just like a common man. There is no mirage of snobbery and so called supremacy over the ruled. They live in common houses, eat simple food and wear simple dress. The difference between an Islamic ruler and an emperor is that the former behaves like a natural man and the latter acts like a delirious demon. Judiciary is the most powerful organ in an Islamic state. Hazrat Ali stood before a judge like a common man by the side of a common plaintiff. Hazrat Umar bin Abdul Aziz ordered his victorious general

Qutayabah to present himself before a judge because he could not act upon his treaty made with the people of Samarkand, a conquered nation. The Muslim Qazi delivered the judgement against the triumphant army and censured the commander in the favor of the conquered person. This is the character of the Muslim rulers and function of an Islamic state.

May I question the super powers about their behavior with poor and weaker nations. Are these technologically advanced nations not sucking the blood of the smaller nations like leeches. What sort of civilized states are these? Fie upon their mean and selfish designs and frame works of exploiting the other peoples. Islam does not permit to exceed limits and exploit any man or any nation. It wards off exploitation and enormity. It orders for the establishment of justice. In Surah "Al-Maidah", the Qur'an says, "Believers, be fully conscious of your duty to Allah and bear true witness. Let not your hatred for people reduce you that you deal unjustly. Deal justly, that is nearer to piety. No doubt Allah is fully aware of what you do." Islam believes in fairplay in international political relations. The western diplomacy and duplicity has no place in an Islamic state. Plato in his book "TheRepublic" regards the concept of justice as the pivotal force of human civilization. What a beautiful interpretation of the word justice springs up for the divine words of the Qur'an when it names justice as piety. It is the duty of the Muslim Ummah not to be reformed only but to reform all other nations. In the Holy Qur'an this Ummah has been described as balanced nation to be a witness over mankind, and as the best nation that has been raised for the benefit of mankind. An Islamic state provides all facilities and protection to its inhabitants. Hence as a token of reciprocity it is the religious duty of the Muslims to leave no stone unturned for the solidarity, integrity, unity and progress of the Muslim State. People who do not pay taxes in Islamic states and try to avoid taxes by many illegal methods can have no place in an Islamic state. In Islam, "Zakat" is neither a tax nor a penalty but is a religious duty as well. Every Muslim pays it happily and considers it the blessing of God. The laying down of life in the way of God is a cherished desire of every Muslim and no other society has such glorious concept of martyrdom except Muslims.

A true Islamic state bridges up the gap between the ideal and practical aspects of life. It the society is not run according to Islamic principles then individual can act upon Islam in its totality. Piecemeal performances of religious obligations make life either arduous or hypocritical. There are no contradictions and double standards in an Islamic state. What one says one means and what one means one acts. Islamic state prohibits the use of liquor, gambling, adultery, fornication, rape, theft, adulteration, bribery hoarding, black marketing, smuggling, murder and backbiting. It is the duty of an Islamic state to look after the interest of pious and charactered people and crush all evil forces. It provides basic facilities to all citizens and makes them respect its laws and regulations. Epicureanism and Mammon-worship which have dazzled the eyes of the westerners has no weight and value in the eyes of a revolutionary Muslim. These negative habits of human conduct have turned a European into a cheat and a coward fellow. The apparent reaction of such demeanor had made some westners to be hippies and ascetics which is also contrary to Islam as it hurts man's social participation for the uplift of human culture. An ascetic can not be a Muslim because he shirks from his job of reformation. An Islamic state produces the men of vitality and action who eliminate injustice and endeavor for a pure and progressive society. It would be unjust if I do not say a few words about the Islamic concept of "Adl" for it is the pivot of Islamic state. "Adl" (Justice) is the basic pillar or root of Islam In an un-Islamic state people run after people. The Holy Prophet has said: "Neither he believes in God, nor in the day of judgement, he who eats his fill at night and his neighbor is reached with hunger." There are many types of justice such as, economic justice, social justice, political justice and ideological justice. Justice in itself is a vast term having multifarious facets. Whether it is formed or spiritual justice Islam ensures it for the needy ones, for the laborers, for the peasants and for the oppressed and for the weaker ones. In an Islamic state justice not only rendered to the human beings but even to the animals. We are exhorted to be kind to all kinds of animals as they have life in their limbs. So far as natural equality of man is concerned all Muslims are equal, just as the teeth of a comb is the Hadith of the Holy Prophet and it is sufficient to exhibit the social justice of Islam.

In the legal domain the Holy Prophet established the authority of law by presenting himself for corporal punishment when a man claimed in the mosque that he was hurt by the Holy Prophet in the rush of public. Another instance is of the recommendation of Ummah of the Banu Makhdum who had committed theft. The Holy Prophet did not listen to any recommendation and angrily admonished "Would you intervene in the punishment setforth by God. Then he turned to his followers declaring, "What has been the downfall of nations before you is that when a thief of noble origin was caught, he was allowed to go free without punishment, whereas the thief of humble origin was submitted to punishment. I swear by all the oaths of God that if Fatima, the daughter of Mohammad, committed a theft, I would have her hand cut off". This episode demonstrates the truth that Islam establishes justice irrespective of creed, clan, class and color differences. In an un-Islamic state law does not apply upon the law makers but in an Islamic State the source of law is God and hence nobody can escape from the tight grip of law.

In our age the maintenance of economic justice has become the dire need of the time. The communists are exploiting the proletariat and the imperialists are suppressing them. Islamic State can not tolerate a gulf between the haves and have-nots. In Islamic Jurisprudence there are many methods of meeting the economic needs of the Government and the public. Besides Zakat and "Sadaqat" the income of awqaf (holy foundations) and Khairat (the general charity) also fulfil the needs of an Islamic state and society. Ibn Hazm is of the view that besides 'Zakat' the Islamic regime can levy other religious taxes upon the people whenever the need arises. In this regard Ibn Hazm has commented upon a Hadith stressed by Hazrat Ali which states: "God makes it an obligation for the rich of a country to provide for the needs of their poor. Authority must collect them where the sources of the Zakat are insufficient." Public ownership is another source of income for an Islamic state. Though Islam believes in private ownership yet it does not permit the private ownership of the natural sources of production. It does not permit the accumulation of wealth in the hands of oligarchic plutocracy. Dr. Kenze, an authority of modern western economy condemns hoarding and lays stress on the need of circulation of money. Islam had strongly abhorred the act of hoarding fourteen centuries ago in the Holy Qur'an. The rich living in opulence and luxury whilst the poor bearing the pangs of destitution can be the members of western society. Islam does not permit the possession of extra wealth and orders to surrender more than need. Surplus value is the share of the other members of the Muslim society. Poverty is a curse and the Holy Prophet has disliked its existence in an Islamic state. The Prophet said "I am in the hands of God with regard to poverty and infidelity." In America and England many old people or beggars die because of hunger or cold. They claim to have modern welfare states and are not ashamed of their naked lies. We the Muslims who have failed in establishing an Islamic State are even worst than the westerners. Our streets demonstrate the most atrocious poverty along with the most scandalous opulence in the palacious dwellings of the elite. About justice Ibn Al Qayyim had aptly said: "Where justice reigns there also reigns the law of God."

Does justice rule over the majority of the existing Muslim States is the question which lowers our heads with shame and sorrow. In the same vein Seyyed Qotb in his treatise "Social Justice" writes: "In this world which is called the Islamic World, you look and then you are a social reality which is not pleasing. Then you were to open your eyes and ascertain that there are social institutions which do not guarantee justice". This citation from the work of Seyyed Qotb is sufficient to prove that the majority of our Muslim States are unIslamic for they do not pratice Islam in to and have diverted from the Islamic concept of sovereignty. After discussing the general features and objectives of an Islamic State it seems proper to discuss the meaning of sovereignty in Islam. The word "Sovereign" has been derived from the latin "Superanus" which stands for the supremacy of one over others. The Islamic concept of sovereignty of God means that no body has any right to rule over any other person except Almighty Allah. God is the highest authority and no man has any natural right to make laws for others or command over others. Sovereignty is indivisible. No human being is supposed to share the divine authority of Allah. The four essential elements of a state i.e. the people, territory, government and unity or sovereignty exhibit that each element of State is essential and has specific discrimination for its unity.

The Holy Qur'an is the only book which discards every other concept of sovereignty than the sovereignty of Allah. In the words of Von Kremer "a rubbish leap of divine names" of idols was well known and Allah had been thrown in the background. Lat, Manat, Uzza were considered the daughters of God. In such conditions Prophet Mohammad (Peace be upon him) stood for the concept of God. The Qur'an announced: "To Him belongs the dominion of the Heavens and the Earth. It is he who gives life and death, and he has power over all things." The Qur'anic terms "Malikul Mulk (the owner of sovereignty) "Malikul Haq (the true king), Qadir (All Omniscient) etc., signify His glory and grace as an omnipotent, powerful, majestic, mighty, supreme, great, grand, greater, all-pervading, omniscient and omnipresent. How tragic it is that the western political thought has utterly ignored the sovereignty of God and has emphasized the sovereignty of man. Austin emphasizes the supremacy of a determinate human superior and considers him the sovereign in the society whom he shapes or influences. Robert Filmer's theory of the divine Right of kings and Hobbes book "Leviathan" are considered the instruments of enslavement. The earlier western concept of sovereignty can be fully comprehended if we have a deep perusal of "A History of political philosophy" written by Vaugham and "Principles of politics" written by Lord. Apart from these despotic concepts of sovereignty the liberal and democratic concept emerged by the theory of social contract of Rousseau and John Locke is acclaimed to be the charter of freedom. Mr. Carenter in the introduction of Lockes on civil Government writes: "The great merit of Lockes political theory is in his denial that sovereignty can exist any where except in the community as a whole. This is the original and supreme will which organizes the Government and defines its powers in the State. The supreme power of the people which may be called as a political power; the supreme power of the legislative which may be called as the legal power; the supreme power of a single person, which may be called as the executive for titular or nominal sovereign.

This signifies that the Muslim emperors who changed the concept of Islamic caliphate into monarchy and announced to be the "Shadows of God" were imperialists and despotic sovereigns just like the callous and crooked ancient emperors of the west. The rise of democratic spirit in west slowly and steadily broke the spell of one man's sovereignty and delegated these powers to community and law. Montesquieu in his book "Spirit of laws" admits the sovereignty of law and the sovereignty of God. He approvingly quotes Plutarch as saying, "Law is the king of mortal and immortal beings". Thus he admits his right as a lawmaker and the sovereign of the heavens and of the earth. Rousseau's criticism of Christianity and of all other religions and his appreciation of Islam, shows that he was impressed by the idea of consensus and the concept of sovereignty of Islam. He discarded other religions on the basis of their being non-social and having no particular relation to the body politic. While in Islam contract is the basis of Muslim social, religious, economic, moral and even political life. As Rousseau was a naturalist he had to laud the spirit and system of Islam. Rousseau was highly impressed by Islamic concept of State and his natural political conclusions won the hearts of giants of philosophy such as Kant, Hegel, Green, Bosanquet and Bradley. They all have accepted Rousseau's contention that the chief quality of man is moral freedom and it cannot be achieved in demonic or despotic societies. Any system which worships State or the ruler of the state is idol-worship. Islam is not nationalism. It is universal. In Islam State is not an end in itself. It is merely a means to an end and that lists the obedience to the canons of Allah. Allah is the core of all activities in an Islamic State. Islam deprecates nationalism and preaches humanitarianism. Allama Iqbal considers state worship to be a new God. He says: "Even the Muslim has created his own Kaaba seperately. The Azar of civilization has carved other idols. In these new gods the biggest is the father land that which it is apparel is the coffin of religion. In Islam there is no loyalty to anything except the loyalty to Allah. Islam means submission to the Will of God. Even the prophet of Islam was commanded to be the first to submit; "Say I am commanded that I should serve Allah, being sincere to Him in obedience, And I am commanded that I shall be the first of those who submit". Thus we conclude that the sovereignty of Allah in Islam is unlimited, undivided, unshared and inalienable.

Every state is a unity and no element out of its four elements is divisible. In the light of modern political theories sovereignty is absolute. It is universal or all-comprehensive. With the change of Government the state does not change. The sovereignty is permanent. It can never be divested. It is inalienable and original. Jean Bodin of France and Hobbes of England are the exponents of the concept of sovereignty in modern political philosophy of Europe. The term "Sovereign King" is also the outcome of imperialists creative evil genius. Islam does not believe in the sovereign power of any king. In Islam sovereignty lies with Allah. The Qur'an has discussed the concept of God's sovereignty when the whole Europe was rambling and loitering in the God's dale of dark ages. The Muslim writers like Ibn-Ali-Al-Rabi, Al-Farabi and Ibn-Khaldune had discussed in detail the doctrine of Islamic sovereignty. P.W. Ward in his book Sovereignty has traced the history of this doctrine in three stages as follows:

1. Its emergence from the complex materials of ancient tradition and late material usages.

2. Its enunciation and application by the absolute monarchs of the early modern period.

3. Its repeated interpretation since 1699 with the historic rise of responsible government in England.

A Muslim ruler must possess the consensus of vision (Ijma al-Ruyal): the consensus of determination (Ijma al-Iradah) and the consensus of action (Ijma al-Amal). By the consensus of vision means that a Muslim ruler must possess the systematic knowledge of the value whose sources are the Qur'an and the Sunnah. A Muslim ruler must have the natural gift of inferring, discovering and establishing a structure of ideas in the light of reason and inquisition. He should get light from the Qur'an and solve the problems of Muslim Ummah according to the need of time. He should be a seasoned jurist and a scholar. Allama Khomeini in his book 'Hakumat-e-Islam' has presented the concept of 'Walayat-e-Fiqih' on the same basis.

The people unaware of Islamic tenets can never establish Islamic Society. The study of Logic, Epistemology, Metaphysics, Anthropology, Psychology, Economics, History, Ethics, Mathematics and Physics are essential for a jurist. A fiqih is not a traditional priest adept in Sectarian discussions or gorgeous gossip. A Muslim ruler must have speculative as well as Inductive insight to visualize the future of his country men.

A Muslim caliph must be progressive and dynamic in making intellectual decisions. His analysis of historical anecdotes must be scientific. Open mindedness is the basis feature of a Muslim ruler. A man with prejudicial blinkers over his eyes cannot be a successful Muslim ruler.

The second trait of a Muslim caliph should be his power of making decisions and infusing a vital spirit in his followers to act according to his higher ideals. It is the "Sensus communis". The whole of the community is activitized and mobilized for a common cause. The sense of social cohesiveness, utility and unity is the vortex of the consensus of power.

A Muslim ruler should be a vigilant and valiant administrator. He should be a steel nerved man. A fickle minded man having no perseverance and mettle can destroy the whole nation. Psychologically deranged person or a man addicted to narcotics can be highly harmful for the existence of a community. A Muslim ruler must have positive points to his credit to guide the strayed masses.

These criteria lead a Muslim Caliph towards the aura of sanctity and sagacity. This is the reason that a 'Mujtahid' has more rights to harness the packing steed of politics lest it should move towards the dale of destruction. The Holy Prophet on the necessity of Ijtehad said; "Whoever does Ijtehad but arrives at error has nonetheless earned a measure of moral merit whoever does Ijtehad and arrives at truth has earned double".

Ijtehad is an empirical and dialectical process which is the orbit of our Islamic state. When in social and political matters the whole society exercises this dynamic principle, it is known as Ijma. Ijtehad is for special minds and Ijma is for the whole society. But both must go side by side and people should use their mind in solving day to day matters. Human life is supersonically fast and changing. Any system that does not absorb any change in it can not survive. Does it mean that the system should also change with the change of life; or the life should be modulated according to the demand of system. In my opinion both should act in such a way that the flow of social changes should neither stop nor it should over-flow from the brim of its flowing stream. The foundations of religion can not be changed but the storeys should be made according to the need. Syed Jamal Uddin Asad Abadi was a great pioneer of pan-Islamism. Iqbal being his ideological follower held after the banner of Pan-Islamism. In his sixth lecture in his famous book, "Reconstruction of Religious Thought In Islam" writes: Fort he present every

Muslim nation must sink into her own deeper self, temporarily focus her vision on herself alone; until all are strong and powerful to form a living family of republics. A true and living unity, according to the nationalist thinkers, is not so easy as to be achieved by a merely symbolical over lordship. It is truly manifested in a multiplicity of free independent units whose racial rivalries are adjusted and harmonized by the unifying bond of a common spiritual aspiration. It seems to me that God is slowly bringing home to us the truth that Islam is neither Nationalism nor Internationalism but a league of Nations which recognizes artificial boundaries and racial distinctions for facility of reference only, and not for restricting the social horizon of its members. Islamic state is not territorial in western sense. It is an ideological and all people believing in Islam are one Ummah. Their faith cannot be divided by Territorial or social divisions. The divine oracle of Islam utters that all humanity is one and various communities are like the beads of one cord and that cord is the Cord of Allah which must be tightly held. The concept of Tauhid in Islam signifies the universal brotherhood of mankind. The loyalty to territory is tantamount to idolatrous worship in Islam. Islam prohibits land-worship and stands for the higher and nobler ideals of mankind under the canopy of Godhood. Islam believes in social-cum-spiritual democracy in which every body is economically and politically free to exercise his right of vote and acts under the moral laws which make him strong and untrammelled by the molestations of fear and force.

Here it won't be out of place to mention that a Muslim ruler can never be narrow-sighted to plead the cause of Nationalism. He can be a patriot. In Islam, patriotism does not mean that we should support our government whether it is right or wrong. The slogan 'My country' right or wrong, is a western slogan and does not coincide with the message of Islam. The Muslims must follow the foot prints of righteousness and truth. It is the moral duty of the Muslims of a country to raise hue and cry against their own aggressive regimes if they are in conflict with another country; whether Muslim or non-Muslim. If any country wages war against any Muslim state with out any genuine grounds the inhabitants of that state must stand against their own un-Islamic tyrannical regimes. Aggression must be boldly checked and the aggressors must be penalized and persecuted.

Iran is the victim of Iraqi aggression and it is the religious duty of Iraqis to retaliate against their aggressive regime and assist Iranians who are sincerely striving for the establishment of an Islamic State. There is no religious obligation upon the Muslims of an aggressive regime to follow its orders for these orders are at war with the teachings of Islam. The Holy Qur'an says, "You are the best of Ummahs who are sent out to transform the life of the people by administering them to do the right and avoid the evil." Islam claims for the sovereignty of God and the application of divine rule through his noble representatives. The Earth belongs to God and its inheritance is for the noble ones who establish divine kingdom upon the earth.

Allama Iqbal had envisaged the future glory of Islam and yearned to see Tehran as the core of Muslim Unity. He had said; "If Tehran becomes the Geneva of Eastern Peoples, then the fate of the whole world can be changed." For this prediction he announced that the long-awaited person has come to break the shackles of slavery.

By all that has been said about Islamic state, features and objectives, one thing which has distinctly cropped up is the universal spirit of Islam. For this system a pious man full of knowledge is needed. Whether it is "Walayat-e-Fiqh" or a council of scholars or the head of senate or chief justice of supreme court, there should be a man or a body which should be powerful enough to check what is Islamic and what is un-Islamic. The Islamic Republic of Iran is the only state amongst all present Muslim states which has eliminated the hoax of sectarianism and is striving for the real Islam.

ISLAMIC RENAISSANCE

In the revival of Islamic values lies the survival of Muslim Ummah. The Muslims are facing grim and grave problems which need proper attention to free them from the fetters of backwardness and slavery. Islam is a misunderstood religion. Though it has been attacked from every side, yet it survives and calls our attention for its proper study, analysis and implementation. The crisis of the Muslims is the outcome of their failure in understanding and implementing Islam as a complete code of life. Before discussing the nature of present crisis of the Muslims and suggesting solutions I deem it necessary to say a few words about the Islam which was brought by the Holy Prophet Muhammad (peace be upon him) and is still lying in its pure form in the pages of the Holy Qur'an. We will have to dive deep into the ocean of the Islamic Philosophy and pick up the gems of wisdom for the solution of our day-to-day issues. We have immensely suffered at the hands of non-scientific and irrational commentators of the Qur'an. They have diverted us from the right path. The rapid outpouring of westernized politicians and emotional speeches of sectarian Muslim theologians have played havoc with a common Muslim. The materialists and pragmatists deal with human life, human history and the material world through dialectical materialism. While the purely mythological creeds and other religions besides Islam negate material forces and take refuge in a self-created world of spirituality. Islam keeps a balance between matter and spirit. It rejects both extremes. It considers material forces as the co-workers in the shaping of spiritual society. It goes beyond the limits of matter and seeks divine help and guidance for the prompt regulation of human society. The finality of the Prophethood in Islam means the closure of Revelation and an opening of the vistas of reason. The spiritual interpretation of the cosmos signifies the fact that the spirit dominates the matter. The constant stress of exercising reason in the Qur'an saves us from annihilation and destruction. Superstitions have no place in Islam. Opaque images must be set aside and reason should be used to seek truth. Islam distinctly reminds us that we are the best creation of God and we have to master the objects of Nature. We are not born to worship any non-godly force.

God must be the Centre of our spiritual, material, individual and social activities and pursuits. The travesty of the situation is that the Muslims who were asked by the Qur'an, "Ye who believe; shall I point to a bargain that will save you from a painful punishment? That you believe in Allah and His Messenger and strive in the cause of Allah with your wealth and your persons. That is better for you, if you did but know." These verses of the Holy Qur'an demand our property, our lives and everything to be sacrificed in the name of God. But what is our conduct? We are away from Jehad and are madly accumulating money to facilitate ourselves. Neither do we spend a penny on Islamic cause nor do we shed a drop of blood in the way of Allah. Then how can we survive? Personal petty interests impel us to make stupid decisions and incorrect verdicts even if the Muslim nations existence and integrity is at stake. All this is done with a purpose to serve and that malicious purpose is to play with the spirit of Islam to keep ourselves spirited in securing our calculated designs. This national tragedy occurs only and only because we have failed to understand the purpose and spirit of Islam. The real Islam has been corroded by the imperialistic interpretation of Islam. The need for introducing real Islam should be the only priority of the Muslim thinkers of our era. The real Islam keeps an eye upon all eventualities and actualities of human life and presents their realistic and scientific solution while the unreal Islam has taught us the so-called mystical and metaphysical fancies and fallacies. The greatest crisis we are facing today is the lack of right understanding of the message and mission of Islam. Islam frees man from the yoke of man. All man made systems have badly failed in providing peace, tranquility, justice, equity and fraternity to Mankind. Islam is the greatest and the latest of religions of the world which provides scientific solutions to all human problems. It does not permit conjectures in religious matters. It is based upon logic, wisdom and reality. The concept of Islamic faith does not permit the exercise of doubt or denial. Faith in Islam is based upon concrete and rational outlooks. I would like to discuss the nature of our crisis from the concept of Tawhid in Islam. Tawhid is such a vast concept that it serves two main purposes at a time. On one hand it teaches us complete submission and surrender to God and on the other it preaches us human values through an everlasting message of peace and prosperity. Tawhid is the bedrock and quintessence of Islam. It rejects social superiorities, blood differences and creed-contrarieties.

It is the most revolutionary concept that frees mankind from the serfdom of all earthly self-made gods. From Adam to the Holy Prophet of Islam all Prophets came with the message to reform mankind. The Qur'an says: "He hath ordained for you (O Mohammad) that faith which he commended into Noah and that which we inspire to thee, and that which we commended unto Abraham, Moses and Jesus, saying "Establish the faith, and be not divided therein." In the words of Bertrand Russell Islam is a militant force and intends to establish its sovereignty. Dr. Iqbal also believed that Islam was a polity with distinct political, economic, moral and social principles. Bernard Shaw in "The Genuine Islam" opines: "I have always held the religion of Mohammad in high estimation because of its wonderful vitality. It is the only religion which appears to me to possess that assimilating capacity to the changing phase of existence which can make itself appeal to every age." There is not a shred of doubt in it that Islam is a religion of intelligible and practicable provision. The hierarchy of priests, far-fetched abstractions, irrational rites and rituals, baseless tabooes and double standards are anti-Islam. The Qur'an exhorts man to pray: "O! my Lord: Advance me in knowledge". Knowledge has been considered the basic quality of caliphate in the Qur'an while describing the purpose of the creation of Adam. On different occasions the Holy Qur'an has repeatedly expressed the importance of knowledge. The following verse: "Are the men of knowledge equal to the men who have no knowledge" clearly portrays the value of knowledge. The constant stress of the Qur'an upon the significance of knowledge condemns the duality between life and life-hereafter. Religion cannot be separated from life.

There is no place for asceticism in Islam. Life can not be divided into watertight compartments of matter and spirit. Islam does not renounce life-fulfillment. Life denial is not the motto of Islam. The division of spiritual and mundane is the product of Greek philosophy. Christianity erred on negating material and social aspect of human life. Hence enlightened Christians revolted against it. Lord Snell in his book "The New World" writes: "We have built a nobly proportioned outer structure, but we have neglected the essential requirement of an inner order: we have carefully designed, decorated and made clean the outside of the cup, but the inside was full of extortion and excess, we used our increased knowledge and power to administer to the comforts of the body, but we left the spirit impoverished."

Christianity like Hinduism ignored life and the problems of life. It ignores social justice and political freedom. On the other hand the communists and the materialists not only marred the moral values but also spelled drastic disaster. The French scientist Dr. De Brogbi truly says: "The danger inherent in too intense a material civilization is to that civilization itself; it is the disequilibrium which would result if a parallel development of the spiritual life were to fail to provide the needed balance. The western isms and religions have failed in establishing an equilibrium between the material and the spiritual needs of mankind. Islam stands for the middle path. It makes us mighty to keep the supremacy of right over might. But an other serious crisis took birth in the Muslim world when our Ummah was ensured into the discussion of "Shariah" and "Tareeqah." The believers of former cult still lay emphasis on the need and performance of religious acts and the believers of the latter stand for spiritual elevation without even caring for formal religious practices. This dichotomy actually resulted in because of our failure in understanding Islam. The group more careful about "Shariah" ignored the spiritual aspects and the group standing for "Tareeqah" ignored the practical aspect of Islam. Hence there was a tug of war between the mosque and the Shrine. Monasticism, undoubtedly elevated the majority of Muslims but shunned their struggle for triumphing over life problems. This crisis is yet to be tackled. The Muslim sufi runs away from the battlefield of life and seeks shelter in remote caves for spiritual elevation. This all happened because of mis-understanding of Islam. The mosques became the centres of sectarian discussions and dialogues and the monasteries became the abodes of secluded rigorous spiritual practices. Now it is the right time that the exploiters boasting in mosque and monasteries should bring their followers out of death-cells to the open fields of life. This is the lesson which we can learn from the sunnah of the Holy Prophet. He used to go to the cave of Hira for meditation and prayer. But from the cave of Hira he climbed over the mountain of Faran addressing the Meccans to embrace Islam. From the mountain of Faran he is seen in the battlefields of Badr, Ahud, Ahzab and Khaiber crusading against the evil forces. This vividly manifests that Islam is a journey from cave to the mountain and then onwards from mountain to the battlefield. Islam should not have been divided into bits. Its division has divided Muslim Ummah into pieces. Islam must be taken in totality. It is a unique system having unity of purpose. If we implement one portion of Islam and ignore other, it means we are betraying ourselves. This hypocritical bent has been condemned in the Qur'an when it reproaches the mentality of those who believe in and practice some of its verses and ignore other ones.

The message of Islam is universal as God, in Islam is the God of the Universe. The Holy Prophet is said to be "The warner to all nations" (The Holy Qur'an, 25:1). The oneness of God means the oneness of humanity. The Qur'an says:"The whole of humanity is one community." It means that Islam is international in its outlook and removes all the barriers and impediments of language, race, status, wealth, cast, clan and color. The Holy Qur'an says: "This day have I perfected your religion for you, completed my favors upon you, and have chosen for you Islam as your Deen." The perfection of Islam means the perfection of human values. Islam represents the whole man. The word religion does not express the man as a whole. It represents an ideology which is one sided. The Arabic word Deen is used in a broader sense. But it is highly tragic that the nation which was appointed to spread virtue and abolish vice is being swayed by the fluxes of indecency, immodesty, indiscipline and ignorance. All and sundry must benefit, not a few. Islam does not permit class society. It gives respect to the men of wisdom and piety. The alpha and omega of Islam is the faith in God and love for mankind. The Muslims, presently, are at sixes and sevens because they lack a scientific attitude and this is one of the basic causes of their being between the devil and the deep sea.

Another evil which cropped up in the minds of Muslims is personality cult. Islam being a solid and sound ideology was not given serious thought. The Muslim theologians either made the personality of the Holy Prophet as an apple of discord or they wasted their time and energies in the fruitless discussions of the self created war between the companions of the Prophet. Instead of doing as the Prophet did his personality was unduly debated. Islam stresses to project model Muslims who by acting upon the sunnah of the Holy Prophet can revolutionize the world. It is an ideology which embodies persons into personalities.

We have been unnecessarily dragged to personality debates. Islam is neither liturgy nor theocracy. We are living in a waste land burying our talents into sand dunes. The Muslims spreading from Indonesia to Morocco are under the spell of pugilistic writings and fiery speeches of the theologians but the ray of wisdom is missing everywhere.

A Muslim who should have the proud privilege to lead mankind is straying in the dark and dreary deserts of ignorance, slavery and inferiority complex. Let us brood over this tragedy. Every sane person can easily conclude what is the cause of this crisis. At the early period of Islam the Muslims achieved victories in every walk of life because they had full understanding of Islam and sincerely adhered to it. They had accepted Islam after serious and sincere comprehension. They were not born Muslims. They had embraced Islam after great sacrifices. Unlike us they did not get Islam by inheritance. They underwent painful toil. For them Islam was an ideology and a mission. We are Muslims because we have been born in Muslim families. We consider Islam as a caste. This is an other serious blow which Islam has received. The Holy Qur'an clearly said that the Muslims were the brethren in faith. Islam is a faith and intends to raise a community fully inspired by faith in Allah. In the short life period of the Holy Prophet a community was formed which had unflinching faith and blotless character. They had earnestly and consciously accepted Islam as a divine code of life and were ever ready to lay down their lives for the sacred mission of Islam. They aspired to establish the rule of Allah upon the earth. They knew that they were the vicegerents of God. They were self-conscious. They never loved the idols of monarchy, greed, fear, lust, tyranny and oppression. They worshipped God and were not scared of death or imprisonment. They were committed to the mission of Islam for realization and the sense of realization quickens and deepens the sense of commitment. A non-conformist attitude is a modern shape of opportunism. A true Muslim can never be a non-conformist. This selfish and materialistic trend had entirely perished the sense of social responsibilities. Michael Green, an enthusiastic pioneer of Christian Renaissance wails over the degenerating conditions of Christian Youth in these words: "Our generation certainly knows what it is to be lost. No over riding aim in life, no enduring relationships, no deep satisfaction."

This is not only the position of the Christian Youth. The Muslim youth is also leisurely and lazily drifting down the dale of purposelessness. They don't have any goal, any target, any interest in noble ideals. In this connection it can be said that the tragedy of Islam is two fold. Firstly: it has been accepted by few persons with sincerity and secondly a few people have its clear understanding. The Muslims as a whole have failed in understanding the true spirit of Islam. Islam is lonely. It needs men of sincerity and wisdom. Bertrand Russell in his book "The Principles of Social Reconstruction" discusses the nature of "Isolation" and "Loneliness" which portrays the causes of the formation of social and mental edifices of a society. Russell's philosophical connotations are not without reason. Society is integrated with the uniqueness of purpose. We have isolated Islam from our society, hence we have been isolated from the civilized and advanced world. Islam feels loneliness and consequently we are lonely. The whole world is against Muslims. The irony of fate is that unconsciously the Muslim themselves are working against the mission of Islam. The real mission of Islam lies in Jehad and Ijtehad. We are away from these two basic principles of Islam. The imperialists inoculated the germs of indolence and inertion in us. Our basic concepts were changed. They were given new meanings and self styled interpretations. For example, "Salat" or the prayer in Islam means the prostration before God, and negation of non-godly forces. The head that bends before God can never bend before any despot or tyrant. But unfortunately the imperialists misguided the simple hearted Muslims through their agents who taught them to remain away from state matters and keep on praying all the night. Five times daily prayers candidly portray the spirit of Islam. Prayer in Islam includes both, the physical exercise and the spiritual uplift. It shows that Islam is temporal as well as spiritual. The regular performance of the prayers teaches us discipline. All the objects of Nature are under natural law. They cannot move away an inch from their appointed course. They do not enjoy the facility of free will. In Sura-e-Noor Almighty Allah says, "Every object of nature is well aware of its nature and law". All the objects of nature perform their natural duty but man has to perform divine duty assigned to him. Man possesses the boon of free will. He instinctively knows what is good and what is bad. But this instinct must tally with the demands of revelation to keep man on the natural, rational and right path, otherwise man becomes worse than an animal.

Islam directs our wishes, thoughts and deeds. It waxes our humanity and wanes our animality. If the element of rationality is detracted from man then there is no difference between man and animal. If we need houses to protect us from the strokes of scorching heat or rainy climes birds also make nests and beasts live in caves for the same reason. Whether these are littorals or ledges, ridges or plateaus, shrubs or bushes, the birds, the beasts and the reptiles make places to reside in. If we need food; birds also need food. If we care for our progeny and manage to protect them from every kind of attack, harm or loss; the birds also strive hard for the protection of their family.

The experts on animal psychology write that when a vulture pounces upon a chick, the hen reacts wildly to it and does her best to protect her chickens from the attack of the vulture. The animals feel happiness and unhappiness in different situations. The only thing that discriminates man from animal is the rational faith. This exercise of reason creates the sense of logical and illogical, legal and illegal, natural and unnatural, moral and immoral. Being endowed by God with such rare gifts of conscience and consciousness a Muslim was asked to master the objects of Nature. A scientist who seeks the latent mysteries of the universe and studies the properties of matter is a true Muslim if he does this with the noble purpose to serve mankind and knows the creator through his marvelous creation. Science is not anti-Islam. The Qur'an has reiterated time and again to study the movement of the stars and think over the secrets of the cosmos. Gallellieo and Kepler were severely tortured for their scientific notions but Islam encouraged scientific inquiry and investigation. No Qur'anic order or claim, hitherto could be proved unscientific. The Muslim scientists have rendered remarkable services in advancing human knowledge. The Qur'an has laid great stress on concrete and factual analysis. It has outright denounced conjectural and unsubstantial methods of studying universe and human life. The basic difference in Greek philosophy and Islam is the method of their treatment. Islam is inductive and Greek philosophy is deductive. Islam is objective and Metaphysics is subjective.

H.G. Wells in his "Outline of History" states: "The thoughts of the Greeks were hampered by a want of knowledge that is almost inconceivable to us today. The Greek intellect is based on abstractions. Their astronomical and cosmological conclusions and calculations ramble in the stale state of rudimentary speculations. Oswald Spengler in "The Decline of the West" writes:

"The Greek, through out his culture, preferred abstract thought to the study of concrete facts." Mr. Lange in "The History of Materialism" and John William Droper in volume 1 of his History of the Intellectual Development in Europe are of the opinion that throughout the Dark Ages in Europe Science was under the spell of obscurity and subordination. The Byzantine, the Roman, the Greek and the Italian early periods were quite sterile and stubborn in their contribution of scientific knowledge. It was the highest of the crescent of Islam which enlightened the whole world. Jabbir-bin-Hayyan, the father of Chemistry is still a shining star in the firmament of science. Before Islam the objects of Nature were worshipped and looked upon as some thing possessing supernatural powers. The objects were defied and adored. Abraham challenged the worshippers of idols and the adorers of the Moon and the Sun. His mission was brought into full lime light by the Prophet of Islam who succiently proscribed idol-worship. The Holy Qur'an laid stress on observation and experimentation. The Holy Book of Allah says: "Most surely, in the variations of the night and the day and what Allah has created in the heavens and the earth, there are signs for a people who think" (10:16). So much was the influence of Islam in the West that Roger Bacon and Martin Luther were branded as Muslims by Christian theologians for their scientific and revolutionary ideas. When the Muslim Spain was splendidly marching upon the roads of civilization, Europe was lingering in dense darkness. Stanlylane Poole in his work "Moors in Spain" depicts the position of that epoch in these words: "For nearly eight centuries under her Mohammadan rulers, Spain set to all Europe a shining example of a civilized and enlightened state. Mathematics, Astronomy, Botany, History, Philosophy and jurisprudence were to be mastered in Spain and Spain alone." The names of Averroes, Avicenna, Ibn Khurdabaih, Ibn Rusta, Al Kindi and Ibn Rushd are imperishable. Cordova, Basra, Baghdad, Cairo, Alexandria and Damascus were once the centers of learning throughout the world.

Mr. Abbot in "The Expansion of Europe" and Phillip K. Hitti in "The History of the Arabs" admits the technological and scientific supremacy of the earlier Muslims. These occasional laurels of excellence by the earlier Muslims are the result of their mission as Muslims. Dr. Iqbal about this scientific mission of the

Qur'an observes. The Qur'an sees the signs of the ultimate reality in the "Sun", the moon, the lengthening of shadows, the alternation of day and night, the variety of human color and tongues, the alternation of day of successand reverse among peoples. In fact the whole of nature as revealed to the sense perception of man. And the Muslim's duty is to reflect on these signs and not to pass by them as if he is deaf and blind, for he who does not see these signs in this life will remain blind to the realities of the life to come. "The Qur'an has emphatically condemned this spiritual deafness and blindness. Islam warns us to open the eyes and read the book of Nature.

What could be a graver situation than this that the Muslims are lagging behind in the race of scientific achievements and discoveries. They are too blind to read the gravity of the present situation. The Qur'an while condemning the non-believers had said: "Allah has set a seal on their hearts and their ears, and over their eyes is a covering, and for them is a great punishment." Of course the infidels are blind and deaf to see the realities and are deaf to listen to the message of Allah. They are spiritually blind and materially sharp sighted but we are blind in both ways. The infidels will be punished on doomsday but the Muslims are being punished in this world. In Lebanon, in Palestine, in Chad, in Afghanistan, in Kashmir, and where not?? We have been deluded by the concept of personal salvation and redemption by spiritless incantations. Our self made Islam starts from life-hereafter. This is an other challenge wisely to be faced. This negative approach towards redemption in life hereafter has highly damaged the material progress of the Muslims. We have left "Jehad" against oppression and injustice. Predeterminism is the material offshoot of this inertion. We have failed to promote positive and progressive values. We have a negative concept of salvation. We do not leave backbiting, fornication, forgery, adulteration, black marketing, the use of narcotics but even then we boast to be Muslims and expect salvation on doomsday. This can be a Judaic notion but atleast it is not Islamic. This is another serious crisis which we face. Islamic concept of salvation is quite scientific. The dictum "what you sow so shall you reap" exhibits the law of Nature and the concept of salvation.

In the subcontinent the majority of the Muslims are still acting upon some of the unIslamic rites and rituals. The influence

of Buddhism and Hinduism is deep-rooted in the form of mythological whims. Our superstitions have perfidiously and pugna-
ciously kept a tenacious grip over our thoughts and deeds. The
Hinduistic caste system, old Arab Tribalism, and ethnic prides
and prejudices have totally corrupted the Muslim society. It
seems to me as the lack of proper education on Islamic patterns
is also one of the causes of the crisis that the Muslim Ummah is
facing. The Western imperialism took the benefit of our traditional and retrogressive educational system and in the name of
scientific progress and rationalism deprived us of higher ideals.
Our traditional system of education also overlooked scientific
and national bents of the west while our modern educational
system introduced scepticism and faithlessness to us. Both systems are lopsided and need complete overhauling. We need a
balanced system which can promote our mundane and spiritual
values at a time. The Western educational system introducing
secular trends has done irreparable damages to our polity. No
sane person would deny the need of humanistic, realistic, and
liberal re-awakening. But the negation of spiritual and moral
values can never be plauded in a Muslim society. The Qur'an
equally lays stress on the need of study of soul and science. Science and Islam are not antagonistic to each other. Islam is not
anti-Science. The modern scientific discoveries have brought immense wonder to human mind and all these latest discoveries in
the realm of science have proved the truth of the Qur'an as the
word of God. The Bible, the Qur'an and Science is a remarkable
book of Maurice Bucaille, a French writer testifying the scientific
truth of the Qur'anic theories.

It can be said that we have failed to appreciate the true Islamic spirit and could not implement Islam as a system of life.
Whatever has been stated above is responsible for confusing issues. Willingly or unwillingly we have segregated Islam as a
purely imperialistic movement which has not awakened the sense
of polity among the masses. What an else tragedy could be that
now the Muslims consider Islam as their private affair. This
Christian concept of religion has crept into Muslim society, what
a downfall!! Under the imperialistic influence the common people
were entangled into sectarian webs cleverly woven by the callous and crafty emperors to grind their own axe. Even today
these sectarian tendencies and vicious imperialist designs con-

tinue to hold the Muslim masses in their tight grip. The social, political and economic exploitation still prevails.

The aftermath of such misconception turned to be so serious that the Muslims entirely forgot the mission of Islam. Loyalty to God was overlooked and selfishness became the fashion of the day. Instead of producing missionaries we produced mercenaries. In India the Muslims had been fighting under the command of the Marhattas and the British colonialists for bread and butter. What a decline? Only the intelligentsia of the Muslim world is conscious of the crisis. The common folk are generally not serious about the plight in which the Muslim Ummah is unfortunately placed and the adverse results which they may face in the future. Because of illiteracy and ignorance, the common Muslim is not alive to what collective issues are at stake.

I call this unawareness of collective spirit a crisis, as crisis is a state or a situation which involves departure from normality threatening the collapse of a particular situation or social order. The awareness of a crisis involves both the emotional and intellectual understanding of a particular state of affairs which ultimately leads you to take practical step to cope with difficulties. The Muslims all over the world are partly aware of the crisis and partly ignorant of it. The intelligentsia intellectually feels concerned about this crisis while the masses are emotionally involved to untying the knot of the crisis. The masses have emotional and vague apprehensions of fundamental causes which touch the roots of the matter. Their emotional understanding, doubtlessly speaks of their sincerity of purpose and loyalty to their religion. But the lack of rational approach has bewildered them and they are fumbling in the darkness but sincerely desire to reach the desired destination. The common run of the people are not conversant with the real Islamic values, their nature, their relations and the teaching of the Qur'an. As I had already mentioned the majority think that they are Muslims because they have been born in Muslim families. I observe with deep pain that the true understanding of Islamic values is quite inadequate Islam, as a social system has advocated two most important human values to which we have turned our backs. These values are brotherhood and equality. Any way these values are interrelated because in the absence of the one the other cannot be realized. The sense of brotherhood inspires us to cultivate equality and the presence of equality fortifies the ties of brotherhood. The Communists are very loudly crying for social justice and economic equality but without political justice and spiritual light they have completely failed in establishing a contented society. I consider economic justice to be one of the greatest issues of the time which the whole world is seriously facing.

The capitalists own the natural and the unnatural means of production while the communist state keeps both in its hands. In the opinion of Dr. Iqbal, Islam is neither communism nor capitalism. Islam permits individuals to possess unnatural means all alone by themselves. The whole public must be equally benefitted from the free gifts of nature. No economic exploitation or political subjugation is permitted by Islam. It is neither monarchy, nor one party rule, nor western democracy. Islamic political system only permits the men of wisdom, piety and character to be directly elected. No party and no sect is allowed in Islam. No question of Government servant or non-government servant. Everybody is the servant of Allah and loyal to the ideology of Islam. In such a dazzle of imperialistic grandeur and glamour a common Muslim is dazed. Without a harmonious and natural system a simple hearted Muslim, in the words of T.S. Eliot can be described as a person with divided aims and split personality. Islam intends to turn persons in to sound personalities: not into split personalities. If we examine this tragedy we conclude that in old literature of the Muslim sages and their commentaries on the Qur'an, we find the influence of the Greek and Judaic metaphysical and mythological controversies which have confused values and misrepresented Islam. Moreover, speeches from pulpit and the religious platforms have tended to arouse sectarian and emotional feelings among the Muslims with the result that ought-to-be Islamic values and principles were thrown over board. They side tracked the real issues and failed to create true Islamic spirit which was so essential for character building of Muslim Ummah in the Islamic ways. We have failed to present models on the pattern of the character of the Holy Prophet. I must mention here that the Arabic speaking Muslim countries did not take the trouble of understanding the spirit of Islam and remained involved in the jugglery of grammar and punning upon the words. They segregated the Sunnah of the Prophet from the verses of the Qur'an and gave new meanings to the verses according to their own thinking, interests, situations and needs. This was a great blow which Islam received at the hands of unwise commentators of the Qur'an. It is said that once Hazrat Aisha, the wife of the Holy Prophet, was asked by a "Sahabi" about the character of the Holy Prophet. She said, "Have you not read the Qur'an?" He replied that he had. She said that the Holy Prophet was a living Qur'an. This shows that the Quranic verses must be tallied with the life of the Prophet. If we do so we will automatically come out of the gamut of every kind of crisis. We pay lip service to Islamic values and do not practise them as they ought to be practised.

The non-Arabic speaking Muslim states had been swept and swayed by the pre-Islamic Persian sufistic ideas and reveries. Iqbal was diametrically opposed to the Persian influence upon Islam. How tragic it is that the non-Arabic speaking read the Holy Qur'an without understanding even a word of it. They have to depend upon theologians for its understanding, and the narrow-minded and self-conceited theologians find themselves at liberty to exploit them.

In my opinion the teaching of Arabic should be encouraged in non-Arabic Muslim countries to have direct approach to the meanings of the Qur'an. In so far as our application of Islamic values at present as well as in the past are concerned we have only restricted ourselves to the performance of certain acts of worship such as prayer (Salat), Fasting (Saum), and Pilgrimage (Hajj), but have not succeeded in adopting the true spirit of Islamic values in our everyday lives in total. This tragedy has its roots in the misconceptions of our history. We have neither analyzed nor grasped the true concept of Islamic history. Ibn-Khaldune emphasized the objective analysis of history. History is not only the record of certain tales and wars. It reaches lessons and provides light for future line of action. Generally speaking Muslim history is a chronological record of state craft, caliphs and monarchs. We share the pride of victories, conquests of lands and vast kingdoms and regard the history of kings as Islamic history. But the real history of Islam which introduces Islam as the greatest revolution of the world aimed at the uplift of the downtrodden humanity who were being crushed under the heels of the savage emperors, tyrants and despots. Those noble personalities were tormented and assassinated but the crimson drops of their blood still shine and show us the right faith in the dreary desert of life. Islamic history is the history of those selfless martyrs who laid down their lives for the will of God. Until we draw the line of demarcation between Islamic history and the imperialist history, we cannot revive the Islamic spirit. Lastly, I deem westernization as a radical cause of the Muslim crisis. Our too much dependence upon western technology has thrown us into the chasm of backwardness and slavery. The Muslim regimes are divided into two blocs. The Imperialists and the communists are exploiting us. Unless we are self sufficient in industry and technology we cannot free ourselves from the bondage of super-powers. The Muslims are lagging behind in science and technology, while the aim of Islam is the conquest of inner and outer world. It lays stress on space conquest and accelerates human endeavor to achieve better and positive results. We depend upon the west for weapons. We can't crusade against tyrants of the time as we depend upon their arms and diplomacy. For an Islamic Renaissance, hence it is imperative to be free from the clutches of sectarianism, imperialism and communism. All Muslim states must revive the concept of caliphate.

They should have one central assembly, one central army, their own press media and market. Geographical boundaries should be wiped off and ideological ties should be strengthened if we want to survive honorably in world. Let us all sincerely strive for Islamic Renaissance as therein lies our survival.

ISLAMIC POLITICAL THOUGHT

Any edifice erected on the frail and sandy pillars is bound to collapse by the stormy winds and swaying sleet. Culture based on vicious desires, selfish ends, stagnant ideas and hollow rites swiftly lurches down from the pitch of time. A social set up having no moral, human or spiritual foundations can never survive. Such an aimless society is of serpents and scorpions. Diogenes, a Greek philosopher, went out of his home in broad daylight to fetch a man in the jungle of humans with a burning lantern in his hand. When mocked at by short sighted worldly wise men he said that the light of the sun was insufficient to find a human face in the city full of so called human beings. In this way he slapped on the shameless faces of so called civilized and cultured people. Any society missing the grand human values such as nobility, virtuosity, decency, civility, sacrifice, simplicity and sincerity is the society of beasts masqueraded in the shape of humans.

The Western countries make tall claims for liberty but practically they have sucked the blood of the weaker Asian nations like leeches. Colonialism is a gift given to all Asians by the Westerners. Islam neither believes in expansionism nor in colonization. It preaches respect for all mankind whether they are Muslims or non-Muslim. Islamic political thought is democratic. It fully negates selection, nomination or dictatorial attitude in national matters. According to Hobbes the sovereignty lies with the ruler. Locke believed that the power must belong to the majority.

Roussue opined that sovereignty lies with the masses. Karl Marx believed in the government of the proletariat. Plato stood for a philosopher king but in Islam society is only a custodian of the laws of God. They are supposed to implement the laws of God. In Surah Yusuf the Qur'an says: "Judgment is only of Allah." It means that nobody can make law for human beings except God. God is the creator, sustainer and law-maker. The same proposition is again repeated in the 62th verse of Surah Anam (The cattle) of the Qur'an. It says: "His is the judgement". No one can lay down the rules what is good and what is bad. An Irish scholar Professor Clive Staples Lewis in his book, "The Case for Christianity" very lucidly discusses the divine and natural standard of right and wrong. He is of the opinion that like the laws of nature, human nature also has some permanent and universal laws which discriminate man from animals. Islamic culture is based on such positive and progressive laws which keep an equilibrium between its mundane and moral life. On one hand it encourages scientific and rational inquiry and on the other, it enhances man's spirituality. The concept of spirituality in Islam is altogether different from obdurate Christianity, Hindu or Judaic concepts of asceticism or monasticism. Islam is a practical and political religion. It believes in power to implement the rule of God on earth. You cannot enforce Islamic laws and tenets in an un-Islamic society. Islamic culture is a pre-requisite for Islamic polity. The advent of monarchy in the Muslim society was not an adventitious act. The family of Abu Sufyan tactfully mannured demolishing the fabric of Islam.

Islamic spirit of political freedom was fully crushed by these callous tyrants who played havoc in the sacred name of Islam. Even today the Muslim monarchs are playing in the hands of their foreign masters who are bent upon crushing the Muslims. Islam provides full liberty to all whether they are Muslims or non-Muslims. It does not crush human ego. The great Muslim reformers such as Jamal-ud-Din Afghani, Shah Wali Ullah Delhivi, Mohammad Abdahu, Kokabi, Nirwak Mustafa and Dr. Allama Iqbal had been trying to reawaken the slumbered ego of the Muslims and sharpen it against colonialism and imperialism. Not only political liberty, Islam ensures religious freedom to all mankind also. The 256 verse of the Surah Baqara (The Cow), says:

The right way has become clearly distinct from error; therefore, whoever disbelieves in Satan and believes in Allah, he indeed has laid hold on the firmest handle, which shall not break off and Allah is hearing, knowing."
The Qur'an asks the mankind to use reason and lets them free in making that choice. In the 29th verse of the Surah Kahf, (The Cave), the Qur'an says:

"And say: the truth is from your Lord, so let him who pleaseth believe and let him who pleaseth disbelieve."

According to the Qur'an men are free in believing or disbelieving. There is no compulsion upon them. They are only ordained to ponder over the realities and seek for themselves what is good and what is bad. This is the reason Islam does not believe in priesthood as the Christians considered them the custodians of faith in the Medieval Ages. Europe saw the rays of reason after renaissance when puritanism miserably failed. The rational waves blown in Europe led it to the zenith of material and scientific progress. The Muslim world till today is groping like a blind man in the dark dungeons of retrogressive culture based on monarchism, fascism, feudalism, fatalism, quiet and inactive Sufism, parasitism and sectarianism. The Christian priests prohibited people to learn science or use reason. They kept them incarcerated in the suffocating cells of monasticism and ritualism like Hindu pandits. Supernaturalism and superstitions became the order of the day in such societies.

The European renaissance is the product of the Islamic teachings Islam stressed on reason, realism and rationalism. It emphasized on scientific culture. Undoubtedly the Greek civilization was based on democracy and intellect. And the Roman civilization based on militarism and materialism. Any thing out of the range of sense meant a reverie, mirage, hoax or superstition for the Romans. They had materialistic and pregmatic approach towards life. The Greeks believed in intellectual, hellenic and intuitive forces. Plato considered intuition the source of supreme knowledge while Aristotle believed in intellect. Bergson fused both powers and concluded that intuition was a higher form of intellect. But Islam believes in material, intellectual and intuitive powers and gives the due share to all.

Islamic culture is a culture of the full utilization of material forces and spiritual excellences. Revelation is the special trait of the prophets. It is not granted to the non-Prophets as an instruction or as a message to be followed. The materialistic and atheistic theories propounded by Hegel, Darwin, Marx and Sigmond Freud brought upheavels in the moral, psychological and political lives of the people throughout the world.

These immoral theories brought a swarm of oddities and absurdities in human life in the name of so called modern scholasticism and modern ethics. On the other hand Islamic culture emanates and culminates didactic uplift and spiritual apogee. The Holy Prophet says:

"I have been made a prophet to consummate ethics."

In Surah Baqarah (The Cow) in verse 82, the Qur'an announces:

"And (as for) those who believe and do good deeds, these are the dwellers of paradise, in it they shall abide."

The main purpose of the prayer, the fasting and the pilgrimage described in the Qur'an is to purify one's soul and crusade for the establishment of clean, just and pious system and society. The prayer is a means to an end. The end is the establishment of a just and democratic society. Social justice and political freedom are the main sacred ends which Islam desires to establish. There is no room for dogmas and rituals in Islam. Islam is a revolutionary and progressive code of life. In the verse 90 of Surah Nahl (The Bee), Allah ordains:

"Surely Allah enjoins the doing of justice, and the doing of good and the giving to the kindred, and he forbids indecency, evil and rebellion."

In Islamic political system right is might while in an un-Islamic society Might is Right. The Holy Qur'an time and again emphatically announces that the main purpose of the prophet is to establish justice and uproot tyranny and injustice. Nearly about forty four times the word justice has been used in the Qur'an. In the 47th verse of Surah Maidah, the Holy Qur'an says:

"And whoever did not judge by what Allah revealed, those are they that are the transgressors."

The Qur'anic political thought completely vanishes every kind of blemish and smirch from the bright brow of society. Islam is diametrically opposed to fascism, subjection and servility. Islamic culture negates repression, oppression and suppression. It grants liberty to every individual within the frame work of divine law and enhances the spirit of scientific inquiry and democratic culture. Plato in his treatise "The Republic" emphasizes over the maintenance of justice and the Qur'an is very vocal about the supremacy of Justice, hence it says:

"O David! Surely we have made you a ruler in the land, so judge between them with justice and do not follow desire lest it should lead you astray from the path of Allah."

At a place the Qur'an clearly ordains that justice should be done even with enemies. Justice is very dear to God. Justice is the hub and core of the teachings of all prophets. When Hazrat Ali was the Caliph of the Muslims he had to present himself in person before the judge against a Jew. The judge decided the case against Hazrat Ali for the lack of solid evidence. Hazrat Ali kept silent and accepted the judgment. The Jew felt ashamed on his false plea and embraced Islam seeking apology from the Caliph. Such is the spirit of Islam and must be maintained in all cases. Islam does not allow the political victimization of the ideological or political opponents. The history of Muslim monarchy is replete with bloodshed and barbarities. The Muslim monarchs have been mercilessly assassinating their political opponents. There is no trace of stone wall of monarchy, Islam and monarchy and poles apart. They are anti to each other. They are antagonistic in spirit. Alas! The Muslim monarchs have disfigured the pretty face of Islam.

The Qur'an ordains the Holy Prophet for consulting the Ummah in their matters. Islam does not allow dictatorship rather it strictly condemns despotism and monarchism. General consensus is very essential in general affairs. The Qur'an in Surah Aale Imran says:

"And take counsel with them in the affairs."

This Qur'anic verse succinctly shows that the opinion of people in social and political matters is very imperative in a Muslim society. When Hazrat Ali was pressurized to accept caliphate after the assassination of Hazrat Uthman he flatly refused to accept this highest portfolio under dourest or in camera. He said that let all the people gather in the mosque and openly declare their allegiance. "Baiat" means free and fair acceptance of leader or ruler without any greed, fear or pressure. The Holy Qur'an gives us some salient features for leadership. Piety, knowledge, administrative qualities, sound health, bravery and honesty are the basic characteristics of a Muslim leader or ruler. There is no dichotomy between political and spiritual leadership in Islam. Church and state have different functions in a modern Christian society. In modern Muslim societies and states the role of religion has been deleted in State affairs. It is true that Islam does not permit and permeate the role of priesthood in State affairs but it should not be forgotten that any state which does not implement the Qur'anic injunctions in toto is an un-Islamic State. Whether it is a modern or a classical State. The Shia concept of "Imamat" also means the rule and leadership of the progeny of the Holy Prophet for they consider those Holy personalities quite fit on the given merits of the Qur'an. But the concept of their nomination or heritance is objectionable by other Muslim sects. Similarly the concept of "Ijmah" (consensus) or "Jamaath" (party) in the Sunni sect means the rule of the majority which is more a democratic concept but unfortunately the monarchs got support of the Sunni Sect. Islam supports the idea of election through open consensus as Hazrat Ali practiced it in the mosque of Medina on the eve of his caliphate. Under the umbrella of strict meritocracy the righteous people come into power. They neither embezzle nor oppress. They maintain justice.

In Surah Hajj (The Pilgrimage) the Qur'an says:

"Those who, should we establish them in land, will keep up prayer and pay poor rate and enjoin good and forbid evil; and Allah is the end of affairs."

Hence in an Islamic society the culture of spirituality and justice is established. It is a society wherein the poor people are looked after well and they receive their due share for their maintenance and nourishment. Good is promoted and evil is eliminated. Now let us honestly have a look at all Muslim states and find out how many of them are providing economic and social justice to the people and are keeping the standard of virtue up. There is no place for hereditary rule in Islam. The Qur'an says in the Sura Shura (The Counsel),

"And their rule is to take counsel among themselves." Democracy honors the opinion of every individual. In the words of Abraham Lincoln, "Democracy is the government of the people, by the people, for the people". Hence, every individual should be freely permitted to exercise his right to vote anyone whom he likes. Dr. Khalifa Abdul Hakim in his book, "Islamic Ideology" on Page 197 about the freedom of an individual in Islam rights, "Man, therefore, for Islam, is a social and political being; his welfare is in every respect bound up with the welfare of society. The highest organization of society is the state. Islam had to found a state and give to the world in practical form the ideals of statehood." Islam is a social religion. The development of individual ego is of paramount importance but its ultimate aim is to establish a just society. Islamic culture and political thought provide grounds for the establishment of noble and pure society. The theistic culture of Islam negates every kind of idol-worship. The idols of power, pelf, clan, color, creed and class are shattered to pieces. The theistic system of Islam spurts out the light of humanism discarding all inhuman forces. Monotheism in Islam actually means the oneness of mankind. At a place, the Qur'an says:

"The whole of humanity is one community".

The concepts of blind mechanic forces and materialistic dialectics are totally rejected by Islam. Materialism permeates fascism and despotism. When a man thinks that there is no life hereafter then no law and morality can check him from crimes and atrocities. Islamic culture is based on divinity and spirituality which stop man to commit heinous acts and odious schemes. Islamic culture promotes material progress but it rejects matter adoration and material history of mankind. Marxian notion of history has no place in Islam. The Qur'anic explanation of human history is ideology oriented record of mankind. Without vision and spiritual uplift there is no concept of nation in Islam. Man plays vital role in the making of mankind but man is not an object of adoration. Man is the best creation of God and enjoys pivotal reverence in the universe. He is a co-worker with God and master of the natural objects but he must not overlook the reality of being subservient to the will of God. As soon as the stars obey the Natural law man has to obey the divine law. If he is led astray from the right path or casts aspersions on the sacred mission of the prophets then he is doomed to condemnation. By acting on divine law it can be said that Islam is a social and divine democracy. Socio-divine democracy is a term which may aptly suit the Islamic political system. When we say Islam is a social democracy by this it is meant that Islam rejects monarchy and despotism and promotes social justice and freedom respecting all individuals. When we say that Islam is a divine democracy by it we mean that Islamic values and laws must be established in a Muslim polity and no party, parliament or person can change the fundamental laws of the Qur'an. Islamic jurisprudence can only bring change or introduce innovations in the social, political or economic matters according to time keeping the universal and everlasting message and laws of the Qur'an. "Ijtehad" is very essential factor of Muslim society. Islamic culture remains intact and fresh if the principal of movement exercises. Stagnancy and ignorance are social evils and must be abandoned in an Islamic society. The Muslims and non-Muslims enjoy the fruits of justice in an Islamic society. The men and women have equal rights as human beings and there is no racial difference in Islam. Islam has given great respect and protection to women folk. If there is any apparent difference in some matters such as the law of inheritance and evidence or some other matters it is because of their physique, psychology and social requirements. As there is difference between the physical constitution of male and female, similarly there is difference between the psychology of man and woman. Hence their tastes, needs and jobs are different. The law of primogeniture, according to which only the eldest son inherits the entire estate is abolished in Islam. Hoarding, accumulation of wealth, bribery and adulteration are strictly prohibited in an Islamic state. Noble and just culture greatly and gravely influences the Islamic polity.

Besides social and economic factors the idea of the finality of prophethood of Hazrat Muhammad provides the foundational stone for the formation of Muslim culture.

After shutting the door of revelation, the doors of reason and scientific inquiry and inquisition have been opened. Allama Iqbal about the finality of the Holy Prophet of Islam comments in his famous English treatise, "The Reconstruction of Religious Thought in Islam" that after shutting the door of revelation God opened the door of reason. Inductive intellect has been introduced by Islam to solve the time to time problems. Islamic culture is a scientific culture. Whims, whimsicalities, rites and rituals have no room in an Islamic society. According to the Qur'an, Nature, History and Reason are the main inductive and scientific sources to learn and act. The Greek culture was based on speculation and deduction. But unfortunately the Muslim states have been under the evil spell of Greek fatalism and obscurantism. Gib in his book "Islam" and Watt Montgomery in his famous books "Muhammad at Mecca", and "Muhammad at Medina", elaborately discuss the primitive Arab tribal society. The Arabs were proud of their tribalism but Islam broke all the fetters of tribes and introduced monotheism and universalism. The tribal culture is still a great hindrance in the way of genuine and ideal Islamic democracy. In a nutshell it can be deduced that Islamic culture is based on humanism, spiritualism, rationalism and provides grounds for Islamic political thought.

ISLAMIC CULTURE

So far as the quest for sublimity of the culture of labor is concerned Islam stands quite distinct on the dignity of human labor. The concepts of culture, civilizations, art, artisanship, intellect and labor are so variegated that it needs the Marathon to elaborate. Art and artisanship are universal phenomenon but their expression and manifestations change in different connotations lending themselves to various doctrinal, practical and ideological expositions like Islamic culture, Marxian culture and European culture. In West Spengler, Sigmond Freud, Bertrand Russell, Land Toynbee are known stalwarts for their cultural theories. Culture and civilization are two different things. Civilization is a progressed and advanced stage and shape of culture. The cultures which keep pace with this progressive movement flourish, grow and advance. But the cultures lagging behind ultimately extinct like the traces and tracks on sands. Such non-progressive and retrogressive cultures are called fossilized, representing the cultures of antique rustics who lived in the caves in the Stone Age.

Culture is like a forest and civilization is like a cultivated farm or like a well trimmed garden. Any act or activity which is unpolished and is in primitive form is the part of culture. But when we cut and polish the rough and rugged diamond of culture it becomes the part of civilization. Nature provides us raw material like clay but we make utensils out of that clay. When we co-work with nature and create, we pave the road of civilization. An artisan shapes the rough and raw material and makes beautiful objects by the magic wand of his skill and brilliance. Cultures which are non-progressive, non-revolutionary and unnatural are like the out-dated and out-worn relics preserved in a museum. Simply it can be said a culture grows like mushrooms and herbs but when the grass is mowed and the lawn is decorated, beautified and trimmed by a gardener it looks beautiful like an advanced and modern civilization.

In our native language we use the word "Thaqafat" for culture and Tahdhif for civilization. "Tamaddan" is also used which has no proper equivalent word in English. The Arabic word "Tahdhib" means to beautify, embellish or improve a thing. It is an external experience which is called extroversion. The Arabian word "Thaqafat" means acquisition of all higher learning, both arts and sciences. It is related to the mental, psychic and intuitive aspects of man and is closer to the introversion. "Tamaddan" includes the culture and civilization of a nation and is the highest and the finest stage of human development. When the external and internal aspects mix at nobler, humane and grand level we call that nation a mature, civilized, great and grand nation. The basic culture of all humans is one and the same. It is based on the natural, volitional, instinctive and climatic factors. All humans dress up. But with the change in climate people wear different dresses. Wearing a dress is "thaqafat", i.e. culture but variety in dresses in "tahdhib", i.e. civilization. In the same way we have Islamic culture and Islamic civilization. All Muslims believe in wearing modest dress. They reject and condemn exposure of limbs ordained to be concealed. Obscinity and nudity are strictly prohibited in Islam. To wear modest dress is the common culture of all Muslims. But the variety and difference in the dress fashion of different Muslims inhabiting in different countries is their cultural expression and is not the civilizational difference for Islamic civilization is one and is based on Islamic ideology. The geographical, climatic or the linguistic differences cannot change the basic ideology of Islam. The basic Islamic do's and don'ts remain uniformly same irrespective of change in territory or period of time. Despite the manifestations of external difference or variety of Muslim culture we find complete agreement and unity in Muslim culture and craftsmanship. Islamic culture creates inner unity, unison and uniformity. For instance, a European sculptor carves out a beautiful statue with sexual or esoteric intentions and manifestation. The nudity has been accepted the integral part of Western culture. But when a Muslim sculptor carves out a statue he will not like to exploit the sexual aspect of the art because Islam has strictly proscribed nudity. Similarly the Muslim artisans make handicrafts which satisfy our needs and aesthetic sense but do not violate ethical norms. Islam stresses on the need of unity in diversity for the existence of a healthy and strong nation.

If the Muslim Ummah is united it is a cultured and civilized facet and phase of nation. But if it is disintegrated, disunited and divided into different sections, sets, tribes, clans, classes and cults, it is severely condemned by Islam. The Holy Qur'an says: "How many small groups have conquered larger groups, with the permission of God". It means that a disarrayed and undisciplined nation has no culture. Unity, discipline, modesty and the nobility are the basic traits of Islamic culture. This basic formula unites us all and gives the concept of Muslim community. We are all brethren-in-faith.

In the South Asia the different cultures consisting of different dresses, different languages, different colors, different religions and different nationalities exist. Even in Pakistan and Kashmir we have various cultures. In external manifestation we may differ but in internal manifestation we are one. We have inner cultural cohesion and unity and that is our Pakistani or Kashmiri civilization. Similarly different Muslim countries may have different cultures but their civilization is one and that is Islamic civilization. Here I must mention that some of the Islamic coun-

tries have adopted Western culture and they feel proud of that.
But all the serious thinkers of the West are disturbed on the plight
of so-called Western modern civilization. Dr. Allama Iqbal after
deeply studying the Western culture had aptly said:
"Your civilization will commit suicide with your own hands.
The nest made on a weak birch will be undurable".

Islam has laid great stress on the dignity of man through labor and nobility. A great British writer Ruskin preferred manual
work to intellectual work. He names it as Hand work and Head
work but Islam has its clear concept of labor. It respects both;
manual work and intellectual work. History tells us that Noah
was a carpenter. David was a blacksmith. Our Holy Prophet
used to mend his shoes, sewed his clothes and milked his goats.
He worked with his hands and honored the laborer by saying,
"Worker is the friend of God."

Under the same spell and spirit of Islamic tenets in Spain the
Mosque of Cordova and the palace Al-Homara are the master-
pieces of the Islamic art of the Abbasid period. In the Sub-Continent the Taj Mahal, the Red Fort, the Shahi Mosque and the Tomb
of Jehangir represent the Muslim Mughal Art. In Kashmir Shah-
e-Hamdanfor the preaching of Islam, had brought seven hundred artisans with him.

ISLAM AND PEACE

There are two plausible forces in the world. The force of reason and the force of rod. Man is superior to all other creatures
for being a social or logical entity. Whenever a crisis arises between two persons, if they are reasonable, tolerant, cultured and
humane they will find the solution of that problem in a civilized
and legal way. But if they are illiterate, uncultured, irrational,
immodest and illogical the dagger or gun will decide their future. Similarly, whenever a dispute arises between two nations
they must listen to each other's view-point and act according to
the laws of reason, responsibility and fraternity. If one country
acts aggressively all the other countries should immediately come
forward to cease aggression. Aggression must be stopped by all
means. Peace is the best policy. Peace is religion and religion is
peace. After going through the pages of history one is convinced
that war is not the solution of any problem. War creates more

problems. Hegel's inclination towards war to test the mettle of the nations and to keep up their moral and cognizance is based on militant philosophy emanating discord and bloodshed of mankind. It may be the war of Troy, or Iran-Iraq war, the consequences of war are horrible and disastrous. It suffers the stability, tranquility and peace. Only the logical and humanistic attitude can enhance peace and prosperity. Knot-headed bums and empty minded nuts accelerate and engineer ignorance, cruelty, immodesty and laceration. The whole world can become the cradle of happiness if people learn to live reasonably and honestly. The Islamic concept of Monotheism believes in one God which means all mankind is like one family, Islam has strongly condemned polytheism. The reason being to stop the division of humans on religious basis. All prophets came for the reformation of Man and to link mankind with one God. We are the creatures of one God, then why we should kill others in the name of creed, class, color or clan. These all petty differences must be shunned to uplift the noble and grand cause of humanity.

After the destruction of societies in First World War and Second World War the thinking men all over the world felt the dire need of United Nations Organization. After the failure of the League of Nations the men of conscience and consciousness did not halt and kept on searching means and ways to establish peace in the world. The very idea of UNO signifies the importance of peace through mutual negotiations and conferences. In early days the concept of Jirga in our tribal society fulfilled the requirement. The elderly people used to decide the matters through dialogues and consensus. Today, the disputes of Kashmir, Bosnia Herzegovina and Palestine are like volcanoes which can blast the edifice of human life. The numerous casualties which took place in Afghanistan could not bring the ray of amity and peace but the Geneva Accord lit the candle of peace in the dark dome of affairs. The humans should not act like bullying dogs. They should behave like dulcet doves in the gardens of civility. They can also behave like lions but they should know that the lions never attack unless they are attacked. Man is the vicegerent of God and is bound to love his fellow beings. The arson, loot, plunder, rape, murder and maiming is strictly prohibited in all religions. The spirit of all religions is the same. No religion permits or encourages bloodshed. All interpretations to shed blood are self-coined interpretations. Islam ordains not to kill the children, the women and the elderly lot. It strictly ordains to fight with those who fight with you. It stops aggression and transgression. Even the cattle and fruit trees of the conquered land are not permitted to be cut or killed. The Westerners who brand Islam as a ferocious force or aggressive religion are at fault. The very meanings of Islam are of peace for mankind and submission to God. The whole of mankind is like one community is a glorious verse of the Holy Qur'an exhibiting the truth that we should decide our matters and settle our differences like brothers. We are like the sacred family of Lord. He is our Creator, Sustainer, Benefactor and Master. We are all sons of Adam and Eve and are made of clay. None is made of silver or gold. We must respect and love each other. Money, territory, ideology and apprehensions should not be the cause of conflict. Power should be attained to protect the powerless. Power should not be attained to crush the powerless. Logic must rule. Law must supercede. Missiles, cartridges, bombs and guns must be thrown into the sea. Men should behave like men, not like beasts. Cold war leads to hot war. All prides and prejudices must be shunned. Conference rooms should be erected and battlefields should be turned into playgrounds where in our future generations can skip like fawns without the fear of death.

The worst thing is the narrow-mindedness of the believers of different religions The religious people always try to convert others to their faith. For this conversation they sometimes use propaganda tactics. Sometimes bribe peoples, sometimes convince them and sometimes pressurize them. In my opinion a good Muslim is a good human being. A good Christian is a good human being. Similarly people belonging to different clans and creeds should try to be good human beings. They should protect human rights and human values. The historical tragedy is that people have never acted upon the tenets of their religions but they have always criticized the religion of others and have branded others as non-believers, hence liable to damnation and slaughter. Not only the religionists have condemned each other, they within the fold of their own religion have subdivided their brethren-in-faith. Suppose in Muslims there have been two main sects, viz., the Shias and the Sunnis. They have been criticizing and killing each other for centuries. They never tried to implement Islamic code of life on real and scientific lines. They did not prove to be model Muslims. Their all stress had been on proving each other as infidel or a strayed ones. Nowadays the Sunnis and the Wahabis are at daggers drawn. This is the tragedy with the religion and with the followers of the religion.

Similarly the history of the Christians is full of conflicts on minor sectarian differences. The Catholics and the Protestants had been at loggerheads to prove the verity of their faiths. I believe that instead of striking head with the sandy walls of speculations and beliefs one should elevate the soul with spiritual and human values.

Faith plays vital role in the making of an individual and society, but faith does not mean whims, whimsicalities, cults, rituals, customs and baseless and self-fabricated non-scientific beliefs. Faith in God and Man can save us from the negative approach towards religion. The positivity of religion lies in unity of mankind. Positive faith unites and negative faith disunites mankind. Let all humans behave positively. We should make our character firm. We should not dodge others. We should not speak lies. We should not commit adultery and adulteration. We should not steal. We should not commit murder. We should avoid looting, bribery and backbiting. If we are good human beings we will live like one happy family. If we are not good human beings we will live as the cattle live in a stable. Let the mankind live with peace. Tolerate and respect each others' ideas and beliefs for a lovely and peaceful world.

ISLAM AND UNIVERSALISM

The origin of Islam is "Salama" which means peace or obedience. Islam is neither a dogma nor a vague vagary. It is a complete code of conduct. "Verily, the whole of humanity is one community" is a verse of the Holy Qur'an, portraying the ultimate goal and introspective spirit of Islam. Islam grants justice and uproots inequity. It is severely inimical to all the foes of mankind. It does not permit inequity of the weak by the strong. It ensures dignity and freedom to every individual. It has no boundaries, discriminations and distinctions on the basis of color, creed, caste or class. The concept of oneness of God actually means the unity of all people. I would like to quote a verse of the

Holy Qur'an that succinctly exhibits the cosmopolitanic verity of Islam.

"Surely, the believers and the Jews and the Christians and the Sabians whichever party from among these truly believes in Allah and the last day and does good deeds shall have their reward with their Lord, and no fear shall have come upon them, nor shall they grieve." (The Holy Qur'an, 2:62). The critics who have not understood the humanistic message of Islam, unfortunately have tried to deride its actual position by giving derogatory comments about it. But it is the matter of great dishonesty on the part of some occidental writers on Islam that they have deliberately distorted its message for their inherent spite and scoff against Islam. I am also aware of the fact of Islam's presentation in the form of conglomeration of spiritless rites by some of our Muslim theologians which resulted in the form of general boycott and departure from religion of our younger generation and scientific minded people. "Time is God, do not vilify it", is a famous saying of the Holy Prophet depicting the progressive attitude of Islam about our day-to-day life. The majority of our priests like the priests of other hollow religions have fallen a prey to orthodoxy. The hegemony of hetrodoxy is the dire need of our era to implement the true spirit of Religion. If we give a serious thought to the message of the Qur'an, we would not find a shred of doubt in its being a universal code of conduct. Islam is not Mohammadanism as described by some of the western writers. Buddhism is called after the name of Buddha and similar is the case with some other religions. But according to the Qur'an Hazrat Abraham (Peace be upon him), gave the name Islam to the divine code of Allah.

Even the message of Adam, Jacob, Moses, David, Noah and Jesus Christ was the message of Islam because it was the revealed code of God for mankind. As these prophets came in different ages hence according to the needs of time they brought new commandments based upon the ultimate truths which had been the same throughout. The Qur'an is the last message of God having sound foundations and basic Principles for all times to come. The principle of movement in Islam is a vital factor to keep it in pace with the fast moving steed of time. The basic laws of Islam are invariable. They cannot perish by the strokes of time and clime. They have to be implemented if we want constant peace and parity. All the prevalent conflict and conflagration is because we have coined an imperialistic Islam which is quite contrary to the Islam of Allah. Its all injunctions and precepts are natural and humane. It wanes the animality in man and waxes the human instinct. Its universality lies in its being the soother of all mankind.

Bilal Habashi was a colored slave but for his richness in faith and firmness of character, he became the caller of the prayers and was very dear to the Holy Prophet. He had a special place in the heart of the Holy Prophet and a distinguished seat in the companions of the savior of Humanity. The sermon delivered by the Holy Prophet on his last Pilgrimage is an insurmountable testimony and testament of the universality of Islam. In his last sermon the Holy Prophet clearly proclaimed: "No Arab has any superiority over a non-Arab and the white have no superiority over black. If there is any superiority of one over the other, it is only and only because of piety." Can the philosophers of the east and west present better motto than this? Can the world bring more precious words than the words of the Holy Prophet which reflect the rays of the universal glow of Islam?

Islam is a peace loving religion. The Holy Prophet had never attacked any tribe. He never initiated war. He was forced to fight against the enemies of Humanity and Justice who were the leaders of their tribes and were exploiting the illiterate paupers in the name of idols. The Holy Prophet always avoided war and when ever war was thrust upon him, his sincere and brave companions fought but he never took the sword in his own hands claiming that he had been sent by God to be kind and merciful to the whole of humanity. His peace loving policy was the product of the following verse of the Holy Qur'an in which Allah has clearly announced: "And if they incline towards peace, incline then also toward it, and put the trust in Allah. Surely, it is He who is all-hearing, all-knowing." There are some western critics who scathe Islam by branding it a militant and aggressive religion and propagate that Islam has been spread by sword. Actually they forget the fact that when the Holy Prophet announced the divine mission the demagogues and plunderers stood against him. They knew that he had stood for justice, freedom and truth. All worshippers of the Gospel of Mammon mustered to eradicate the sapling of Islam which they knew eventually would take the form of a fruitful tree. Time and again the Qur'an has reiterated its claim to have peaceful negotiations with the mischief-mongers. On the day of "Mobahila" when the famous Jew scholars wanted to have a dialogue with the Holy Prophet they were tongue-tied and amazed to see a divine grace on the countenance of the Holy Prophet. Peace is indivisible and if we want to have a balance between our material and spiritual needs we must look for the high ideals of Islam. It takes us to the dale of purity and parity. It aspires to fathom the secrets of the seas and capture the glisten of the stars and the rays of the sun. Undoubtedly science has a universal appeal and importance. Scientific discoveries are not the asset of one group of people. It is for the benefit of general mankind. Science has a universal outlook. Islam is a scientific religion. On one hand it tells us how to exercise command over the heavens and the earth. On the other hand it gives us the principles of politics, economy, law, jurisprudence, ethics and sociology. Islam teaches discipline and self-evaluation. It proscribes sloth and prescribes love. It tarnishes Nationalism and enhances cosmopolitanism. The universal spirit of Islam accelerates its followers to strive for the maintenance of justice and peace.

The idea of one state propounded by Bertrand Russell is not his original idea. It is in fact, the preaching of Islam to have one state, on the basis of natural necessity. Hegel's theory of necessity ejects untoward consequences if it is implemented with out caring for negative and positive values. Any thing which harms the personality or an individual or damages the higher objectives of society is sin and must not be permitted to flourish or flower. Every pioneer of humanity is bound to flunk and fluctuate without standing over the sound grounds of natural positivity. The dream of universalism can never become a reality unless we draw the line of demarcation between Vice and Virtue. "Nothing is good or bad only thinking makes it so" is of course a beautiful poetic line of Shakespeare, but it is not a logical maxim. Good is good and bad is bad. In Jew of Malta, Shakespeare deriding religion says: "I count religion but a childish toy, And hold there is no sin but ignorance?" undoubtedly ignorance is a sin but it is not the only sin. There are other sins also which Shakespeare overlooked.

A malevolent act cannot be applauded whether committed

overtly or covertly. If poison is fatal for one man, it should also e fatal for the life of another man. By applying inductive method we can deduce the indifference that the majority of men die by taking poison. If some one does not die by taking poison or poison helps him in getting rid of his disease he may be treated an exceptional case with a disease. All healthy men are bound to have bad effect upon their health by taking poison. Exceptions can not be the base of general laws. There can be no exception in the laws of nature except the show of a Miracle which is super natural outwardly but quite natural inwardly. Miracle is not a fantasy. It is a reality. Suppose we read in the history of the prophets that when Hazrat Abraham was thrown in flames he was not burnt and the fire brands were turned to ashes. Is it scientific? Yes it is. According to the physicists every flame has three layers. The outer layer gives heat, the central layer ejects smoke and the inner most layer produces coldness. Had not this layer existed in every flame the fire brands would never have turned to ashes. When the intensity of outer layer is deeper than the intensity of the inner most layer the fire remains burning otherwise it goes out. When Hazrat Abraham was thrown in fire the creator of all elements and substances ordered the outer layer to eject less heat and the inner most layer was ordered to eject more coldness. In a twinkling of an eye, the fire went cut. Now a question arises that if it is a material world being run by a blind force and no sane designer is controlling it then the flames should have burnt Abraham. The control over all natural laws by a super power clearly tells that there is a creator who can make and unmake, shape and reshape. If somebody says that the event of Abraham is just false story and not a fact then he is denying the history of sages. But as I have already mentioned that exceptions cannot be taken as rules, hence we have to construct our fabric of society on the pillars of natural principles. For example in taste or liking we can have differences or variations but that is the second nature of man which is actually the outcome of his environments, climate, diet and social taboos. The laws of human nature are unchangeable like the laws of Nature. We can find some difference in the degree of their appliance but generally there can be no difference in their kind. For example, when a kettle is put on fire the water in it is bound to boil at a certain degree. The difference of boiling point can differ with the difference of place or height, but it is beyond question that water boils up when given heat.

In the same way there are certain things which belong to the first nature of man and others that belong to his second nature. Every man likes mercy and peace because it is in his first nature but why then do people behave mercilessly and barbarically. It depends upon the external forces that force him to behave inhumanly. Islam lays special stress on man's first nature and also provides all facilities to keep the second nature in harmony with the first nature. This is the reason there is no dichotomy in Islam. The laws of vice and virtue apply to the first nature of man. As the first nature of all human beings is one and the same throughout the world, hence Islam lays down eternal and universal laws which are beyond the strokes of change. Appetite is a human instinct. When a man feels hungry he has to take some food. Now what he eats depends upon his taste. So far as taste is concerned he is free to eat whatsoever he likes. But whether he eats something that benefits his body and mind or harms his body and mind is that important point from where the question of good and bad arises. In life one has to be very careful about his deeds. The deeds which harm us are illegal and the deeds which are advantageous for our personality are legal. Islam intends to establish a universal society on the basis of natural and legal deeds. Everything un-Islamic is unnatural because Islam is a natural and scientific code of life. Universality is harmed if we mix unnatural with natural; vice with virtue and good with bad while harping on the idiotic strings that nothing is good or bad only thinking makes it so. Every action has a reaction and no cause is without effect. If we sow wheat how can we harvest barley? Good deeds sooner or later effect humanity positively and bad deeds ultimately mar the whole circumference of civilization. In the light of negativity and positivity of ideas and deeds we can establish a universal society.

For that universal community we will have to step forward in the light of the Islamic principle of movement. For the replenishment and revival of the Islamic spirit the modern commentator of the Qur'an should not ignore the promises of our supersonic age. The religion which is stagnant or retrogressive dies its own natural death. Most probably for this reason "Ijtihad" is one of the fundamental principles of Islam. As the edifice of

Islam stands on sound foundations, the construction of further storeys must not be suspended. Islamic concept of universalism lies in its being a dynamic and vital code of conduct. The fundamentals had been given in the light of first nature which is universal and everlasting but the subsidiary tenets can be altered with the alteration of time. It has full faith in the basic and natural needs of men. It neither believes in asceticism nor encourages the greed of pelf and power. Islam stands for the legal and natural fulfillment of every man's basic needs. It neither crushes man's individuality like communism nor exploits the poor class as the capitalists do. It does not provide illicit methods or means for their satisfaction. Under the parasol of law man has full freedom to act according to his free will. When a man starts curbing or annulling the will and freedom of others to satiate his roguish desires in the name of so called liberty, Islam does not appreciate such kind of derision and delusion. Liberty is not without limits. A river flows freely but has certain limits to make a river and keep it flowing forever. When a river crosses its limitations it sways the menfolk like the straws of dry grass towards the dale of death.

The modern western concept of liberty is a big farce and a malignant conspiracy against the existence of every civil and human value. Islamic concept of liberty is universal because it is based on the innate positive values. It goes side by side with the individualistic uplift as well as with the sense of social responsibility. If the western thinkers and governments permit open kissing of girls and boys even in the university campuses as I have seen in England and America then what can be the next step of this so-called liberty except open sexual intercourse on the road sides or in the class rooms. Some of the so-called free thinkers of the world do not like that there should be any impediment of free sex. Russell even did not believe in wearing dress. His naturalism has badly effected some of the younger generation of the west.

I am told that in California there is a place where some of the young American couples ramble nakedly and they have made their society in which any man can become a member, provided he puts off the clothes. A friend of mine was just joking with me last night, persuading me to go and talk to the members of that society. I said: "Am I supposed to talk to them in dress, or without a dress?" He laughed and said, "They won't talk to you unless you are undressed." Now my friends you tell me where to go and what to do? The simple answer to all these questions is that we will have to establish an Islamic society in which natural and universal rights are ensured.

A libertine can say what is the harm in having a naked society or doing sex openly? The short answer to this question is "Are we trying to become gentle and good human beings or are we following the foot tracks of animals?" I believe that man has a part of animality in hum but he can not be graded as animal for that part while ignoring the major part of humanity in him. If the sexual desire in man is taken as the main drive and center of his deeds and personality and we boast to be the Freudian even then sex has certain rules and responsibilities. We can never establish a universal society on such ignoble and immoral concepts. Have you ever noticed so many dogs running after a bitch for sex? Have you ever seen the way pigs behave for sexual satisfaction?

If some of the so-called modern thinkers have decided to change our society in to dogs and pigs, then they should be ready to meet the fate of pigs and dogs. Universality lies in the respect of other's freedom with the freedom of every individual. It is an axiomatic fact that Islam has strongly abhorred the idea of amputating humanity into bits on such trivial and foolish concepts. The Holy Prophet once said: "We all belong to Adam and Adam was made of Clay." This saying means that the whole of humanity is one and must have one code of life. The Islamic concept of fraternity lies in its demand for one society on the basis of natural rules. No other religion or ism has given us crystal clear rules and regulations about life as Islam has done. The motto of Islam is that we all are the sons of Adam and Eve and must live like brothers. At a place the Holy Qur'an exhorts: "Lest the enmity of one Tribe or nation keeps you away from the path of justice and righteousness." Islam wants to see justice to be done even with one's enemies. The first and the foremost principle of Islamic universalism lies in its concept of "Tawhid". Oneness of God vicariously serves the purpose of oneness of Mankind. By bowing before God one is freed from the worship of all demigods. When the whole of humanity is supposed to prostrate before one God then there should be no reason for division and dissension of Mankind.

Communism raised the slogan of God's negation by taking it the root cause of all strife's and problems but it also failed in establishing any universal society. It may flower or fade out the future of Mankind is not in the hands of communism for its spiritless and dictatorial set-up. I am of the opinion that the negative concept of God has provided that chance to the communists to utter slander about God. For the same negative approach towards God we are lagging behind in achieving our spiritual destination. If we are serious in establishing a universal society we all will have to take permanent refuge in the universal message of Islam through the service of Mankind and positive concept of Almighty Allah. When we worship the gods of money, power, state or self made idols we actually incur vindictiveness and violence for each other. Islam gives great importance to man by nominating him as the vicegerent of Allah upon the Earth. Man is more important than the dogmas. Man must not bow before man. We all are the servants of God and no one is the serf of the other. Islam diametrically opposes the idea of political subjugation or economic exploitation of man by man.

An Islamic concept of universalism lies in keeping a balance between political and economic system. The world divided into two super blocs in a lop-sided world. The capitalists claim to grant political liberty but without granting economic parity. The communists boast of their so called economic equity but are mute over their political accessories. Islam provides natural justice to everyone irrespective of the fact who they are and to which race or territory they belong.

FRATERNAL ELEMENT IN ISLAM

It is customary in the occidental circles to brand Islam as a militant religion assaulting upon other people and forcing them to succumb to its tenets. But it is totally the wrong interpretation of Islam. It is only done with ulterior motives. Islam is a very tolerant and peace abiding religion. It is an accommodative cult having religious coexistence. It is not a religion in Western sense in which dogmas and superstitions are taken as religious rudiments. It is a code of life unifying all its various standards we are able to visualize as a code of conduct. This code of conduct enables the whole world to pay its liege to this sanctimony bestowed to the Holy Prophet's life. There is a great charade in the world about the inherent character of this God chosen, man-proclaimed religion. But no one can deny the fact that the world was sunk in a camouflage of sin, sacrilege, idolatry, prejudice and grief at the advent of Islam. The practical life of the Prophet of Islam is a beacon of light for the dark and dreary menfolk till doomsday. The last sermon of the Holy Prophet is the beginning of the first step of every man, woman and child. As such, it was the declaration of freedom for the masses for the uplift of character to revolutionize the whole world. A believer is a man who has his own share of the divine. Divine only ALLAH is but the believer is the base. He is capable of creating that fundamental framework from which has arisen every Islamic glory and grandeur. The Holy Prophet of Islam was very atrociously treated by his brethren in Makkah but see his munificence and amnesty how he forgave each and every one after conquering Makkah. He marched into Makkah as a citizen not as a Lord. As such human values which had degenerated and decomposed due to the valueless civilizations of the others under the guidance of the one who was fatherless, brotherless and sonless, the world gained the shadow of benevolence that can never again be created in this selfish and servile world of give and take. The prophet enlivened the deadened spirit of the female species and bestowed that flamboyance of cordiality and civility which is unprecedented. Hazrat Bilal was a Negroid. He was a slave also but when he entered the fold of Islam, all were like brothers. His voice even made the stars to weep at night. As such who can deny the fraternal bond that the Holy Prophet tied to elevate the burden of the strangulate of animosity, hatred and discord that had torn the fabric of human relationship to tatters. The women who used to throw garbage upon him when he saw she did not throw dirt upon his pathway, he visited, inquired her health and thus won her to the fold of Islam.

The personality of the Holy Prophet was such that in that vast, deep desert of Arabia a place which was filled with greatness, grace, peace and liberality won the whole area as his friends and compatriots. What could be a more open impression of his universal religion and personality which to the dead shrubs of human passions gave the water of his benign character and raised up the tree of Islamic universal idealism. This idealism is a subsidiary development which embraced the whole world in the clasp of its verity, vision and validity. The Holy Prophet was a man alone in the vast aura of existence, a torch bearer to all who summoned not only men but angels and genie to the worth of his teaching. He never preached, he taught and practiced. He was a living example. His exemplary life is a model for mankind for ever. The example of right conduct and upright character that he has left as an emblem of divine guidance is the one that shall remain till the end of time. The Prophet's exceptional being was such that fraternity, brotherhood and love grew out of the relationships of human beings. They turned into a unity, one unity. One I say because prior to Islam there were minor unities now a major and single devoted assembly arose in the human fold that is called the Ummah. The word Ummah is derived from the root "amm" which has the sense of path and intention. We are Muslim Ummah. We are not Islamic Ummah as we have, hitherto, have not implemented Islam as a complete code of life. As being the last Prophet, he is the leader of all mankind. As such who do not follow his footprints are strayed and lost in their own blind alleys. So the fraternity created by Islam is a fraternity that shall remain forever. He is a leading light not only to the Muslims but those not under his shadow to ask for his light. Thomas Carlyle in 'Heroes and Hero worship' places this last prophet as the only hero who has left his mark upon history. Goethe, a great German poet and philosopher and Bernard Shah, a successful English playwright paid rich tributes to the philanthropist in the personality of the Prophet.

Islam preaches tolerance. It does not oppress or subjugate any people. If a nation is over run by a militant Muslim power they are dealt with humanely. The humanism and love of man that is a Muslim criterion is all alone in the world of religious discrepancy. For example, in Spain no church was desecrated when the Muslims gained power. The poor and the citizens of the land were dealt with as men, not as animals. The Christian women were neither insulted nor molested. The children were spared and no non-Muslim was incarcerated or killed.

In Al-Baqarah, verse 62, the Qur'an ordains:

"Surely, the Believers and the Jews, and the Christians and the Sabians whichever party from among these truly believes in

Allah and the Last Day and does good deeds shall have their reward with their Lord and no fear shall come upon them, nor shall they grieve."

Islam enhances and furnishes an evidence of universal attitude. Ethnic and racial prides of prejudices are completely exterminated. The Holy Prophet proclaimed:

"No Arab has any superiority over a non-Arab and the white have no superiority over black. If there is any superiority of one over another, it is only and only because of piety".

We can reckon the degree of Islamic fraternity by the fact that the Holy Prophet wrote numerous letters to different rulers including the rulers of Rome and Persia exhorting them to maintain justice in their states and immediately end aggression upon their subjects. For his followers, he also said:

"The Muslim is one from whose tongue and hand all mankind is safe."

The people who criticize Islam by branding it the religion of sword actually shun their eyes from realities. Islamic concept of "Jehad" or crusade is only defensive. Islam is not an offensive religion. It preaches kindness, parity and piety. The Holy Qur'an ordains:

"Call them to the way of the Lord with wisdom and good admonition" (16:125).

Rational and scientific approach to solve the human problems is the hub and crux of all Islamic teachings. Islam stands for Justice. The Qur'an says:

"O, believers, be securer of justice, witness for God. Let not detestation for a people move you not to be equitable. Be equitable that is nearer to God-fearing" (5:8).

For maintaining justice the Qur'an is very particular. It ordains to do justice not only to human beings but to cattle, chattel, birds and trees as well. Islam says when you confront an enemy fight with steadfastness but do not follow the man who flees from the battle field. Do not cut the fruit trees or spoil the crops of the conquered nation. Do not kill their children or women. Do not insult anyone. Only fight with their youths who fight with you. Can any religion or ideology present a better code of war than presented by Islam? It is a living miracle that people are attracted to Islam by its pure, inherent, magnetic, rational, natural, logical and humane appeal while it cherishes no backing of huge missionary corporations. Islam has fallen a prey to inner conflicts and clashes. Sectarianism is the greatest ailment, which is weakening the healthy body of Islam. We will have to hold the cord of Allah collectively and tightly. As the teachings of Islam are in complete compatibility and consonance with the laws of nature the people all over the world are being gravitated to its simple and logical principles. It is not a new religion but it is a divinely executed combination of all old revealed and divine verities and tenets. The very Arabic word Islam is derived from 'Salama' which means obedience and peace. Obedience means that its votary should only obey the commands of Allah and should surrender his will before the will of Allah. None should be adored except God. NO one is his partner. He alone is the creator of the universe. We seek succor and guidance from Him. Peace means that the followers of Islam should foster and maintain fraternal relations with all human beings. This peace is two fold. On one hand, it provides its followers moral, spiritual and psychological peace and on the other hand it makes its followers to achieve the utmost progress in all world matters and material sources. If we go through Torah (The Old Testament), Zaboor (Psalms) and Injeel (The Bible), and the Holy Qur'an with the desire to deduce the cardinal codes and the spirit of these revealed books we find that these scriptures have candidly given the message of God's adoration and Man's service. The people like Karl Marx, Hume and Russell discarded religion on the basis of its being injurious for a healthy human society. They were of the opinion that religious dissects, disrupts and divides mankind. So they opined that religion should be finished and let the coming generations be free from the fetters of religions. To this humbly I would like to submit that religion is not the factor of dissent or dissention. It is the misuse of religion that has created all disturbances. If you have a gun in your hands, you can face aggression or kill an innocent man. It is the use of gun that matters. There are several factors such as color, class or country which have brought havoc to mankind.

These are the real factors which damage the noble cause of the unity of mankind. Religion is an artificial factor. The misuse of religion by its sham custodians is negativity of religion that breeds prejudice, discord, division, bloodshed and injustice, while the positivity of religion burnishes love, fraternity, virtue, peace and human dignity. The Monotheistic concept of God in Islam fortifies the concept of oneness of all human beings. There can be no permanent peace without sticking to the concept of God. All believers must adhere to the common factor of faith and that is obedience to God and service to man. We must tolerate and accommodate each other. Hostility will throw us in the ambit of travails and pit of travesties. The ideological differences should not lead us to bloodshed. It will be then the mockery of religion. The Qur'an succinctly says, "For thee your religion and for me mine", (109:6). This means no interference in the religion of others. It is the universal spirit of Islam. No one is permitted to impose his ideas or ideology upon others by force. Islam has encouraged the forces of reason and discouraged the force of rod. The Qur'an exhorts its followers to call others to Islam amicably, modestly and reasonably. The Qur'an abhors the tyrants and sinners who render injustice, indecency and imbecility. It says in Sura Baqarah:

"And when he is in authority, he runs about in the land to create disorder in it and destroy the crops and the progeny of man; and Allah loves not disorder."

The Qura'n announces: "Mankind were one community, then they differed among themselves, so Allah raised prophets as bearers of good tidings and as warners and sent down with them the Book containing the truth that he might judge between the people where in they differed." (2:213)

To achieve this humane, fraternal and universal spirit of Islam, people like Jamal-ud-Din Afghani, Kawakbi, Allama Iqbal and Mohammad Abduoh throughout their lives have been struggling. All efforts to unite the Muslims through Arab League, OIC, Rabita-e-Alam-e-Islami, Al-Motamir and International Islamic Forum are bright omens. The Muslims all over the world are seriously trying to unite for their safety and security. After the dismemberment of the Soviet Union, now America is the only sole and solo power in the region. The unipolar system of America has announcd for New World Order. What is this New World Order, the time will tell. Let us be positive and hope for better future of mankind. Communism is a negative ideology. It wanted to crush Capitalist or democratic ideologies. Islam is not a negative or a reactionary ideology. It wants its implementation not through the exercise of force. When the Holy Prophet conquered Makkah and entered the city as a conqueror, he pardoned even his deadliest enemy like Abu Sufyan. If we put a cursory glance over Muslim history we see that even in the regimes of Ummayyads, Abbasids, Fatimids and Ottomans, there was no persecution of the Christians or the Jews. Islam has formed a special code of conduct for the "Zimmis", the non-Muslims. They have their social, religious and political rights in an Islamic state. No Muslim government is supposed to tease, torture or trouble them. In the pre-renaissance period the crusades fought between the Muslims and the Christians were the result of religious prejudice. But when the fatal enemy of the Muslims Henry Frederick fell ill, Salahuddin Ayubi sent his personal doctor to treat him. He showed Islamic tolerance. We should not repeat the unwanted experiment of the crusades.

The Western powers consider Islamic Renaissance as a challenge and threat to them. This is very negative approach. Islam has condemned expansionism and colonialism. America and Western countries should extend the hand of friendship to all the Muslim countries. Their self-imagined fears will lead us to some serious clash. Let us forget our bitter past and all believers of God should unite under the canopy of human respect and love.

ISLAM AND RATIONALISM

Islam is a religion based on Rationalism. Superstition has no place in Islam. Islam nowhere stands on the pillars of miracles. Though the Holy Prophet (peace be upon him) had shown some of the historical miracles whenever needed, yet no where in the Qur'an people had been asked to enter the fold of Islam on the basis of miracles. The Holy Qur'an has not even mentioned any miracle of the Prophet of Islam but had always asked the unbelievers to accept Islam on the basis of its being a natural, just, rational and peace-loving doctrine of life. Islam has given a clarion call for the exercise of intellect. I must mention here that though the book of any religion is not supposed to be an exhaustive note on Inductive or Deductive logic, it should not be devoid of reasonable concepts and rational precepts. Intuition in the words of Bergson is a higher reasoning. Revelation or "Wahi" is an absolute reason and is imperative for the positive action and noble contemplation. Prophets were the torch bearers in the dark and untraversed deserts of life. The superiority of Religion over philosophy is based upon the fact that the latter gives "Tasawwar" (concept) and no "Tasweer" (Model). Islam has given us ideology in the form of the Holy Qur'an and model in the form of the Sunnah of the Holy Prophet. After the demise of the Holy Prophet we had been obligated to use intellect for the solution of our day to day problems of life. Intellect is the only measuring yard between the men and the beasts. It is of course tragic to mention that the majority of the Muslim theologians along with the nasty imperialistic and dictatorial designs of savage and callous emperors, Islam has received fatal blows and still the Muslims throughout the world are the victims of decadence and degeneration. It is the right time that like Dr. Iqbal we should launch the crusade of Islamic Renaissance. Anything that is unreasonable is un-Islamic and we must eradicate its sapling from the soil of Islamic free inquiry based on intellect. If we look at the constitution of our physical structure we will bear out the reality that the creator has poised the brain in the skull of man which is the safe seat of intellect and is the top most organ of all other parts of body.

Hikmat (intellect) and 'Hakumat' (power) go side by side in Islam. This is the reason as to why Adam was assigned the duty of Vicegerency and became the caliph. This episode depicts that Islam does not enhance blind faith but faith based on reason.

Islam is the religion of rationality. Time and again it reiterated the importance of sound faith based upon logic and sense. Before the advent of Islam the whole world was driven into the shabby cells of inhumanity, immorality, indecency and irrationality. People were in the iron chains of dogmatic rites and rituals. Gambling, lechery, debauchery, brigandage, fornication, theft, arrogance, pride, snobbery, robbery, sedition, usury, usurpation, murder and deceit were in vogue. People used to bury their daughters and insanely drew the swords out of the sheaths on trifles and trivialities. Tribal taboos and sectarian trifles were generally influencing the course and direction of Arab's convictions and actions. Under such inhuman and unreasonable circumstances arose the sun of nobility and knowledge. The Prophet of Islam lit the candle of wisdom, piety, justice and liberty. The aim of Islam is the intellectual mobilization of all thoughtful minds and peace-loving souls. Allama Majlisi writes that once Hazrat Imam Jafar Sadiq had stated that after creating Adam, God put three things before him and asked him to choose one. The three things were faith, nobility and intellect. Adam chose intellect. This metaphorical episode manifests that who so ever possesses the boon of intellect is bound to have sound faith and character. Thomas Carlyle did not like atheism on similar grounds for intellect enhances one's insight to study the causes and factors lying beneath the purpose of all creation. After reading a translation of the Qur'an, the greatest German poet Goethe abruptly exclaimed: "f this is Islam, every thinking man among us is, in fact, a Muslim." Isn't it a tragedy that Goethe considered the Qur'an as a compendium of wisdom but we have not done justice to this source of inspiration and wisdom. The Qur'an is a complete code of life meeting man's bodily and spiritual needs on positive, progressive, natural, moral and rational grounds. Mr. Pickthall in his famous treatise "Islamic Culture" has beautifully enumerated the ultimate scheme and purpose of Islam as: "The leader is the Prophet, the Guidance is the Holy Qur'an and the goal is Allah".

Islam has sufficient grounds to provide us the modus operandi of purification in the guise of the Holy Prophet who said, "Verily, Allah doth not keep knowledge as a thing apart that he withholdeth from his servants, but he doth keep it in the grasp of man of knowledge, so that if he shall cause not a man of Knowledge to remain, mankind will take foolish heads, and they will be questioned and give 'Fatwas' and they will err and lead others to errors."

Islam does not give leadership into the hands of knowledgeless ninnies and mummies. Islam is a religion of rationality and faith. It does not draw of line of demarcation between faith and reason. Anything that is unreasonable is un-Islamic. St. Augustine has said: "I believe because it is incredible". In Islam such baseless claims have no place at all. The Qur'an outright denounces irrational cults and appeals for the free exercise of reason. Why don't you meditate?, is oftly repeated in the Qur'an. "My verses are for thinkers" is another verse of the Holy Qur'an depicting the significance of rational attitude in solving the complex problems of human life. Islam does not support the idea of blind faith. Bertrand Russell could not appreciate religion for its being the replica of obscurantism. Had he studied the Qur'an with impartial mind he would have come to some other conclusions. Islam believes in an unseen entity but gives us solid proofs in believing the absolute cause and ultimate principle. About the creator of the universe Islam exhorts us to brood over Nature and the laws of Nature which are set and tell that no creation is without a creator. So far as the human life is concerned it swings around the orbit of justice and wisdom in an Islamic society. The moral and immoral in Islam is based upon reason. The Western empiricists after strenuous struggle and experiments are concluding the same that had been revealed upon the Prophet of Humanity in the form of Qur'an.

The Holy Prophet time and again had been emphasizing on the need of reason and intellect. Once he said: "An hour's contemplation and study of God's creation is better than a year of adoration." One can image the importance of research and scientific study from the above mentioned hadith of the Holy Prophet in an age when people were only and only given to idol-worship.

Except for Islam no religion has considered scientific research as an "Ibadat" (the worship). "To listen to the words of the learned and to instill into others the lessons of science is better than religious exercises" is a well-known saying of the Holy Prophet. Islam has laid down the basic principles which are universal and eternal. The whole edifice of Islamic values stands on the foundations of reason. Islam can never die because it enhances and encourages the principle of movement. Ijtahad is a dynamic and rational mode of inquiry in Islam. "The scholars of my 'Umma' will be like the Prophets of Bani Israel", a saying of the Holy Prophet manifests the value of scholarly pursuits and intellectual inquiry in Islam. After these solid facts the critics who detach Intellect from faith should seek the latent spiritual mysteries in the light of reason and rationality, for Islam is the religion of Rationalism. In the end it seems necessary to mention the basic difference between Scepticism and Rationalism. Scepticism is the philosophy of doubt and Rationalism is the Philosophy of reason. The modern occidentalists are the great pioneers of scepticism. The question is why does the doubt arise? It arises with the creation of a sense of Good and Bad. Suppose a man is a dead drunkard. He takes liquor by habit or by fashion. One day he suddenly starts thinking whether he should continue drinking or leave it. This moment or pause in which he has to decide what to do has created doubt in his mind about the act of drinking. This skeptical approach is not bad. It is a step towards something other than present state. Either he decides to continue taking liquor or he will immediately discard wine forever. When he discards wine he comes to the stage of repentance. But the taste of sin is preserved in his conscious or sub-conscious mind. It can never be eliminated because the man had the experience of wine drinking. This process because of the skeptical approach resulted, in the form of a healthy omen. But as a prophet never tastes the fruit of sin, the taste of sin is neither found in the conscious mind or the sub-conscious mind of a prophet. Hence a prophet is above skepticism. He is always at the stage of firm belief. A man who believes in the Prophet of Islam can use reason to test and justify his beliefs but is not supposed to doubt the authority for this doubt would become the part of state of solid believers. Islam enhances Rationalism but discourages skepticism. The nation lingering in the nebula of doubt remains away from action. Islam hence cannot afford the permanent inactive state of doubt. Faith based on reason and scientific enquiry is Rationalism and that is the kernel of Islamic philosophy.

CLASH OF CIVILIZATIONS

Professor Huntington of Harvard University thinks that after the failure of communism in Soviet Union now there will be a clash between Western and Islamic civilizations. America and the West had basic differences with socialist state. The communists do not believe in God and interpret history and human life in the light of materialism. Their political system is Fascism. Islam grants social, economic and political freedom and justice but rejects atheism, materialism and communism. The believers of Judaism and Christianity believe in the basic teachings of Abraham as the Muslims believe in him. Our sources are one and the same. We have doctrinal or religious differences but they are to be tolerated. The Quran in Sura Al-Kafirun says: "For you your religion and for us mine" (109:6). It clearly means that we should not spill blood in the name of religion. Some Christian fundamentalists believe that Jesus Christ will resurrect in Israel when all Muslims will be finished in that land. They are supporting the Jews in Israel on the plea of religious dogmas. Similarly some Muslim Fundamentalists believe that the presence of Jews on the sacred land of Palestine is impermissible and unwanted. But the enlightened Jews, Christians and Muslims want the Israelites and the Muslims to live peacefully and respect the rights of each other on human grounds. Instead of enhancing the spirits of clash we should support the mantra and mission of congruence. Actually the clash of civilizations is the clash of Fundamentalism. The fundamentalists from all sides are fanning the flames of discord.

Dr. Iqbal S. Hussain in his recently published book entitled "Terrorism in Action" writes: "Thus for the West it has emerged over the past decades as the most challenging ideology with great civilizational fundamentals. Despite Huntington's theory of the "Clash of civilizations" and Berlusconi's tirade against Islam the inherent ingredient contained in the religion of Islam remain as imbued with inspirational purity and consistency that even massacre of millions of Muslims cannot reduce their impact." In this book Dr. Iqbal Hussain discusses the hostile attitude of the West towards Islam. He writes that Islam is a target of Western imperialism. In his opinion Islam is a moderate code of life and is universal and natural in its theory and practice. Dr. Iqbal Hussain further opines; "Muslims are convinced that it is a divine religion and has arrived to prevail over all other codes and ideologies. Even Samuel Huntington recognizes the reality of Islamic values which he condemns for their "revulsion of the West's materialistic, corrupt, decadent and immoral hegemony, as Islam claims the universality of its values." Though it is true that the Muslim world lacks liberty and social justice but Islam is not at fault, these are the Muslims who do not practice the real Islam. The Muslim monarchs and rulers belong to capitalist class. They are mostly cruel and callous. The Muslim history is replete with bloodshed but it is also true that Islam strictly prohibits injustice, slavery, dictatorship, inequality and monarchy. The time is coming when the Muslim masses will end capitalism, feudalism, fascism and imperialism. On the same grounds we find that the American constitution guarantees liberty and social justice which is a golden principle. But what liberty means? Only to write and speak freely does not mean we are a free nation. The true liberty means when all people have equal opportunities and equal resources to live and to compete. In America ninety percent people are living hand to mouth. A few monopolists enjoy the boon and fruit of free economy. To make it a welfare state so many social and economic changes are required. Islam strongly condemns capitalism. If by the clash of civilizations Professor Huntington means a clash between money and mind or a clash between capitalism and social justice then he may be right but this is not the clash between civilizations, this is a clash between systems. The preaching of clash is a crime. It breeds extremism and terrorism. We must preach peace and tolerance for each other. We should neither condemn nor criticize other's system of beliefs. If we desire peace we will have to maintain Justice. We will have to announce justice for Israelites, justice for Palestinians, justice fro Kashmiris, justice for Chechens and justice for all - which is American slogan as well. Let this slogan be given practical shape. Then no body will pose the question: "Why people hate the Americans"? Let us preach dialogue of civilizations. To end clashes and initiate dialogue and harmony Dr. Iqbal Hussain suggests: "dogmatism in tolerance and bigotry are the dominant features of fundamentalism. Fundamentalists, whether Christians or Muslims are inspired by the evil instincts whenever a situation gets out of control. In such environments fundamentalism assumes added dimension of divisions and dispersion. With the rise of schisms extremists on both sides share a common bond of irrationality and stupidity. Experiences of excessive and emotional expression confer on fundamentalism a bad negative image."

The Quran appreciates diversity of views and considers it a happy sign for mental nourishment and development. It says; "Had your Lord so wished He could surely have made all mankind one single community but they continue to hold divergent views" - It teaches us the lesson of co-existence. We reject the virulent theory of clash of civilizations propounded by the most vitriolic exponents like Huntington and support the views of tolerance, moderation, peace and harmony.

EIGHT AREAS OF EXPLOITATION

Unfortunately mankind's track record in the area of human rights is deplorable. Those with power have been exploiting, enslaving, shedding the blood and trampling upon the dignity and rights of those unable to defend themselves. Such behavior is a cruel mockery of the noble station of human beings.

Although the arenas of exploitation and abuse are legion, the following eight are prominent among them and are crying out for reform.

The first is religion. In the name of religion the human blood had been spilt like water. The Jews killed the Christians. Then the Christians attained power and they executed and persecuted the Jews. The Hindus killed the Buddhists and the Sikhs. The Muslims and Christians during the crusade for two centuries killed millions on both sides. Today, sectarian clashes in which innocent people are killed still beset us. When we study the divine scriptures of these religions, we find only admonitions to peace, purity, piety and care for those who are weaker and less fortunate. The divine books give the message of love, why then, do the followers of these religions behave so abominably toward each other? Then why the followers of these religions hate each other and regard each other as infidels, heretics and pagans? It is a big question and needs to be answered. Either we like Atheists, Marxists, Materialists and Communists and totally reject religion or we accept the message and spirit of all religions and love and respect all human irrespective of their color, class, creed and country. We must condemn religious extremists and terrorists. We must change their curriculum. We must introduce scientific, logical and rational methods to guide the religious students. We must abandon sectarian education in our Islamic schools and mosques. The moderate, humane and universal spirit of religion must be imparted and imbued; otherwise human life will become hell over the globe.

The second area of exploitation is skin color. The prophet of Islam in his last sermon on the mount of Arafat categorically proclaimed that no Arab has any superiority over a non-Arab. The standard of superiority could only be measured by righteousness before God. In ancient days all over the world the blacks were mistreated. They were made slaves. They were used as beasts of burden. Event today in parts of America and Europe they are considered second-rate citizens. Although the American Constitution grants equal rights and freedoms to all people, inequalities and abuses still exist. We must love and respect all humans despite color differences. The color of blood is red, whether it is the blood of the white or the black.

The third area of exploitation is race. When we brag and boast about our lineage, race and tribe we negate the existence of other people. Racial prides and prejudices are toxic to the fabric of society. The Arabs were always proud of Arabism. Firdusi who wrote "Shahnama" shared the pride of being Persian. Hitler inculcated pride in the German nation. These racists hurled the world in to the chasm of division and destruction. Nationalism in a great curse. It breeds mental neurosis. It corrupts the society and divides humanity in to fragments and segments.

The fourth area of exploitation is language. Basically all languages have developed according to the technique of phonetics. Different sounds and then alphabetic played the basic role in the making of different languages. Some languages are developed, some are underdeveloped and some are undeveloped. Languages like English, French and German are known as modern languages as they are impregnated with scientific knowledge. Some are still dialects and need special attention to achieve the status of a language. There was a time when the Arabs used to consider the non-Arab as Ajami, meaning by the dumb people. Of course, Arabic is such a developed language that its literature is marvelous and unprecedented when compared to any language of the world. But unfortunately it lags behind in science and technology. It needs special attention to enrich its sources on scientific lines. What I intend to propound is that we should not hate or kill each other in the name of language. I see people coming close to each other when they express themselves in the same language. When I meet anybody who speaks Urdu I feel comfortable. It is because of necessity as well. We must not hate the people who do not speak our native language. About the variations of languages and colors the Quran in the Chapter The Roman Empire says: "And among His signs is the creation of the heavens and the earth, and the variations in your languages and your colors: verily in that are signs for those who know." (30:22) In Karachi we had miserable experience of language riots. The Urdu speaking and the Sindhi speaking groups massacred each other which is shameful and must be condemned.

The fifth area of exploitation is gender. For centuries the women folk had been the victim of discrimination. They were made concubines and hand-maids. The kings and moneyed people used them like cattle and chattel. They were denied equal rights. The rights of education, property and freedom were denied to them. They were used as sex symbols. In modern societies of America and Europe they have been given basic rights and equal status which is praiseworthy step. But in the whole history of America, France and Germany no woman ever became president or prime minister. In the name of so called freedom and modernity the ladies are being misused as a symbol of sex on television and in advertisement companies. The clubs and brothels are stigmas on the face of modern civilization. The sexual perversion in the shape of gays and lesbians ridicules our claims of modernism. The excessive divorce rate laughs at us. We should bring harmony between masculine and feminine gender by introducing moderate and moral values.

The sixth area of exploitation is economics. In a capitalist economy there is a big gulf between the rich and the poor. The feudal lords suck the blood of their tenants like leeches. The capitalists and the industrialist exploit the poor workers. In a socialist society the ruling class crushes the ruled ones. America represents capitalism and Russia represents socialism. Both are extremes. England is a welfare state and keeps balance between social justice and political freedom. We must introduce social justice to fill the gap between the rich and the poor and provide democratic culture throughout the world.

The seventh area of exploitation is dictatorship. The military rulers, the monarchs and autocrats are the worst type of adversaries of mankind. We must introduce democracy in the whole world. We cannot provide freedom and justice until we abolish dictators.

The eighth area of exploitation is nationalism. One must be loyal to his country and even lay down his life when his country needs it. But the slogan: "My country is superior" is a wrong slogan. I agree with Bertrand Russell who preached cosmopolitanism. Let there be one state and one government all over the world. The Americans, the Russians, the Chinese, the Indians, The Pakistanis, The Iranians and the Arabs must respect each other without considerations of nationalism. We all are made of clay and we hail from Adam and Eve – we are one – we stand united. We are humans. We must finish the factors of exploitation.

FASTING IN ISLAM

Fasting is a test of patience and perseverance. It teaches self-restraint. Fasting means to control your base sentiments purify your soul and abstain from eating, drinking, smoking and sex from dawn to sunset. Before the advent of the Prophet of Islam the earlier communities like Jews and Christians also used to fast. The Quran testifies this in these words: "O ye who believe! Fasting is prescribed to you as it was prescribed to those before you, that ye may (learn) self restraint." (2:183). Self restraint is not something physical or ritualistic. If we abstain from our physical drives or needs its purpose is to attain moral and spiritual uplift. The purpose of patience through fasting is to be a tolerant and moderate man. Anger, agitation, fury, frenzy, hastiness, intolerance, impatience are abandoned. One learns noble values and shuns vices. This is the reason that the Prophet of Islam is recorded to have said about the month of Ramadan: "A month of endurance (sabr) and the reward for endurance is paradise. A month in which a believer's provisions are increased." Ramadan is the ninth month of the Islamic calendar in which the Muslims are obligated to fast. But the people who are sick, traveling or frail due to old age are exempted from fasting. Tallal Alie Turfe in his book entitled "Patience in Islam" writes: "However, missed fasts must be done at another time when the Muslim restores his health or completes his travel." Some Jurists are of the opinion that seriously sick people or very old persons who cannot fast should offer ransom as prescribed in the Quran. About the basic aim of Fasting Dr Saleem Ahmed in his book entitled "Beyond Veil and Holy War" writes: "Fasting is supposed to be a soul-purifying and body-cleansing experience; it is also to inculcate discipline, compassion, and piety among us. Seeing others eat and drink should not affect our fasting. After all, Muslims in non-Muslim countries fast while others around them carrying on life as usual." On this point we are divided. Some people opine that during day time in Ramadan in Muslim countries people should not openly drink or eat even if they are sick or are traveling. Some others believe that we should not make life hard. The sick people or the travelers have all religious sanctions to eat or drink secretly or openly. These people cite a Hadith which says: "Neither should those fasting criticize those not fasting, nor should those not fasting criticize those fasting" (Bughari and Muwatta). By mentioning this Hadith what is concluded is that there is flexibility and tolerance in Islam. It is reported in news papers often that some people were beaten or even killed by some others as they did not fast and ate something on roadside. Islam prohibits extremism in rituals as well. It grants flexibility and easiness in religious matters. If you cannot pray while standing, sitting or prostrating you can pray while lying on bed with the gestures of fingers or eyes. Islam is a practical and easy code of life. It is a mercy. It is not a botheration or burden. Besides the moral and spiritual elevation, fasting teaches us social equity and parity. A king has to fast. A capitalist has to fast. Fasting is obligatory to all Muslims whether rich or poor. The rich experience thirst and hunger. Hence they practically realize the problems and miseries of the poor. Fasting permeates both aspects of self denial and repentance. The month of Ramadan is a sacred month for Muslims. First time the Quran was revealed in this month. The Quran says: "Ramadan is the (month) in which we sent down the Quran, as a guide to mankind, also clear (signs) for guidance and judgment (between right and wrong). So everyone of you who is present (at his home) during that month should spend it in fasting"(2:185).

The Month of Ramadan is the month of repentance and prayers. We should recite the entire Quran during the month of Ramadan. Once Prophet Mohammad (PBUH) in a sermon in the month of Ramadan said: "The month of Ramadan is the best of all months, its days the best of all days, its nights the best of all nights, and its hours the best of all hours." The prophet reminded the Muslims to pray, to recite the holy Quran, refrain from what Allah forbids, repent and ask for Allah's forgiveness. It is actually the month of moral training. Mahmoud Abu-Saud in his book entitled "Concept of Islam" writes: "Muhammad related that God ordained that everything a person does has consequences for him, or is done for him, except fasting, which is done for God's sake." The faster through obedience and submission achieves self-restraint, spiritual elation, moral stability and social equality. The month of Ramadan is a great boon and blessing for all believers.

Besides the logic and purpose of observing fasts there are some other related points. In Sura Baqara there are some instructions about Fasting. The Quran says: "(Fasting) for a fixed number of days; but if any of you is ill, or on a journey, the prescribed number (should be made up) from days later. For those who can do it (without hardship), is a ransom, the feeding of one that is indigent. But he that will give more, of his own free will, - it is better for him. And it is better for you that you fast, if you only knew." (2:184). In verse 187 of Sura The Heifer the Quran permits approach to wives but during Fasting sexual act with wives in prohibited. About 'Sahar' and Iftar the Quran says: "And eat and drink, until the white thread of dawn appears to you distinct from its black thread; then complete your fast till the night appears" (2:187).

In Sura Maida (The Table Spread) for the breach of oath three days fasting is recommended as expiation. In the same Sura the expiation of killing any animal is the sacred precincts of Kaaba is prohibited and equivalent fasts are recommended as ransom. In Sura Ahzab (The Confederates) in verse 35 Allah gives glad tidings of reward and salvation to the men and women who fast.

Then in Sura Mujadila (The woman who pleads) from verse 1 to 4 the Quran tells us about a case of a woman. If someone in anger says to his wife: "you are like my mother." Then he desires to have marital relations with her the Quran ordains that such a man should observe consecutive fasting for two months as expiation. Hence we see that fasting besides the source of piety, equality and patience is also the source of ransom and expiation for sins and errors. It may not be out of place to mention here that the month of Ramadan is a lunar month; not a solar month. It is also for equality and justice for all people worldwide. The lunar months keep on changing climate wise. Sometimes Ramadan comes in winter and sometimes in summer. Hence it adjusts all months and all nations. Had Islamic calendar been solar then Ramadan would have come every year in the same month. Hence people living in hot countries would have complained. Ramadan comes in rotation to all nations which is also the sign of Islamic universality and equality.

Similarly about Hajj season it can be said that it is in rotation climate wise and provides equal opportunities of climate to all its believers living in different countries and climates. Lunar system is practiced in the Muslim world for all its events and rituals. The universality of this system is portrayed in the month of Ramadan as well.

FUNDAMENTALISM OR FORMALISM

The Muslims are being branded Fundamentalists. Is it a fact or only an allegation? I intend to shed some light on this issue. Fundamentalism is of two types. Positive Fundamentalism and Negative Fundamentalism. By positive Fundamentalism I mean that every ideology, science or religion has some fundamental principles, articles or tenets. These fundamentals are also called as foundations. As no building can be constructed without foundations, similarly no religion can function without fundamentals. These fundamentals are also called as foundations. In my opinion some religions are positive religions and some are negative religions. The religions standing on the pillars and principles, which are humane, rational and natural, are positive religions. And the religions or isms preaching inhumane, irrational and unnatural modes and codes are negative religions. When we say Islam is a natural religion by it we mean that Islam is a progressive religion preaching peace. When the westerners criticize some Muslims for their irrational, bigoted, rash and terrorizing attitudes and name them as terrorists or fundamentalists they criticize their non-progressive attitude. The Westerners should not criticize the fundamentals of any religion rather they should criticize the formal approach of some hard liners towards religion. It is called Formalism. Even Muslim Sufis have been criticizing the spiritless approach of the formalists for centuries. The formalists have been bearing the brunt of harsh criticism by the Muslim Sufis. These Sufis were more humane, secular and liberal in their attitude and rejected the retrogressive approach of the fanatics and hard liners in the matters of religion. They said that the priests and clerics believe in "Form" and the Sufis believe in "Spirit"- By form they meant "Shariah" (The Law); and by spirit they meant "Tariqah" (The spirit). Then a third group emerged who claimed that the real Islam is both; the

Shariah and the Tariqah. They are known as Ahl-e-Haqiqat; (the realists). They claim they have found the ultimate reality.

Let us now briefly discuss what are the fundamentals of Islam. In Sura Heifer the Quran announces; "It is not righteousness that you turn your faces toward East or West; but it is righteousness – to believe in Allah and the Last Day, and the Angels, and the Book, and the Messengers; to spend to your substance, out of love for Him, for your kin; for orphans, for the needy; for the way farer, for those who ask, and for the ransom of slaves; to be stead fast in prayer, and practice regular charity; to fulfill the contracts which you have made; and to be firm and patient, in pain (or suffering) and adversity and throughout all periods of panic. Such are the people of truth, those who fear Allah"

These are some of the fundamentals of Islam mentioned in the above verses. What is wrong with them? These are the basic principles of justice, freedom, equality, humanity, fraternity, liberty, rationality and equality. Islam believes in divine and human values. It is the other name of positive Fundamentalism. What is Negative Fundamentalism? It is belief in whims and rituals. It is belief in unnatural way of life. It is retrogressive way of conduct. Formalism ultimately turns into Negative Fundamentalism. I would like to make this point more vivid through some examples. The Quran ordains us to offer regular prayers. But what is the meaning, purpose or spirit of the prayer. The Quran in Sura The Spider says; "Recite what has been revealed to you of the Book and establish regular prayers. For prayers preclude indecency and wrongdoing"(29:45) Just to pray as a habit without any improvement in character is formalism. But when we abstain from evils we serve the purpose of prayer. The real purpose of the prayers is announced in Sura Al-Maun as such; "Do you see one who denies the religion. Then such is a man who repulses the orphan (with harshness). And does not encourage the feeding of the indigent". Besides prayer we lay much stress on Fasting. The Quran in Sura The Heifer in verse 183 says; "O you who believe! Fasting is prescribed to you as it was prescribed to those before you, that you may (learn) self-restraint". It is clearly mentioned in the Quran that purity and piety are the basic purposes of the prayers. The Gnostics claim that they believe in formalism as well as in spirit. Islam believes in Middle course. It rejects extremism. Even while offering regular prayers the Quran exhorts; "Neither speak your prayer aloud, nor speaks it in a low tone, but seek a middle course between (17:110).

The formalists keep the people entangled in the webs of juristic turns and twists. They will discuss the matters of beard and moustaches. They say as the holy prophet used to mount the camel, they will not appreciate aeroplane. They do not like to wear suit as the prophet did not wear suit. They do not like to use tooth brush and use stick as a dentifrice as the prophet did not use tooth paste or tooth brush. These hard liners do not understand that these modern inventions were not in practice in the times of the holy prophet. Islam stresses on the need of inquiry and invention and keeps pace with the time. Let us not condemn Fundamentalism but curse false Formalism.

HUMANITY AND ISLAM

The Holy Quran expressly declares that the human race is one family. All of us are the children of Adam and Eve, whether our skin is white or black. At various places it says: "All human beings are a single nation" (2:213). "All human beings are naught but a single nation and yet they disagree" (10:19). "And verily this your nation (human beings) is a single nation" (21:92) and (23:52).

The differences in our physical features, colors, complexions, languages, dresses, customs and the ways of living arise due to different climates and geographical territories. Those who settled in hot tropical zones grew to be black, and those who settled in cold climates remained white in their complexion. The people living in hot climates are hot-headed and the people living in cold climate have cold temperament. The diet also affects the color and temperament. The Mongolians, the Semites, the Darvidians and the Saxons took pride in tribalism. The lust for property, power and pelf made one tribe the enemy of the other tribe and led to bloodshed and battles. Such savage and illiterate people fashioned idols with their hands and worshiped natural phenomenon such as the sun, fire, bodies of water and snakes and other elements and creatures which could harm them. They believed that they could obtain protection from such material objects, creatures and elements of nature the river, the snakes and other objects which could harm them. Hence out of fancy and fear they made their gods. But the prophets always guided them and instructed them to worship one God –

The prophets, the guides whom God sent to all people, instructed these people to worship the one God, Who is omniscient, omnipotent and all merciful. These individuals, who were ruled by fear and stuck in their beliefs, frequently tortured, teased and persecuted these divine reformers known as the prophets. God never left humankind without guidance through prophets.

Adam was the first man as well as the first prophet. He guided his wife and children. The Quran tells us, "every people had a prophet" (10:47) "And certainly we raised in every people a prophet" (16:36). And there is not a people but a Warner has gone among them" (35:24). "And we did not send any apostle but with the language of the people, so that he might explain to them" (14:4). The advent of the Holy prophet of Islam is described in the Quran: "Those who follow the Apostle, the Ummi, whom they find written down with them in the Torah and in the Bible" (7:157). The Holy Bible also mentions about the advent of our prophet. It says: "For Moses truly said unto the fathers, a prophet shall the Lord your God raise up unto you of your brethren, like unto me, unto him shall ye hearken in all things whatsoever he shall say unto you. And it shall come to pass, that every soul, which will not hear that prophet, shall be destroyed from among the people." (The New Testament Acts 3:22-24)

Moses is prophesying about a prophet who will give them law as he gave them divine law. Prophet Mohammad endorsed the Law of Moses and presented to him in the Quran. Hence no one else save Prophet Mohammad is the prophesized one by Moses in the Torah. About Hazrat Abraham the Quran says: "And when his Lord tried Abraham with certain words, and he fulfilled them, He (God) said, 'I will make thee an Imam (a guide) for mankind . . . and of my offspring?' then the Lord said "my (covenant) shall not reach the unjust." (2:124)

About the eminence and guidance of Abraham the Bible says: "And I will make of thee a great nation, and I will bless thee and make thy name great; and thou shalt be a blessing" (Genesis 12:2-3). About Ishmael the Bible says: "And as for Ishmael, I have heard thee; Behold I have blessed him and will make him fruitful, and will multiply him exceedingly; Twelve princes shall he beget and I will make him a great nation" (Genesis 18:20)

Ishmael, Moses and Jesus Christ announced twelve successors. The Holy Prophet Mohammad also declared "Twelve Imams: after him and they are from Hazrat Ali to Hazrat Imam Mehdi. When Abraham left his wife Hagar and Ishmael at Mecca it was a barren and waterless desert. Hagar searched from water from hillock to hillock. Ishmael was thirsty and near to death. Through a miracle, a spring gushed out known as the well of zam zam. It is mentioned in the Bible and in the Quran. Abraham and Ishmael raised the House of God known as Kaaba. While raising the walls of the Holy House, Abraham prayed to God to accept this humble and sincere service. He said: "And when Abraham and Ishmael raised the foundations of the House (saying) our Lord! Accept from us; surely Thou art the knowing. Our Lord! And make us both submissive (Muslims) to Thee and (raise) from our offspring a nation submitting to Thee, and show us ways of devotion and turn to us (Merciful), surely Thou art the oft-returning (to mercy), the Merciful- Our Lord! And raise up them an Apostle from among them who shall recite to them Thy communications and purify them; surely thou art the mighty, the wise" (2:127-129)

God tested Abraham by asking him to sacrifice his beloved son Ishmael. He told about his vision to his son saying: "O, Son! I see in vision that I slay thee." (37:102) Ishmael, an obedient and dutiful son replied: "O, Father! Act as thou hast been bidden (by the Lord) and thou wilt, if God willeth, find me of the patient one" (37:102). When Abraham laid down his son Ishmael and tied his hands and legs lest the boy should struggle while being slain and blind folded himself with a piece of cloth, passed the knife across, cutting the throat. When he uncovered his eyes he found a lamb laid slain and Ishmael safe and sound standing nearby. Abraham got worried. He thought his sacrifice was not accepted by God. But God has substituted lamb for Ishmael. The Quran says: "O, Abraham! Of course thou hast faithfully fulfilled the dream, thou art of the truthful ones, but verily it is an open test, we have substituted it with a greater sacrifice. We have transferred it to later generations." (37:105-108).

The Bible relates that it was Isaac who was offered as a sacrifice, whereas the Quran seems to relate that it was Ishmael who was offered as a sacrifice. Whichever son it was, the point is that Abraham was willing to do what God asked of him, even at supreme personal cost.

The Quran and other divine scriptures testify this verity that humanity is the core message of prophecy. Some non-believers maintain that religion is the apple of discord. But is it not the mind's inability to understand and the selfish and greedy passions that cause the discord, not the Truth given by God through the prophets? The prophets rendered great sacrifices. John was beheaded with a saw. Jesus Christ was tortured and crucified. Muhammad was teased and attacked. Thy tyrants and tribal chiefs troubled him, but the prophets tolerated all trials, for God and humanity. Humanity is the message of all religions.

ISLAM AND DARWINISM

Islam believes in the theory of creation and Darwinists believe in the Theory of Evolution. In this article briefly it is discussed that the life on earth is created by God; it is not accidental or by chance. The atheists and the materialists negate the existence of God and consider human life and even mind to be a form of matter. Darwin's theory of Evolution has influenced the minds of people and their character has been influenced as well. Such people do not believe in divine morals and values. They do not believe in God, soul and Hereafter. Islam says that God has created this universe and Humans with a specified goal. In Sura the Heifer in verse 117 the Quran says: "To Him is due the primal origin of the heavens and the earth: when He decrees a matter, He says to it: "Be", and it is." Similarly in Sura Yasin in verse no. 82 the Quran announces: "Verily, when He intends a thing, His command is, "Be"; and it is". The Quran has used two words for creation "Khaliq" and "Amr". "Amr" is immediate command and immediate creation. Suppose about the creation of soul the Quran says: They ask you about soul, say; the soul is the command of my Lord" – All humans and the cosmos has been regarded as "Khalq". The man comes in to being through a proper natural system. Without sexual intercourse and conception no life can take shape. But when the Quran refers about the birth of Jesus Christ; it is not natural or usual way of birth. It is through special command. Similarly the mothers of Yahya and Ishmael had gone old and barren and could not produce children. But the Quran mentions about their birth through special command. The natural laws and usual system of creation is regarded as Khalq. Hence the Quran in Sura Al-Imran in verse 190 says; "Behold! In the creation of heavens and the earth, and the alternation of Night and Day – there are indeed signs for men of understanding." There are many verses in the Quran dealing with the subject of creation. Then there is also the concept of evolutionary process in creation but it is not in Darwinian sense but in the sense of developing stages of cosmos. The Quran in Sura The Height in verse 54 announces; "Your Guardian – Lord is Allah, who created the heavens and the earth in six days." Then in Sura "the cattle" in verse 2 the Quran says; "He it is who created you from clay; and then decreed a stated term) for you). An there is in His presence another determined term; yet you doubt within yourselves". The six days and stated term indicate the process and stages of creation by God. The creation of the universe in six days is the Biblical concept as well. Man is the blend of Matter and Soul. When God created Adam out of clay he infused his spirit in it. The Quran very explicitly narrates the story of the creation of Adam. The materialists do not believe in creation and spirit and regard the universe only the product of blind material forces. Now let us discuss what Darwin propounded. Darwinism bases on materialism. The ancient Greek materialists like Democritus believed in Evolutionary Naturalism. Besides the British scientist Charles Robert Darwin (1809 – 1882) and the British philosopher Herbert Spencer (1820 – 1903), a number of other eminent philosophers supported the theory of evolution. Hegel's theory of cosmic evolution is its offshoot. Nietzsche applied the concept of evolution to ethical theory. Karl Marx and Engels adopted it to socio – political philosophy. Thomas Henry Huxlay humanized it. Henri Bergson became one of its most influential exponents and Samuel Alexander developed it into his novel theory of emergent evolution. French Zoologist Jean de Lamarck (1744 – 1829), in 1809 presented his pioneering theory of evolution. Charles Darwin, in his "The Origin of Species" 1859) and "The Descent of Man" 1871), presented his theory of evolution. He presented the theory of the Mechanism of Natural Selection or survival of the fittest. Darwinism maintains that living things were not created but came into being by chance. Darwinism, materialism and communism believe in matter not in spirit. Darwin himself regarded his theory based on assumptions. Darwinism has been scientifically rejected. The defeat of Darwinism in the faces of science can be reviewed under three basic topics:

1- The Darwinism theory cannot scientifically explain how life originated on Earth.

2- No scientific finding shows that the "evolutionary mechanism" proposed by the theory have any evolutionary power at all.

3- The fossil record provided proves the exact opposite of what the theory suggests.

The evolutionists' claim that the universe started from "first atom" and life started from "first cell". Who created the atom and cell, the evolutionists cannot answer. Inanimate matter must have produced a living cell as a result of coincidence in the belief of the evolutionists. Modern biologists have rejected this claim. Life comes from life has been proved. The theory of "spontaneous generation", which asserts that non-living materials came together to form living organism has been rejected. In a lecture at the Sorbonne in 1864, Pasteur said; "Never will the doctrine of spontaneous generation recover from the mortal blow struck by this simple experiment." The great evolutionists like Russian biologist Alexander Oparin and American chemist Stanley Miller experimented to prove that a living cell could originate by coincidence but failed and they admitted their failure. Oparin in "Origin of Life" and Stanley Miller in "Molecular Evolution of life" discuss it in detail. Jeffery Bada in his book "Earth" admits: "we still face the biggest unsolved problem that we had when we entered the twentieth century: how did life originate on earth." The conditions required for the formation of cell are too great in quantity to be explained away by coincidences. The DNA molecule is so complex that it cannot be accidental or coincidental. Mechanism of evolution has been also rejected. No deer becomes horse and no ape becomes man. It is a fallacious theory having no historical and scientific evidence.

Lamarck and Darwin believed in the transferring of traits of one species to the other. They maintain that living creatures passed on the traits they acquired during lifetime to the next generation. Giraffes evolved from antelopes and bears transformed into whales. However, the laws of inheritance discovered by Gregor Mendel (1822 – 1884) and verified by the science of genetics have nullified the theory of evolutionary mechanism. Neo-Darwinism advances the Modern synthetic Theory". Mutations, i.e.; genetic disorders do not cause living beings to develop on the contrary they are always harmful. The fossil record theory of Darwin, which was a basic contention, has been rejected on scientific grounds. According to this theory, every living species has sprung from a predecessor. No "Transitional Forms" have yet been uncovered. On the contrary, the British Paleontologist, Drerk v. Ager in "The Nature of the Fossil Record" admits that the fossil records shows not gradual evolution but the sudden explosion of one group at the expense of another. This is just the opposite of Darwin's assumptions. Douglas J. Futuyma, an eminent evolutionist biologist in his book, "Science of Trail" announces organism as the creation of some omnipotent intelligence. Fossils show, writes Harun Yahua, in his book, "The Importance of Conscience in the Quran", that living beings emerged fully developed and in a perfect state on the earth. That means that the Origin of Species, contrary to Darwin's suppositions, is not evolution, but creation." On the wonders of creation the Quran in Sura Rehman aptly announces: "He has created man. He has taught him an intelligent speech." Then in the same Sura in verse 13 God announce; "Then which ot the favors of your Lord will ye deny."

ISLAM AND MODERN SCIENCES

Christian church throughout history had been quite antagonistic to scientific enquiry. This was the reason when Galileo announced that the Earth is round he was punished. Kepler also met the same punitive fate. The Muslim clergy even today discards scientific enquiry. These clerics are anti-science. They are prone to mythological and super natural matters. In Muslim world great philosophers like Avicena and Averroes were condemned and criticized by the clergymen. These traditionalists known as conservatives are anti-reason and anti-rationality. Eminent Britain philosopher Bertrand Russell at a place admits that the wave of Renaissance in Europe came through the Muslim World.

The Muslim scholars imbibed the spirit of Greek philosophy and fully drank from their tavern. The Sufistic trends came through Plato and the rational through Aristotle. The Muslim culture became an amalgamation of mysticism and logic. The Greek philosophy used Deductive method. It was more abstract and metaphysical than concrete, pragmatic and logical. But the Muslim mind made improvements on it and developed an Inductive method that is rational and scientific method. Here it is sorrowfully mentioned that hitherto the Muslims could not develop scientific method neither in the matters of Natural Sciences nor in Social Sciences. The Muslim world lacks logicians and philosophers. Reasons of this intellectual catastrophe being two. First: the Muslim monarchs crushed independent enquiry lest their thrones be at stake. Second; the clerics did not encourage independent dialogue and closed the doors of "Ijtehad". But even then some great sages kept aloft the standard of Independent Enquiry and laid down the foundations of scientific Method in Muslim scholastic centers. American historian Dr. Philip K. Hitti in his book entitled "The History of the Arabs" and the founding premier of India Jawahar Lal Nehru in his treatise entitle "The Glimpses of World History" admit that it were the Muslims who introduced Scientific Methods to the rest of the world.

The famous book entitled "The Bible, The Quran and Science" written by Dr. Maurice Bucaille explicitly discusses the scientific truths narrated by the Quran. In a chapter under the heading "The Quran and Modern Sciences" on page 121 he observes: "The association between the Quran and Science is a priori a surprise, especially since it is going to be one of harmony and not of discord". The book of Mr. Yamin entitle "God, Soul and Universe in Science and Islam" throws much light on this subject as well. It is a customary belief that Religion and Science are poles apart. But it is a wrong conception. Actually the incompetent clerics opposed rational and scientific method. The educated and enlightened religious clerics and scholars have always supported the spirit of scientific research even in the theological matters.

In the Quran there are 193 verses about the rights to God: 673 about the rights of humans and 750 about the universe. One ninth of the Quran deals with the creation of the universe. The

Quran tells us that seven skies and planets are not static or fixed. They are mobile and are floating in the celestial spheres and space. The sky is not standing on pillars; it is made of smoke and has layers. The Quran rejects the Aristotilian concept of Fixed Universe. The movement of the cosmos is not circular. It is even not circumlocutory. Rather it is vertex-wise.

Let us briefly annotate the Quranic version on universe. The verse 11 of Sura 41 (Fussilat) reads; "Moreover He comprehended in His design the sky, and it has been (as) smoke". The science believes that the sky is the layers of clouds and smoke.

The verse 30 of Sura 21 (The Prophets) says: "Do not the unbelievers see that the heavens and the earth were joined together, then we clove them asunder and we got every living thing out of water, will they not then believe". Science believes that all creatures were created out of water. The verse 15 and 16 of Sura 71 (Noah) says: "Did you see how God created seven heavens one above another and made the Moon a light therein and made the Sun a lamp?' It is scientifically proved that there are seven layers of the sky. The Moon receives light from the Sun. Besides, there are so many verses in the Quran referring to astronomy, astrology, plants, animals, masculine and feminine genders, seas, stars, satellites, zones, seasons and planets that the Quranic scientific verities are suffice to prove it a book of divine source.

In verses 5 to 7 of Sura 55 (Most Gracious) the Quran says: "The Sun and the Moon follow courses computed. And the herbs and the trees both (alike) bow in adoration and He has raised the Firmament high, and He has set up the balance (of Justice)." In verse 39, Sura 36 (Yasin) the Quran says: "And the Moon, we have measured for her mansions (to traverse) till she returns like the old (and withered) lower part of a date-stalk".
In verse6, Sura 37 (The Saffat) the Quran announces: "we have indeed decked the lower heaven with beauty (in) in the stars".

In sum, in the light of above a few Quranic citations it can be concluded that the Quran is a book which gives fundamental principles of science as it provides foundation for Theology, Psychology, Politics, Economics, Sociology and Zoology. The Quran is a book, which provided scientific and spiritual eternal truths.

ISLAM AND MYSTICISM

In Greek philosophy Plato promoted Gnosticism. The author of Fasusul Hikim and Fatoohat-e-Makkiya, eminent Muslim thinker and saint Sheikh-e-Akbar Ibn-e-Arabi seems under the influence of Platonic mysticism. An eminent philosopher and agnostic of our age Bertrand Russell in his book "Logic and Mysticism" believes in some immaterial powers but names such miraculous forces as mental super activities. The materialists do not believe in spiritual and mystical powers. In the history of Prophets we find Abraham doing miracles with the command of God. He minced the meet of four birds, mixed it, and put it at four mounds and called them and the four birds were raised to life and flew towards him. He was thrown into flames by Nimrod but the fire extinguished and he remained safe. This was a miracle. David used to touch the iron and it melted like wax. Moses threw his staff on the ground and it devoured the rope made snakes instantly. He threw his staff in the Red Sea and it gave way to him and to his people, the Israelites. Jesus cured the blind and the leper. Even he raised the dead to life. Prophet Muhammad parted the Moon in to two pieces. He picked up the pebbles and they recited Kalima. What these miracles show? These miracles tell us that God can interfere in the Natural system. He has the power of changing the Natural rules. The natural law is that Fire burns. But when it did not burn Abraham that proved the supremacy of soul over matter. It is the negation of materialism and atheism. It is not with the Abrahamic or Semitic prophets that they have shown miracles. In Hinduism we read about the miracles of Krishin. Yoga is a rigorous physical and spiritual practice which trains the people to do wonders.

Taoism in the expression of mysticism in ancient Chinese religion, and the Tao Te Ching (The book of the way and the Power) is one of the great mystical scriptures. Buddah was a miraculous personality. These founders of different religions like Guro Nanak of Sikhism with their spiritual message showed miracles. Not only the Prophets, their followers ere endowed by God such miraculous powers that hundred of thousands people embraced their religions after seeing their miracles. They were saints. The Christian monasticism represents mysticism.

Saint Teresa of Avila and Saint John of Cross were great saints. Hazrat Ali is famous for his spiritual and miraculous attributes.

In Islam material and spiritual go side by side. As a human being is compound of matter and soul, similarly "Shariah" (The Law) is the body and "Tariqah" (The spirit) is the soul. The clerics stress more on the law while the Sufis give more importance to the spirit. But there is another group of Muslim Sufis who believe in the amalgamation of the law and the spirit. They are known as Ahl-e-Haqiqah; the people of reality. To them the jurists pay more attention to the religious legalism and the theologians are more concerned with the religious dogmatism while the Sufis believe in asceticism. The people of Reality believe in full truth; not in half truth. The people of the Law and theology are strict about rites, rituals and practices. They are hard liners. They are sectarian and extremists as well. While the people of spirit claim to be moderate, humane and universal. The Sunnis and the Shias believe in Shariah and Tariqah while the Wahabis do not believe in Sufism. There are so many sunni sufistic orders such as Qaderiyya, Naqshbaniyya, Chistiyga and Mouliviyya etc. The Shais believe in the Wilayya of Hazrat Ali. It is interesting to note that nearly all Sunni mystical orders stem out from Hazrat Ali. Sufism has been controversial in the Muslims. The theologians have always opposed it. The Mosque and Monastery have been clashing with each other. Many famous Muslim scholars and poets were Sufis. They believed in Shariah and Tariqah and condemned the clerics for their dry and spiritless religious ritualism. Malcolm Clark in his book entitled "Islam For Dummies" writes; "Sufis played a major role in converting people to Islam in regions such as Sub-Saharan Africa, South Asia (today's Pakistan, India and Bangladesh), and Central Asia." Sufism is a search for God. The Arabic word Tasawwuf is from "Suf" which means wool. The early Sufis used to wear coarse woolen dress and were ascetics. They practiced physical self-denial. Such Sufism of self abnegation and self-denial is prohibited in Islam. There is a famous saying of the Holy Prophet; "no asceticism in Islam" On the other hand there is a sober mysticism and ecstatic mysticism. The former means mysticism of "Salik" or "Arif"; the people who are self-conscious and practice religious rituals with their spirit. The latter deals with "Majzoob" i.e; the ecstatic and engrossed and possessed persons.

These people are mostly naked and ascetics. They are not conscious about themselves and about religious rites. Behlol Dewana is its best example. Such people are not mad. They have spiritual and miraculous powers. Religion is silent on such exceptional cases. The Sufis believe in experiencing God. They claim that merely soulless rituals cannot take you near to God. It is spirit that is more important. In Sura "The Heifer" God says; "when my servants ask you concerning me, I am indeed close to them" (2:186). Then in Sura "The Table Spread" God says: "As to those who turn (for friendship) to Allah, His Messenger, and the (fellowship of) believers, it is the Fellowship of Allah that must certainly triumph." (5:56). The term "Waliullah" (the Firend of God) is used in Sufism. The Sufis believe Muhammad's night journey through the seven heavens to the throne of God as the model for stations of the Sufi path. They use the word Faqir or Dervish which means a poor person. They derive it from the Hadith of the holy prophet; "My poverty is my pride" The holy prophet distributed all his wealth in the poor and needy and that is the spirit of Islamic mysticism. Tawakul (Absolute Trust in God); Sabr (Patience) and Rida (Contentment) are the three golden principles of Sufism. The Sufis reacted against the Umayyad monarchic luxuries and devoted themselves to Jihad-e-Akbar (The greater struggle) by purifying their souls. For this purpose they practice "Dhikr" (recollection and recitation) and Sama (singing of spiritual songs). They have established the Sufi orders, chains or brotherhoods. The Qadiriyya, the Rafaiyya, the Shadliliyya, the Subrawariyya, the Moulavi, the Bektashiyya, the Chistiyya, the Naqshbandiyya, the Badawiyya, the Kubrawiyya and the Tijaniyya are the famous sunni sufi orders. Amongst Muslim Sufis some are following; Hassan Basri, Ibrahim ibn Adham, Rabia Basri, Sufyan Thuri, Abu Yazid Bistami, Junaid Baghdadi, Mansur al –Hallaj, Data Ganj Baksh, Nizam-ud-Deen Awlaya, Boo Ali Qalaudar and Moeen-ud-Deen Chishti Ajmeri. The famous Sufi Muslim poets are; Ibu al-Farid; Farid al-Din Attar; Hakim Sanai; Jalal al-Din Rumi and Yunus Emre. In the end it is necessary to mention that the real Sufi achieves divine attributes and powers. The holy prophet says: Fear the sagacity of the believer for the sees with the eyes of God." In Hadith Qudsi it is said; "When a Believer says Be: it is done: It is an allusion to the following verse of Sura Yasin "verily, when He intends a thing, His command is, "Be", and it is" (36:82) when the Quran regards the pelting of stones by the prophet as the deed of God Dr. Iqbal in a couplet regards the hand of Believer as the hand of God. Maulana Rumi in a couplet also says that when a man attains godly attributes he attains godly powers. It is not infidelity but the sublimity of Man. There is no doubt in it that Sufism is movement of purity and spirituality. But, unfortunately some people made it a profession and are exploiting common Muslim folk in the name of Sufism. Ibn Tamiyya and Mohammad Ibn Abdul Wahhab rejected Sufism and regarded it equivalent to heresy. Sufism has been made a trade which is, of course, un-Islamic. But we should not forget that the Quran announce: "The friends of God have neither fear nor woe". The friends of God are saints and mystics. Islamic mysticism is a vast world having Sheikhs, Qutubs, Abdals, Majzoobs and Qalanders. If there are false prophets we can not reject the true prophets. If there are sham mystics we cannot reject the true mystics. Mysticism is a branch of Islamics and is super knowledge of spirit.

ISLAM AND UNITY

Unity is strength. When the sand grains unite they become a vast desert. When the sea drops unite they become a boundless ocean. The conglomeration of stars in the firmament of sky soothes our eyes. The seven colors emerge in the shape of a bewitching rainbow. The unity of people makes an invincible strong nation. This is the reason Islam lays great stress on the importance of unity. The Islamic concept of Towhid is the other name of the unity of humankind. The corner stone in Islam is the unity of God. Allah's unity teaches us the message that we should not divide humans into sections and sects. Almighty Allah in the Quran says that the division of people in the races and clans is only for their introduction. The best one out of them is the man of piety. Dr. Mohammad Ali Al-khuli is his book titled "The Light of Islam" writes. "Islam is the greatest unifying force in the world. It is a religion to all humans regardless of color, race and language. It is a religion that tolerates other religions and orders its followers to respect and protect all humans." According to a Hadith of the Holy Prophet all persons belong to

Adam and Adam was from soil. The racial discrimination has been strictly prohibited in Islam. In the last sermon from the Mount of Arafat the Holy Prophet had clearly announced that no Arab has any superiority over a non-Arab; or the white over the black. This is the reason that in Muslim countries we do not find racial discriminations. Islam gives clear injunctions for the respect, safety, security and prosperity of the non-Muslims as well. Unity teaches peace, equality and paternity. The absence of unity brings and breeds disruption, devastation and disputes. Islam ordains protection of non-Muslims simply to show the respect for the Canons of divinity and humanity. God is not only of the Muslims. God is the God of all human beings. The unity of all humans is the ultimate aim of the teachings of Islam. The doctrinal and ideological differences should not lead to war or bloodshed. Man is a thinking creature. Aristotle, the Greek philosopher introduced Rationalism in Philosophy. The Quran time and again asserts on the need of cogitation. "Ijtihad" is an analogical and analytical approach towards the matters of jurisprudence. Ashab-e-Suffa were the people of wisdom. They gave more time to cogitate on social and academic matters along with their saintly and spiritual practices. They were praised by the Holy Prophet for their involvement in intellectual pursuit. Once the Holy Prophet said: "The juristic scholar who receives two rewards for every correct decision and even one for every incorrect one, for he is endeavoring with all his effort to reach the correct decision." The difference of opinion must be positive. It should not lead to prides and prejudices of priests. It should be decent difference on the bases of logic like the differences of Philosophers. Aristotle was the pupil of Plato. He differed from his teacher on many points but he never issued the edict of his assassination. Hegel and Bergson differed. Immunel Kant differed with Nietzche. None cursed or condemned the other. These differences were on principles; not personal. But unfortunately the so called scholars and clerics of different religions brought immense misery to mankind in the name of religion. The Jews, the Christians, the Muslims, the Hindus, the Buddhists and others had mercilessly shed the blood of each other in the name or religion. Each of these sects then killed the followers of their own religions on minor interpretative issues. Even to date the bloodshed in the name of faith is rampant. This is the greatest error and must be rectified. The Quran discusses the concept of unity on three levels. Foremost is the unity of humanity. The Quran in Sura Al-Hujurat (The Inner Apartments) says: "O, Mankind! We have created you from a male and a female, and made you into nations and tribes that you may know one another. Verily, the most honorable of you with Allah is the one who has piety." (49:13). The Quran no where addresses the Muslims. Either it addresses the believers (momineen) or the people (Annas). The Quran on second level refers to the unity of the people of the Books: the Jews, the Christians and the Muslims- In Sura Al-e-Imran the Quran says:" O, people of the Book! Come to a word that is just between us and you, that we worship none but Allah, and that we associate no partners with him, and that none of us will take others as lords besides Allah. Then if they turn away, say; Bear witness that we are Muslims" (3:64). The fifth verse of the Sura The Clear Evidence and the forty eighth verse of Sura The Table Spread also shed light on the unity of the people of the Book. Then on third level the Quran asserts on the unity of the Muslims. In Sura Al-e-Imran the Quran says; "And hold fast, all of you together to the rope of Allah, and be not divided among yourselves." (3:103). Then Quran condemns sectarianism and regards it shirk (polytheism). The Quran again in Sura Al-e-Imran says: "O ye who believe! Fear Allah as He should be feared and die not except in a state of Islam." In Mishqat Sharife there is a tradition of the Holy Prophet which says; "The Muslims are like a body; if one limb aches, the whole body aches." Then the Messenger of Allah says; "whoever does not care about the affairs of the Muslims is not one of them." From the above Quranic facts we deduce the result that Islam believes in the unity of all humans and preaches peace, justice and equality. Religion is to serve humankind. Religion has come to reform and unite humans, not to divide them. We must condemn extremism and terrorism in the name of religion and unite humankind if we believe in the unity of God.

ISLAM AND UNIVERSE

The materialists believe that the universe is an automation device. It is an accidental creation having no designer or creator. A blind material force is working and shaping all material objects and forms. They reject the concept or existence of God. They consider matter an eternal entity or substance. Beyond matter there is no other world or entity. This is the basic belief of the materialists and Marxists. Atom, molecule and cell are the basic units of creation and substance. On the other hand Islam believes in the existence of God and soul. It is God who has made this universe on scientific lines. It is entirely based on mathematical calculations. The universe is created by God on exactly scientific principles. Nothing is blind in the creative process. The Quran about the creation of the universe in Sura "The Heifer" says; "Behold! in the creation of the heavens and the earth; in the alternation of the night and Day; in the sailing of the ships through the ocean for the profit of mankind ; in the rain which Allah sends down, and the life which He gives therewith to an earth that is dead; in the beasts of all kinds that He scatters through the earth; in the change of the winds, and the clouds which they trail like their slaves between the sky and the earth; (here) in deed are signs for a people that are wise" (2:164).

In the above verse Allah Almighty has in detail announced the different forms of creation. We cannot make a chair without a carpenter. We cannot make a dagger without a blacksmith. When without a designer nothing can be designed, then how can such a vast universe is made without a Maker? Some scientists believe that all material things are composed of elements. Some others believe that matter is formed by very small or minute things called atoms. Democritus called these parts atoms or indivisible parts. The Greeks considered water, air, earth and fire as simple basic elements. Later some Arab scientists added to these four elements three more elements, sulphur, mercury and salt. Now the scientists have discovered more than one hundred simple elements of which the primary matter of the universe in general is composed. Substances are divided in to two kinds; simple substances like gold, brass, iron, lead or mercury; and composed substances like water and wood. Water is composed of two atoms, one atom of oxygen and two atoms of hydrogen (H_2O). H_2O is the water formula. Wood is composed of three atoms; oxygen, carbon and hydrogen. The atom is the minute part of an element. Rutherford's theory of "Divisibility of Atom" totally annihilated the notion of 'Dialectical Materialism' and opened new vistas about the immateriality of matter.

The division of atom leads to the disappearance of the properties of that simple element. It has been proved that mass is nothing but concentrated energy.

Atom is a universe in itself. The universe has been designed
on its principle. The study of atom is an interesting subject.
Albert Einstein, the father of modern physics in his book entitled "Out of My later Years" writes that this universe is very
scientifically created by God. In the nucleus of an atom there
are electrons, protons, photons and neutrons. An electron is the
unit of negative charge. A proton carries a positive charge equals
to the negative charge of an electrical charge. Similarly we have
three kinds of humans; the male, the female and third sex. In
animals we have male, female and neutrals as well. Horse is
positive and mare is negative and mule is neutral creation.
Hence we have masculine, feminine and neutral creatures. God
is the best creator. The Quran says; "Blessed is God who is the
best of the creators". The change of matter in to energy and of
electrons in to electricity proves the fact that the heaven and hell
may be electric states. There will be different states and stages
of these electric states. As we receive electricity of different watts
similarly people of hell and heaven will receive atmospheric
zones according to their deeds. On the day of Reckoning the
materiality of the whole universe will be converted in to energy
and electricity. As an atom is broken and its diffusion produces
enormous electric waves, similarly the blast in the universe will
be horrible converting matter in to energy. The Quran in Sura
At-Takwir (The Folded up) says; "When the sun is folded and
when the stars darken. And when the mountains vanish" (81:1-
3). In sura Al-Infitar (The cleaving) the Quran announces; "when
the heavens cleave asunder; and when the stars disappear and
when the seas commingled; and when the graves be over-turned;
Then shall every soul know what it hath sent forth and left behind." (82:1-5). In Suras Al-e-Imran, The Cattle, The Repentance,
Yunus, The Thunder, Abraham, The Rocky Tract, The Bee, The
Israelites, The Cave, TaHa, The Prophets, The Criterion, The Poet,
The Spider, The Roman Empire, Yasin, The Crowds and in many
other Suras the creation of the universe is mentioned. And in
the Suras; The Rending Asunder, The Celestial Stations, The
Nightly Visitant and the Quaking the destruction and the end of
the universe is described. Islamic principles are solid and scien-

tific like mathematical propositions. One of the hallmarks of Islam is its complete harmony with science. Whatever science discovers, it only increases our knowledge of God's magnificent creation. Science does not contradict Islam. Muslim scientists study the latent mysteries of the Cosmos and advanced in the fields of Mathematics, Chemistry, Physics, Medicine, Astronomy and Biology. Muslim scientists invented the magnetic compass, the astrolabe, and the clock pendulum, to name a few. Many critical systems such as Algebra, the Arabic numerals, and the very concept of Zero in mathematics were introduced by Muslim scholars. This is the reason that the study of universe in Islam is equal to worship of God.

ISLAM BY SWORD OR BY PERSUASION

The other day a Jew named Martin Moshay called me and asked: "Was Islam spread by sword or by persuasion?" I responded: "Islam was spread by peaceful preaching but the Muslim imperialists expanded their territories through sword." Hence we must be clear that Islam was introduced and preached by Prophet Mohammad (PBUH) himself through character and message. The prophet of Islam peacefully preached Islam in Mecca for thirteen years. There was no battle or sword involved. He was teased and tortured. His companions were executed and persecuted. His adversaries plotted to kill him. He had to migrate to Medina. In Medina he made peace truce with the local Jews and Christians for peaceful co-existence. He did not attack the Meccans. Rather the Meccans under the leadership of Abu Suffyan thrice raided Medina and killed his relatives and companions. His dear uncle Hazrat Amir Hamza was killed in the Battle of Ohad. The people of Medina accepted Islam not by sword but by preaching. During the life time of the holy prophet of Islam he was involved in defensive battles. The anti-Islamic forces desired his extinction with the extinction of Islam. An orientalist has aptly remarked that the error of Mohammad is that he did not offer himself to his foes to be killed. He bravely faced them and dastardly defeated them. What this man meant was that Mohammad was not a lamb but a lion. The purpose of Islamic mission by raising a special "ummah" was just to maintain peace and justice. Islam did not come to shed blood of the people of other faiths. In Sura "The Heifer" the Quran announces: "we have made you a just community (an ummah justly balanced) that you (with your lives) might bear witness to the truth before all mankind and your own Apostle may testify over you." (2:143).

The basic aim of the Muslim community is to spread truth and end falsehood. The Quran at another place says: "Truth has come and falsehood has runaway." Islam is an absolute and final truth. It believes in the motto: Right is Might. It does not believe in the mantra: Might is Right. The earlier Islam battles were defensive. When the foes of Islam saw that a religion claiming freedom and equality is rapidly spreading they attacked both; Islam and the Muslims. Actually these were religious monopolists in the form of priests who opposed Islam.

As Islam does not believe in obdurate theocracy and priesthood, hence the so called custodians of other faiths issued the decree of killing the Muslims calling them heretics and pagans. On other hand the imperialists opposed Islam. The emperors of Rome, Byzantine and Iran opposed Islam. Islam gave the message of political, economic and social equity and equality. The Islamic concept of Caliphate is contrary to monarchy and priesthood. Hence all the priestly and imperialist forces turned against Islam and attacked Muslim territories. As an honest student and analyst of history I admit the bitter fact that some of the Ummayyed and Abbasid Muslim monarchs in the lust of expansion assaulted some non-Muslim countries. They were usurpers and callous emperors. They were not Caliphs. The Western critics take advantage of their period and blame Islam and the whole history and Muslims. Here we must admit that when these emperors attacked some non-Muslim territories these were their military expeditions which in some cases were necessary, otherwise they would have been exterminated and extirpated. Overall every honest and neutral student of Muslim history would agree with me that Islam was not spread by sword but by peaceful persuasion. The tragedy with Islam is that its arch enemies became the rulers of Muslims and the custodian of Islam. They brought bad name to Islam. The religion that had come to exterminate monarchy and priesthood became the victim of both; monarchy and priesthood. Nowhere any Muslim ruler forced his subjects to embrace Islam. Malaysia and Indonesia are examples where the Muslim traders went for business and the locals accepted Islam without any coercion or force. In India the Hindus averted to Islam under the influence of Muslim mystics. The Muslim armies never set foot on these lands. Islam is like a fountain having inner force to flow to heights.

Christianity also spread through the message of peace and love by the selfless and devoted missionaries. We cannot ignore the services of Christian monks and nuns in the spread of Christianity. But it is also true that wherever the Christian colonialists went they preached Christianity by coercion and money. In Sub Continent the British imperialists converted the poor and needy people by offering them money. Dr. Iqbal Hussain in his book entitled "Terrorism in Action". On page 53 writes: "when the Roman Emperor Constantine embraced Christianity, he did so not only for himself but for the whole nation. He made all embrace it. Christianity became the religion of Roman Empire, and imbued with enthusiasm and force. It started spreading all over the neighboring areas." It may be true as far as the Roman Empire is concerned. It may be true as far as the Sub-continent, Asia and Africa are concerned. But does it mean we should say: Christianity spread by sword, fear and money? In my opinion this statement or conclusion is wrong. When Jesus preached the mission of God and so many people followed him, he had no sword in his hand and no money in his coffin. Similarly it is a baseless charge that Islam spread by Sword. Throughout his life Mohammad never brandished or wielded sword. He never killed anyone. He forgave his arch enemies when he was a victor and could have killed them. It is the tragic aspect of history that church and colonialism became one in spreading Christianity in Africa, India and Asian. In 1878, Earl of Carnarvon, secretary for colonies, under Disraeli, declared: "It was the British duty to create a colonial system where by the light of religion and morality could penetrate in to the darkest dwelling places in the world." John Wolffe, in his book, "God and Greater Britain" Observers that the Christian influence on the formulation of policies pertaining to British Imperialism were quite significant. There were still missionaries and others in India who saw Britain as having a "providential Christianizing and civilizing mission in the Sub-Continent. On page 56 of "Terrorism in Action" Dr. Iqbal Hussain writes: "Christian fundamentalism became so profound that many British politicians and dogmatists started believing in some sort of divinity conferred on them. Militarism became an integral part of their strategy. They took it as a missionary duty to occupy foreign lands and disseminate the message of Christianity all over the world. Sir Winston Churchill, the British Prime Minister declared in 1940 that the Battle of Britain must be won for the survival of Christian civilization." The Christian colonialists did their best to spread Christianity in subjugated territories. But Christianity did not spread by sword in America, England, Italy, Germany and France. Similarly Islam did not spread by sword in so many countries. Judaism is a racial religion. The Jews do not believe in conversions and publicity. They are the descendants of the Prophets and have limited number in the world for their own policy. It is their choice. We must find commonalities in different faiths for interfaith dialogue and co-existence. The people who say Islam has spread by sword should seriously study the universal, eternal and humane message of Islam and then they should decide whether Islam has spread by sword or by persuasion.

Islam in many countries was spread by mystics. The saints persuaded people through their moderate, humane and loving conduct and character. Professor Malcolm Clark in his book entitled "Islam for Dummies" observes: "Sufis played a major role in converting people to Islam in regions such as sub-Sahara Africa, South Asia (today's Pakistan, India and Bangladesh), and Central Asia." We can aptly claim that Islam has logical force to spread its message. It needs no coercion and oppression. It is not a militant religion as wrongly ascribed by Bertrand Russell. Here I deem it necessary to cite from a few eminent non-Muslim scholars about the verity, veracity and truth of Islam. De LacyO' Leary writes: "History makes it clear, however, that the legend of fanatical Muslims sweeping through the world and forcing Islam at the point of the sword upon conquered races is one of the most fantastically absurd myths that historians have ever repeated." About the universality of Islam eminent playwright and thinker of Britain George Bernard Shah writes: "If any religion has chance of ruling over England, nay Europe, within the next hundred years, it can only be Islam. I have always held the religion of Muhammad in high estimation because of its wonderful vitality." About the Prophet of Islam Lamartine writes:

"Philosopher, orator, messenger, legislator, conqueror of ideas, and restorer of rational dogmas, of a cult without images: the founder of twenty terrestrial empires and of one spiritual empire that is Muhammad." This was about the vitality and universality of Islam and Muhammad. Let me quote an excerpt from a great British thinker and historian Thomas Carlye who is unforgettable for his renowned books entitled "Heroes and Hero-worship" and "Sartus Resartus". He writes: "Sincerity, in all senses, seems to me the merit of the Quran." We can not ignore the views of great German thinker and poet Goethe about the excellence of the Quran. After these genuine acceptances and acknowledgement of truth of Islam by eminent non-Muslim thinkers we come to the conclusion that Islam is a natural, rational, practicable and universal religion based on freedom, fairness, justice, equality, humanity and peace.

No religion preaches aggression or terrorism. In The Torah in Exodus it is ordained: "Thou shalt not kill." But we find many verses and passages in The Torah which apparently seem inciting the Israelis to kill their foes. At a place it direct Hebrews: "(The Lord said): Now go attach Amalek, and proscribe all that belongs to him, spare no one, but kill alike men and women, infants and suckling, oxen and sheep, camels and assess" (1 Samuel 15:3). Then in "Numbers" in the Old Testament we find these lines: "And the Lord spoke to Moses: "When you cross the Jordan in to the land of Canaan, you shall dispossess all of the inhabitants of the land; you shall destroy all their figured objects; you shall destroy all their molten images, and you shall demolish all their cult places. And you shall take possession of the land and settle in it, for I have assigned the land to you to possess" (Number 33:50-53). Then in Deuteronomy in the Old Testament says: "You shall destroy all the peoples that the Lord your God delivers to you, showing them no pity. And you shall not worship their gods, for that would be a snare to you." (Deuteronomy 7:16). These passages of The Torah portray a specific militant message and mentality. Keeping in view the context it can be said that these injunctions are for particular age and for particular people. The historical record of The Old Testament shows the battles of the Hebrews with some enemy tribes. Such extreme views can not be appreciated in modern age which has taken a staunch stand on human rights. How can you preach the genocide of women and children in this supersonic epoch? We cannot. No sane person can practice any inhuman norm in this modern age of democracy and human rights. The Zionists who are killing the Palestinian women and children are actually acting upon the above cited verses of the Old Testament. They have failed to differentiate and discern that in all divine books some verses are timely and some are permanent. Some verses are abrogated and need not to be practiced.

In the Quran we also find some verses about crusade. The critics of Islam quote such verses to show that Islam believes in bloodshed. Mostly the following verse is quoted: "To those (Muslims) against whom war is being waged, permission to fight is given, because they have been wronged and verily God is most powerful for their aid. (They are) those (Muslims) who have been expelled from their homes in defiance of their right, for no cause except that they say our Lord is God." If God has not checked (the aggressive design of) one set of people by means of another, (then) surely monasteries, churches, synagogues and mosques, in which the name of God is commemorated in abundant measure, would have been destroyed" (22:39-40). Though in the above verse we find the invitation of fighting but it is conditional and defensive. Besides you cannot kill the children and women or the prisoners of war. You are ordained to fight who fight you. In Sura The Pilgrimage, the Sura Muhammad, the Sura Repentance and in the Sura The Heifer we find verses about Jihad. But all these verses show that when the Muslims were exited, terrorized, teased and tortured then they were allowed to wage defensive wars. They are not permitted to aggress or transgress. The Quran grants immunity and asylum to the non-Muslims. If anyone extends the hand of friendship and peace the Quran welcomes such a deed. In Sura Repentance the Quran announces: "If anyone of the (treaty-breaking) pagans ask you for asylum, grant it to him, so that he may hear the word of God, and then escort him to where he may be secure. That is because they (the pagans) are men without knowledge" (9:1). At this point it must be borne in mind that the enmity between Muslims and non-Muslims whether they were pagans of Mecca or Jews or Christian was timely and in certain contexts. Islam is not against Judaism or Christianity. The Battle of Ohud was fought in 2 A.H. The pagans of Mecca had attached the Muslims of Medina. In 3 A.H again the Meccans attacked the Muslims and the Battle of Ohud occurred. The Jews of Medina breached the treaty and helped the Meccans in the battle of Trench. Tabari notes that the Jewish tribe Bani Qurayzah was punished according to their nominated arbitrator Saad bin Maaz. This battle occurred in 6 A.H. The battle of Khaybar was fought in 7 A.H against the Jews of Medina. In 8 A. H, the Holy Prophet sent Harith ibu Umair with a letter of peace to the king of Bosra, but his messenger was killed in a place called Mutah. The Muslims marched towards the enemy and in Mutah they confronted the army of Heraclius, the king of Rome. Byzantinian emperor wanted to attack Arabia. The Prophet sent army on expedition to Tabuk. The King of Byzentine did not come out to face and fight, hence the Muslim soldiers returned peacefully. The Battle of Hunain was drawn without final fate. When Mecca was conquered not a single enemy was killed. The message of peace was given to all and general amnesty was announced. Muhammad was a messenger of peace not of war. He fought all defensive wars. He did not terrorize anyone. Rather he and his companions were terrorized and tortured. The question whether Islam was spread by sword or by persuasion needs neutral and unbiased study of Islam.

The focal point I intend to emphasize is that Prophet Muhammad personally was not against any person. He did not hate any Jew or Christian. He was quite sympathetic towards them. The battles were imposed on him and he had to defend his faith. History testifies this fact. I quote from the authentic book of Hadit Al-Bukhari: A funeral procession passed in front of the Prophet; he stood up. A companion said, "O Allah's Apostle; this is the funeral of a Jew. The prophet responded, "Whenever you see a funeral procession, you should stand up." It was a token of respect for a human being irrespective of his faith. Najashi was a Christian emperor of Abyssinia. When the Muslims were mercilessly being persecuted in Mecca at the hands of Meccan pagans some of them sought refuge in Abyssinia in 615 CE. Then in 616 CE some more Muslims sought asylum in Abyssinia. Hazrat Jafar bin Tayyar headed the victims and pleaded his case before the emperor Najashi. When Najashi heard the verse of Sura Mary his heart was melted and moved. He offered shelter and security to the Muslim immigrants. On the death of this pious and just Christian ruler the Prophet of Islam expressed deep sorrow and grief. He offered his funeral prayers in absentia. Those two episodes mentioned above tell us that Prophet Muhammad had no personal hatred or grudge for the Jews and Christians. In verse 5 of the Sura The Table Spread the food (grains) and the pious women of the people of the Book are made lawful. In verse 82 of the same Sura the Christian have been admired for being devoted to learning and for their piety. Hence we conclude that Islam respects righteous, just and virtuous Christians and Jews. The battles had causes and are the part of history which must not be repeated.

In the end I must mention that some writers are fanning the flames of clashes like Professor Huntington, rofessor Paul Eidelberg and Professor Luous ReneBere. They are poisoning the minds. The article of Professor Paul Eidelberg published in the Jewish Magazine on October 22, 2004 reflects hatred. It is the moral and humane duty of all writers and scholars of all faiths to give positive suggestions to end and eliminate the root causes of conflicts. We must provide justice to all communities irrespective of likes and dislikes. Justice must be done. The culture of hatred must be abandoned. Live and let live must be our motto and that is the message and spirit of all divine religions.

ISLAM CONDEMNS SECTARIANISM

I feel shocked when somebody asks me; what is your sect? I simply say; I am a Muslim. The fact of the matter is that when you say that you are a Muslim, the Muslims don't believe you. They don't understand what you say. The reason is that they are divided into sects. They boast and brag about their sectarianism. When general Zia-ul-haq was the president of Pakistan, on his orders a form was distributed to all government servants. They were asked to fill out the form and mention their sect. I had criticized this government policy which further fanned sectarianism and extremism in Pakistan. Dr. Allama Iqbal through out his life had been condemning sectarianism and crusading for unity. He had been preaching rationality, tolerance, moderation and modernity in the light of analogy and rational Inquiry.

There is a big difference between the approach of philosophers and priests. The differences between two philosophers are academic. These differences are not personal. Aristotle differed with Plato on many intellectual points. Bergson did not agree with Hegel on many issues. Similarly the rationalists, the idealists, the empiricists, the positive logicians, the intuitionists and the Marxists differ on many academic issues but they have never issued the edicts and decrees of infidelity and heresy against each other. They respected each other and learnt a lot from each other's writings. Their method of approach is scientific and objective. But, unfortunately the clerics are hardliners and extremists. On ideological and doctrinal differences the priests are always ready to tear each other into pieces. They issue decrees of killing of the people who do not agree with them. In the name of religion the believers of different cults and creeds had been mercilessly shedding the blood of humans. Recently in Ireland the Catholics and the Protestants killed each other. They belong to the same faith but on minor differences they also acted like diehard Christians. In Nigeria the Christians and the Muslims had fatal fights. Such things are abominable and must be condemned. Islam strongly condemns sectarianism. In the Holy Quran, sectarianism has been regarded as heresy. The Islamic concept of Monotheism teaches the lesson of Oneness of God and oneness of human kind. So for as the Muslims are concerned, the Quran in Sura Al-e-Imran says, " And hold fast, all together, by the Rope which Allah(stretches out for you), and be not divided among your selves; and remember with gratitude Allah's favor on you; for you were enemies and He joined your hearts in love, so that by His grace, you became brethren; and you were on the brink of the pit of fire, and He saved you from it. Thus Allah makes His signs clear to you: that you may be guided" (3:103). These verses clearly depict the truth that unity is the favor and grace from God and division and dissensions are the curses of God. The believers who are united are mentioned as guided ones and the people who are divided are mentioned as misguided folks. It means that Muslims are misguided because of their sectarianism. Five times in their daily regular prayers they beseech God; "Show us the Straight Path". But how can they see the straight with the colored glasses of sectarianism? The Holy Quran in Sura Al- Hugarat (The Inner Apartments) says; "The believers are but a single brotherhood: so make piece and reconciliation between your two (contending) brothers; and fear Allah, that you may receive mercy" (49:10). How the Holy Quran is specific in telling the Muslims to make piece and reconciliation if they want to have God's mercy. Are the Muslims of today under the canopy of God's mercy? What is happening with them in Palestine, Kashmir, Iraq, Afghanistan and Chechnya? They are mercilessly being killed. Who is responsible for this plight? It is no one else but the Muslims them selves. They lag behind in science and technology. They have no rational and scientific culture. Their seminaries, mosques and Islamic centers are imparting sectarian and nonproductive education. The enlightened Muslim thinkers have no place in Muslim society. They are either killed or branded as infidels. The Muslim monarchs deliberately kept the masses ignorant and backward. In this modern age of science and democracy the Muslim masses must revolt against the tyrant rulers and establish an egalitarian society based on democracy and social justice. The traditional and conventional methods of imparting Islamic teachings should be converted into modern methods in which Islam should be presented as a rational, democratic, scientific, progressive and peaceful complete code of life. It wouldn't be untrue to say that even today 99% literature written about Islam is conventional and sectarian. Islam teaches brotherhood and stresses on the need of cordiality. There is a saying of the Holy Prophet recorded is Mishqat Sharif which reads as such: "The Muslims are like a body; if one limb aches, the whole body aches". In another Hadith the Prophet has said; "The Muslims are like the teeth of a comb". It means that they are equal, harmonious and united. From the similitude of comb we must learn a lesson. There are so many other sayings of the Holy Prophet recorded in the Bukhari, Tirmize, Sahih Muslim and Al Kafi, about unity of the Muslims. Unfortunately the Muslims just after the departure of the Holy Prophet were divided into two main sects, groups or parties; The Sunnis and The Shias. Actually they were two political groups which later on turned into religious sects and even today exist. The Sunnis sided with Hazrat Abu Bakar, considering him the genuine and legal Caliph of the Muslims. While the Shias believed in the Caliphate of Hazrat Ali as the true and genuine successor of the Holy Prophet. This difference concerns the political thought of Islam. Presently it is more important to seek and find the Islamic political principles to establish the Muslim Caliphate to end the

monarchic Muslim states. In the light of public consensus on the
Quranic merits of the leadership we will have to chalk out the
political program on universal bases. Besides political differences
there are four Sunni schools of jurisprudence, the Maliki, the
Shafai, the Hanbali and the Hanafi. The Shia school of Jurisprudence is known as the Jafaria. These schools of thought had been
quarreling with each other on minor juristic issues. The principal of Jama Al-Azhar of Egypt Mahmood Shaltoot had issued a
decree of excepting all these five Muslim jurisprudences. He was
of the opinion that a Muslim should take benefit of any decree
of any Imam which suites his/her purpose and facilitates him/
her. By issuing this decree Mahmood Shaltoot actually wanted
to unite Muslims. It was, of course, a positive approach towards
Muslim unity. We are Muslims. Our God is one, our Prophet is
one, our Quran is one and our Kaaba is one. Then why are we
divided? The simple reason of our division is that we are clung
to religious personalities and are carrying the standards of slo-
gans. We should adhere to the Islamic Principles. We will have
to restudy our history in the light of logic and facts. We will
have to interpret the Quran according to the needs of time. We
must abandon the sectarian approach and promote the Islamic
principles of unity.

ISLAM ON HUMAN RIGHTS

The other day I read a book entitled "Islam for Dummies,"
written by an American scholar, Professor Malcolm Clark. It is
indeed a praiseworthy effort. He taught in the Department of
Religion at Butler University for 30 years. The problem with the
author, however, is that he exhibits only superficial understanding of Islamic concepts. He fails to present Islam as a religion
which stresses the importance of human rights and incorporates
many practices to guarantee them. This is a serious failure in
any treatment of Islam which represents itself as balanced. While
it is true that the track record of human rights in the majority of
Muslim countries is deplorable, this is no more attributable to
Islam than abuses within American society are attributable to
Christianity. Abuses of human rights are political and social
issues. They happen because the perpetrators *ignore* the just and
compassionate provisions given by God through the Prophet
Mohammed (PBUH).

On page 280 of his book, Malcolm Clark states, "Provisions of Islamic law sometimes conflict with human rights and international law in the area of due process." This is a false statement. Nowhere does Islam conflict with human rights and international law. If by human rights he means the freedom of expression, democracy, choice and conscience, these all are granted in Islam. If he includes within the subject of human rights condoning such practices as homosexuality, then it is true that Islam disallows it.

Professor Clark further writes, "While international law requires countries to relate to one another on a basis of peace and reciprocity, 'Sharia' according to some interpretations, imposes an obligation on Islamic states to conduct war against non-Islamic states to bring them under the control of Islamic law". This is simply untrue. The religion of Islam is based in the Qur'an and in the practices of the Prophet of Islam. Time and again, the Qur'an states that there can be no compulsion in religion. The Qur'an says; "for you your religion and for me mine." The Holy Prophet was never offensive. His nobility of character was legendary. He was a respecter and protector of women and of less privileged members society. It is highly misleading to confuse Islam with the deeds of evil, imperialist Muslim emperors who acted in the *name* of Islam. Such individuals are a disgrace to Islam and most certainly do not represent it.

Islam means peace. Islam is the religion of peace. Any Muslim who violates the principles of peace and sheds the blood of innocent civilians is a terrorist. He cannot be regarded as a true Muslim. The Holy Prophet says that a true Muslim, one who is surrendered to the Will of God, must not hurt anyone. The true meaning of jihad is to struggle against evil within oneself. Obviously, if the safety of life and faith are threatened, they must be defended.

In his chapter on human rights, Professor Clark has made a point with which I agree. He writes, "Many Muslim countries deny human rights not only to women and non-Muslims, but also to their own Muslim citizens. Human rights organizations are often harassed in Muslim countries, even when asserting the rights of Muslims, including Islamist groups." This statement is true. However, when he presents the opinion of a Gallup poll in the spring of 2002 about the attitude of Americans toward Muslims, he fails to make the distinction that this poll concerns Muslims and Muslim countries as opposed to the religion of Islam. It is probably safe to assert that 99 percent of non-Muslim Americans have not studied the Qur'an. Unfortunately, there are also many Muslims who have not studied the Qur'an. It is tragic that so many believers maintain beliefs which have no foundation in the Qur'an. These people cannot substantiate their beliefs within the Qur'an.

It is alarming that Professor Malcom, who is a scholar and a professor, should make such gross errors in a published book. He should have been careful to differentiate between Islam itself and Muslim states. There is not a shred of doubt for centuries Muslim emperors have been violating human rights. They have silenced people, incarcerated, killed and exiled their political adversaries. They have exhibited callous cruelty and should be condemned for it. We cannot blame Islam for the fact that these monarchs have denied human rights to women, non-Muslims and even to Muslims. Islam has given all rights to women and to non-Muslims as well. Relative to the equal rights of male and female, Sura Al-e-Imran in the Qur'an says: "And their Lord had heard them (and He said): Lo; I suffer not the work of any worker, male or female to be lost."(3:195). The Holy Qur'an at different places has stressed much about the respect and equality of women. When the daughters were being buried alive and they were treated as cattle and chattel, Islam stood for the rights of women. In Sura The Confederates the Qur'an says: "And those who annoy believing men and women undeservedly, bear (on themselves) a calumny and a glaring sin" (22:58). Then in Sura The Women the Qur'an says: "Do not covet what Allah has given to some of you in preference to others – men have a portion of what they acquire and women have a portion of what they acquire; but ask Allah for His bounty. Allah has knowledge of all things (4:32). There is a full chapter titled "The women" in the Qur'an, which deals with womens' rights and other concerns. In the last sermon delivered from the Mount of Arafat, the Holy Prophet exhorted the Muslims about the rights of women. The last sermon of the Holy Prophet is the basic charter of human rights. The human rights charter of the United Nations Organization is an offshoot of the last sermon of the Holy Prophet. Sahih Bukhari records a saying of the Holy Prophet; "The whole of a

Muslim for another Muslim is inviolable; his blood, his property and his honor." Not only the Muslims but the non-Muslims have also full protection and all human rights in an Islamic state.

Mahmoud Abu-Saud in his book entitled "Concept of Islam" on page 131 writes; "every citizen of Islamic state, whether he is a Muslim or a non-Muslim, has the right to live decently. The state must provide the indigent and needy citizens with ample food, decent clothes, a suitable dwelling and opportunities for education. The government is also responsible for providing work for those who have no jobs."

Islam is a complete code of life and is the religion of state and society. It provides solutions for all problems. It is a religion of humanity and human rights. We should differentiate between Muslims and Islam.

ISLAM ON MOSES AND JESUS

A few days ago, I was going through a book titled "The Crusades" written by Harold Lamb. He writes that when Pope Urban stirred the Christian world against the Muslim world he used hot rhetoric. The speech of Urban is also cited in his book. In that speech Urban regards Islam as anti-Christ. Similarly we find some of the Jewish rabbis and Christian priests misbriefing and misguiding the common people about Islamic views on Moses and Jesus. The Quran has mentioned the names of some prophets in Sura "Al-Anbiya" and there are some stories about them as well. Abraham has been given much reverence in the Quran. The Quran at a place says: "Peace Be Upon Abraham." Abraham was not an idolater. He was sincere to God. Such are the tributes paid to him in the Quran. Judaism, Christianity and Islam are the offshoots of Abrahamic faith. He is considered as the Father of the Prophets. The Jews, the Christians and the Muslims can unite on one agenda and that is Abrahamic agenda. What is Abrahamic agenda? Abraham did two things. First; he challenged the tyrannical and dictatorial regime of Nimrod. He said that Nimrod was not God. God is God. He had to tolerate insults. He bravely faced tests, trails and tribulations. He succeeded in his tests. He was thrown in the flames. God saved him. He did not yield to the tyrant of his time rather challenged his power. What is a lesson for us? The lesson is that we should never succumb to tyrants and promote democratic values and stand up for human rights as Imam Hussain did. He did not accept the tyrannical regime of Yazid and laid down his precious life along with his companions and relatives for the glorious cause. The second message from the life of Abraham is that he broke the idols with his axe and announced that none is worthy of worship except God. He gave the message of monotheism. Time and again we find in the Torah and in the Bible the message of monotheism. Moses and Jesus said that they were sent by God to establish His law and kingdom on Earth. What does it mean? It means that Moses and Jesus Christ propounded what Abraham propounded. The Torah, the Bible and the Quran talk very high of Abraham. The Quran is neither Anti-Moses nor Anti-Jesus. I wonder how the people without studying the Quran pass such remarks and such judgments. Moses is the most mentioned prophet in the Quran with immense respect and glory. There is a full chapter named Mary in the Quran dealing with excellence and spiritual sublimation of Jesus Christ. Both the prophets have special mention in the Quran and are highly revered.

Now let us briefly discuss what the Quran says about Moses and Jesus. The Quran honors their message and mission. The Quran gives glad tidings to their followers for heaven and in Sura "The Heifer" in verse 62 says; "Those who believe (in the Quran) and those who follow the Jewish (scriptures), and the Christians and the Sabians, Any who believe in God and the Last Day, and perform good deeds shall have their reward with their Lord on them shall be no fear, nor shall they grieve". The Quran respects the righteous Jews and Christians, how can it be blasphemous about Moses or Christ?

In Sura "Al-Aaraf" in verse 159 the Quran about the Jews says; "Of the people of Moses there is a section who guide and do justice in the light of truth". It is the universal principle of Islam. Islam does honor the man of noble deeds of all faiths. The Quran does not encourage or promote suppression or force rather it believes in inter faith dialogue and mutual respect and tolerance. At a place the Quran says: "For you your religion and for me (my) religion".

In chapter 29, verse 46 the Quran announces: "And dispute Ye not with the people of Book, except with means better (than mere disputation), unless it be with those of them who inflict wrong (and injury); But say, "we believe in the revelation which has come down to us and in that which came down to you; our God and your God is one; and it is to Him we bow". The first Sura of the Quran "The Hiefer" from verse 40 starts the story of Moses and the Israelites ends on verse 61. Then the verses of Al-Maida from 20-29 also discuss the matters of the Israelites and Moses. In the Sura "Aaraf" verse 103 the Quran says; "Then after them we sent Moses with our signs to Pharaoh and his chiefs. But they wrongfully rejected them. So see what was the end of those who made mischief". The verses of Sura Al-Maidah from 103 to 162 deal with the matters of the Israelites and Moses. We find the mention of Moses and the Israelites in the following chapters of the Quran; Chapter 2, 5, 6, 7, 10, 11, 17, 20, 23, 25, 26, 28, 31, 40, 43, 51, 61 and 70. In all verses Moses has been glorified as a great messenger of God. Similarly the Quran eulogizes and praises Jesus Christ. In Sura "Al-Imran" in verse 42 the Quran says: And Lo! The angels said; "O Mary! Behold, God has selected thee and made thee pure and raised thee above all the women of the world". Then in the same chapter in verse 45 and 46 the Quran says: "O, Mary! Behold, God sends thee the gland tidings, through a word from him, (of son) who shall become known as the Christ Jesus, son of Mary, of great honor in this world and in the hereafter. And he shall speak unto men in his cradle, and a grown man, and shall be of the righteous." The verse 50 and 51 of Sura "Al-Imran" say; "(I have come to you) to attest the Torah which was before me. And to make lawful to you part of what was forbidden to you; I have come to you with a sign from your Lord. So fear Allah, and obey me. It is God who is my Lord and your Lord; them worship Him. This is a way that is straight". The verses of Sura "Al-Imran" from 33 to 61 deal with the matters of Jesus Christ. In chapter 3, 5, 6, 19, 23, 43 and 61 of the Quran Jesus is regarded as a righteous Prophet. How can the Quran be regarded as Anti Moses or Anti-Jesus? I request the non-Muslim researchers to neutrally and honestly study Islam.

ISLAM AND NON-VIOLENCE

Violence is the product of ignorance, fury, wrath and prejudice. It is inhuman and irrational attitude. The violent people have brought great miseries to humankind. The tyrants and despots are mostly people of violent temperament. The ancient sages have said that man basically is the product of four elements; water, earth, fire and air. The people who have more fire in their body are fierier than the others. Such people are temperamentally hot and haughty. People having more water in body are lazy and cool-tempered. The eastern sages and physicians used to treat patients according to their nature and behavior. A balanced person is the one who has equilibrium in the quantity of above mentioned four elements. The basic purpose of religion is to maintain a harmonious and balanced society on the basis of universal natural and instinctive laws. According to this philosophy non-violence may be categorized in three classes. First; some people are non-violent by nature or temperament. Second; non-violent by coercion or suppression. Third; non-violent by design. But the real non-violence is the one in which man has the power and authority but he avoids violence and acts upon the good and glorious values of amnesty and forgiveness. When we say Islam discards violence it means Islam preaches some basic ethics of war and administration. It is not only Islam that stands for non-violence but we find that the Torah and the Bible also preach non-violence. In a psalm of David, he seeks peace in these words; "I will lie down and sleep in peace, for you alone, O Lord, make we dwell in safety (4:8). Jesus Christ gave the message of love, peace, tolerance and non-violence. The Gospel of John records the following words of Jesus; "Peace I leave with you; my piece I give you. I do not give to you as the world gives. Do not let your hearts be troubled and do not be afraid" (14:27). Similarly the Quran exhorts for peaceful treaties. In the chapter Well-Expounded the Quran says; "Respond with that which is better, so that he, between whom and you there was animosity, shall be like an intimate friend. And none shall be accorded this rank accept those who have stood fast, and none should be accorded it except one blessed with great good fortune" (41:34-35). All the three Abrahamic religions preach non-violence. What the followers of these religions did with each other? They shed the blood of each other in the name of religion. When Adam was going to be created the angels had said to God that this creature will shed blood. In Sura The Heifer the Quran says: "Behold, your lord said to the angels: "I will create a vicegerent on earth: They said; "will you place there in one who will make mischief therein and shed blood? While we do celebrate your praises and glorify your holy (name)?"- He said: "I know what you do not know" (2:30). My study of scriptures impels me to believe that the followers of different religions have played havoc with human values and human rights. In the name of holy war they have cut their enemies like carrots and cabbages. They beheaded their adversaries and carried their heads on the points of lances and felt pride in this obnoxious deed. What would be the conduct of people two excerpts are cited from the Old Testament? In Deuteronomy we read; "Thou shall surely smite the inhabitants of that city with the edge of the sword, destroying it utterly, and all that is therein, and the cattle thereof, with the edge of the sword." (12:15). In Deuteronomy it is also written: "But of the cities of these people, which the Lord thy God doth give thee for an inheritance, thou shall save alive nothing that breath." These predictions tell about the inhuman behavior of the followers. God never wanted bloodshed. God prophesied about the future behavior of man as the angels had predicted. The human history is weltered with human blood. The Jews mercilessly killed the Christians. The Christians killed the Jews. Similarly in the crusades mercilessly the Christians and Muslims killed each other. What a tragedy! In chapter fifty eight of the book entitled "The Decline and Fall of the Roman Empire", Edward Gibbon states: "The first crusade recorded, in the history of mankind, the most brutal prejudice not only against the Muslims, but also against the Eastern Christians and Jews. Once they took the control of the holy city Jerusalem, the crusaders, who saw themselves as the servants of the lord, decided to honor their lord by offering a bloody sacrifice to the God of the Christians. They slaughtered more than seventy thousand Muslims." Besides the Christian historian Edward Gibbon we find these words of the famous Muslim historian Ibu Atheer (1160 -1234) in history: "The Europeans slaughtered more than seventy thousand in the Al-Aqsa mosque. Many of those murdered were women and children, as well as Muslim

Imams and scholars, worshipers and pilgrims who had come from far a field to this holy site. In the rampage, the crusaders then plundered the mosque of its countless precious Jewelry". The Battles which Prophet Muhammad (PBUH) fought with the heretics of Mecca he never permitted rampage and the killing of women and children. After the conquest of Mecca he announced general amnesty and did not kill a single man. Alas! The Muslims after the passing away of prophet killed each other mercilessly. In the battle of Camel and Siffin they killed the companions of the prophet in large number. To restore his throne Yazid sent troops from Syria to Medina. These so called Muslims looted, plundered, persecuted and raped the families of the companions of the Prophet. According to Tabari for three days the Syrians looted and persecuted the Medinaites. This all was done in the name of Islam. What a travesty! The Quran in Sura the Heifer says: "There is no coercion in religion". (2:256). In Sura Repentance the Quran announces; "(This is) a declaration of immunity from Allah and His messenger, to those of the Pagans with whom you have made treaties" (9:1). In Sura The Spider the Quran says; "Do not dispute with the people of the Book but in the fairest way" (29:46). How tragic it is that the Quran which is the source and spring of non-violence its followers are divided in to sects and are cutting the throats of each others. We need respect for all faiths. We need non-violent attitude of Faith if we want to show respect to religions and the followers of different religions.

ISLAMIC CONCEPT OF CONSCIENCE

Conscience is a judge having spiritual quality that differentiates between right and wrong. Common sense and conscience are given to everyone but their use is not common. People even do not use commonsense and conscience; hence they are strayed from the right path. Conscience is like inspiration. When a man does something wrong, deep in his heart he feels guilty. When a man does some good he feels a queer sense of pleasure and satisfaction. When people like William Shakespeare say; "There is nothing good and bad, only thinking makes it so"; actually they try to mix up good and bad. Good is good and bad is bad. Intrinsically values are absolute but relatively they are relative.

To make it clearer and simpler an example can be presented. Everybody irrespective of creed, class or clan condemns murder. To commit murder is a sin. When Mr. A murders Mr. B without any reason or justification it is to be cursed. But now as Mr. A is a culprit and a murderer, hence he has to be punished. Now to give him sentence to death becomes essential. We have justification for the murder of Mr. A. The act of murder, from one angle is a sin and from the other angle is correct. Hence conscience decides what is good and what is bad. Here it should be noted that Human conscience is of two types; pure conscience and impure conscience. The former in the words of Quran is "Nafs-e-Mutminah". "The contented self" It is a virtuous self differentiating between good and bad according to divine injunctions. The latter is "Nafs-eummarah", the evil self. It does not differentiate between good and bad. It is a demonic and vicious self. The Quran regards such vicious and cruel people worse than animals and hard stones. Such people of hardened hearts are tyrants, oppressors and terrorists. For their petty material and worldly gains they can go to any extent even to kill people indiscriminately. The atheists and the unscrupulous persons have coined the philosophy of relative values. The Theory of Relativity of Einstein has largely influenced the morals of human kind as well.

But they should know that mind and matter are two different objects. There can be no relativity in the matters of morality. Moral and Immoral are absolute values only in relative situations they look relative.

About the conscience or self the Quran in Sura "Shams" says; "And the self and what proportioned it and inspired it with depravity and piety, he who purifies it has succeeded, he who covers it up has failed."

When we ponder on this systematic and harmonious universe our mind and conscience approve of the existence of some designer. Such a designed universe cannot be accidental. The way the cells are formed, planets are made, humans, animals and plants are flawlessly created, and our conscience accepts that these things are the creation of the greatest scientist known as God. Such a perfect universe can not be the creation of chance. The creation of "cell" which is in itself a complete universe leaves no doubt that what a wonderful creator has created this universe. The vast and complex world in an atom having protons, neutrons and phontons mainifest the hidden and mysterious divine spirit. Francis Crick is one of the two scientists who discovered the structure of DNA during the 1950's. The blood culture is also a strange scientific discovery. We have numberless green shades in green color. All leaves of different plants have different shapes and green colors. There are so many green shades of color in one green color. The finger prints of every person in the world are different from the finger prints of the other man. The shapes of all humans are different. The father of modern physics Einstein in his book entitled "Out of My Later Years" writes that the study of universe amazes one and makes one to believe in spiritual excellence. Francis Crick during research on the structure of "cell" became so amazed that in his book entitled "Life Itself: its Origin and Nature" writes; "An honest man, armed with all the knowledge available to us now, could only state that in some sense, the origin of life appears at the moment to be almost miracle, so many are the conditions which would have had to have been satisfied to get it going; Darwin in his book entitle "The Origin of Species" propounded the theory of evolution. The Evolutionists believe in coincidence. They do not believe in creation. Francis Crick was also an evolutionist and atheist but his amazement in the perfect creation shuddered him. Such believers of the theory of "Aliens" are conscienceless people strayed from logical and divine course. The people with dead conscience have been condemned in Sura Al-Jathiyya" in the Quran in these words: "Have you seen him who takes his whims and desires to be his god – whom Allah has misguided knowingly, sealing up his hearing and his heart and placing a blindfold over his eyes? Who then will guide him after Allah? So will you not pay heed? They say, 'there is nothing but our existence in the life of this world. We die and we live and nothing destroys us except for time'. They have no knowledge of that. They are only conjecturing."

Conjecture and conscience are altogether different things. Conjecture has no substantial, factual or logical background. Conscience is a natural gift of God which is a great guide and arbitrator. Conscience draws the line of demarcation between vice and virtue; justice and injustice; beauty and ugliness; logical and illogical. In Sura "The Heifer" such conscienceless people are described as "blind" and "deaf". When the Quran says that their hearts are sealed it means that they have no sense to distinguish between right and wrong. As they do not use their mind and their conscience is dirty, rusty and dead; hence they are blind to realities. Conscienceless people deliberately ignore the scriptures for their base desires. They console themselves by defying the divine instructions and injunctions. In Sura "Baqara" and Sura "Furqan" it is mentioned how people ignore the Quran. The Book of Allah shows the real purpose of life which awakens and fortifies human conscience. In Sura "Al-Muminen? The Quran says; "Did you suppose that we created you for amusement and that you would not return to us." Life after death is also conscience related issue. The wrong doers cherish the delusions of non-accountability after death. When a man dies his soul do not die. In my book "Philosophy of Soul" I have discussed this matter in detail. It is the need of justice that the sinners and transgressors who manage to escape from punishment in this world must be punished in hereafter for their cruel deeds. The Quran names it the "Day of Accountability." In Sura "Johah", the Quran announces; "Each and every one of you will return to Him. Allah's promise is true". Then in Sura "Hud" the Quran says; "Your Lord will pay each of them in full for his actions. He is aware of what they do." When a virtuous man dies, his conscience is clear and he feels no fear. He happily dies. At a place then Quran says; "you desire death, if you are truthful." The pious people receive glad tidings on death bed. In Sura "An-Nahl" the Quran announces; "Those the angles take in a virtuous state. They say, 'peace be upon you! Enter the Garden for what you did." Again in Sura "Al-Anbiya" the Quran declares; "The greatest terror will not upset them and the angels will welcome them; this is your day, the one you were promised."

In case man has passed voluptuous and corrupt life Allah warns these people in Sura "Muhammad" saying; "How will it be when the angels take them in death, beating their faces and their backs." When the death seems close one starts remembering God. When a wrong doer is about to die his dead conscience is awakened and he feels ashamed of his past. Some body asked Imam Jafar Sadiq; where is God and how can we know about God? The Imam replied if you are voyaging in a boat and sudden storm encompasses you and are sure of death. Then in the heart of your hearts you seek assistance from some mysterious power to save you. That mysterious power is God. It is actually experiencing God. We find great lessons in the concept of death but only people with living conscience learn the lesson. The prophets have been regarded as conscientious men. In Sura "Saad" the Quran says; "And remember our servants Abraham, Isaac and Jacob, men of true strength and inner light. We purified their sincerity through sincere remembrance of the Abode. They were in our sight, truly of the company of the Elect and the Good". The men of conscience are instructed to impart justice under all circumstances. "You who believe! Be upholders of justice, bearing witness for Allah alone, even against your selves or your parents and relatives." According to the Quran a conscientious person does not care to please even king. He only strives to please Allah. Hazrat Ali in Nehjul Balagha says; "I do not worship God due to the fear of Hell or for the greed of heaven. I worship Him because he is worship worthy." It means we should sincerely love and worship God, as He has no partner and deserves adoration. It is the voice of conscience which makes you bow before God. The man of living conscience is like prophets. God is the voice of conscience and conscience is the voice of God. In Sura "Al-Muddaththir" the Quran about the conscience says; it is truly a reminder to which anyone who wills pay heed." Let us listen to the voice of conscience because pure and noble conscience is the boon of God, which is the second form of rationality, intuition and even revelation. The living conscience makes a man a living personality close to human kind and God.

ISLAMIC CONCEPT OF EDUCATION

The Principal of Iman School New York Mr. Raza Naqvi asked me to address the students on the subject Islamic Concept of Education. This school is being run under the administration of AL-Khoei Benevolent Foundation headed by prominent religious scholar Sheikh Fadhl Sehlani. On December 19, 2003 I lectured the students on the given subject. I maintained that The Quran believes in the respect and equality of all human kind but it announces the superiority of the class of educated people. The Quran says:

" Are the educated and uneducated equal?" In Sura The Heifer the Quran declares the superiority of Adam in these words: " And He taught Adam, the names of all things; then He placed them before the angels and said: " Tell me the names of these if you are right".

They said: " Glory to Thee: of knowledge we have none save Thou hast taught us, in truth it is Thou who art perfect in knowledge and wisdom". (2:30-32). The angels and Satan failed in the test of knowledge. Hence the vicegerency was assigned to Adam. Knowledge made him superior to all creatures. The first word of the revelation deals with the importance of knowledge. In Sura Al-Alaq it is said: " Read in the name of thy Lord who created". There is another verse of the Holy Quran asking the Prophet (P.B.U.H) to pray: " Lord increase my knowledge". The importance of knowledge is manifest at different places in the Quran. The Quran says that we send the Prophets to teach people wisdom. It further says that only the people of knowledge fear God. In Sura Heifer the Quran says: " But the best of provisions is right conduct so fear me, O ye that are wise". (2:197).

The Arabic word " Olilalbab" (The men of mind), has been used in the Quran maintaining that the verses of the Quran are for the men who cogitate. The animals share humans in sex and stomach. They do not share the humans in intellect. The humans are superior to the animals because of the mind. If we negate the element of rationality from human they are nothing more than cattle and chattel. The Quran time and again says: " Why don't you meditate". Hence we see that the Quran is a Book of wisdom and exhorts to pick up the glistening pearls of wisdom. Besides the Quranic emphasis on education we find many sayings of the Holy Prophet on this subject. A drop of sweat of the brow of a thinker is better than the thousand blood drops of the martyr, is a famous Hadith of the Holy Prophet. The Prophet further said: " Attain knowledge from the cradle to the grave". Then the Prophet said: " Acquire knowledge even if you have to travel to China". In another Hadith the Prophet said: " Acquiring of knowledge is obligatory to every Muslim male and female". The Holy Prophet once issued the orders of release of those prisoners of war who could teach the Muslim children. Hazrat Ali, in his book entitled " Nehjul Balaga" emphatically stressed on the significance of knowledge saying that the one who cognizes his Self, cognizes his Lord. In a poem Hazrat Ali has beautifully portrayed the significance of knowledge saying:

" The beautiful dress does not reflect beauty.
The beauty is the beauty of knowledge and morals.
The one whose father dies is not an orphan,
The real orphan is he who brings bad name to his tribe."

Islam believes in the mastery of matter and mind. In Surah Al-Jathiya in verse # 13 the Quran says: " For you (God) subjected all that is in the heavens and on the earth, all from Him. Behold! In that are signs for people who reflect". The message of God makes us to ponder over the natural objects. It is a scientific enquiry and research, which are made obligatory. The Greek philosophers gave importance to abstractions. Their method of inquiry was deductive. The Muslims introduced the Inductive method, which is analytical and scientific. Dr. Maurice Bucaille in a book entitled, "The Bible, The Quran and Science" proves that Islam is a scientific religion emphasizing on the need of scientific inquiry.

There are four gates of knowledge, Perception, Intellect, Intuition and Revelation. Perception deals with five senses and enhances material research. It provides us information on the matter and the properties of matter. Scientists use this method. Philosophers, Logicians and Jurists use intellect to solve the problems. The mystics and poets are endowed with the boon of intuition. The Prophets have been given the special and chosen duty of reformation through the gift of revelation. Islam ordains to use all these methods for the benefit of humankind. The antonym of " Ilm" (knowledge) is " Jehl" (ignorance). The Quran at a place says that turn your back to the ignorant. It means that we should not strike our head with the stony walls of illiteracy and ignorance rather we should educate the uneducated lot. An eminent Muslim political thinker Al-Mauwardi in his book entitled " The leadership and Politics" writes that four characteristics are essential for a Muslim ruler or leader, Knowledge, Piety, Justice and Administration. Eminent British philosopher Bertrand Russell in his book entitled " Education and Social Order" writes that tolerance is the first step towards learning. The real knowledge makes us tolerant, civilized and rational. In Islamic jurisprudence no one can become Faqih (Jurist) without sound intellectual background. Whether some one is a scientist, a ruler, a leader or a jurist, knowledge is the basic requirement for these positions. Islamic conception of education teaches us to be the master of matter and mind to serve the human kind.

Islamic Concept of Jihad

The Arabic word Jihad literally means "holy struggle". It is not holy war. War is war. No war can be holy. The blood of humans is holy and sacred. The Quran says unjust killing of one man means the killing of the whole mankind. What is just killing and what is unjust killing. When some body kills a man without any reason or justification it is unjust killing. When the judge gives the capital punishment to this murderer and issues the order of his death, it is a just killing. Similarly, when a war is thrust upon you and you become the victim of persecution and aggression, you are permitted to defend yourselves and kill the invaders or perpetrators. There are some Muslims who believe in Jihad in the name of aversion and conversion. They have aggressive attitude. Such extremists divide the world in to two blocs. The House of Peace (Darus Salam) and the House of War (Darul Harab). Wherever there is no Islam as a code of system of life it is Hose of war and we should crusade for the enforcement of Islamic way of life and change it in to the House of peace. Such ideology has created immense problems for the Muslims world over.

In Islam Jihad is of three types. The struggle by Tongue; the struggle by Pen and the struggle by Sword. So far as religion is concerned the Quran time and again announces peaceful preaching through exhortation, love, logic, mercy and example. No where the Quran has said that the people of other faiths should be killed or forcibly converted. In Sura Al-Nahl in verse 125 the Quran says; "Invite (all) to the way of Lord with wisdom and beautiful preaching; and argue with them in ways that are best and most gracious; For thy Lord knoweth best, who has strayed from His path, and who receive guidance." The Jihad by Tongue and Pen means that you preach your ideas and ideology with logic and love. Do not hurt others feelings. Do not sow the seeds of hatred and discord in the name of God. The Quran announces the whole of humankind as one community. We are the members of one human family. Believers are human beings. God sent prophets with books not with swords and guns. Noah, Abraham, Moses, Jesus and Muhammad gave us law and code of life. All preached brotherhood, justice, freedom, equality and peace. The prophets were the greatest champions of human rights. They boldly revolted against the tyrants, oppressors and aggressors.

Jihad by sword is only permissible when you are attacked. It is unfortunate that Islam is being branded as the religion of extremists, fascists, fundamentalists and terrorists. A few days ago some non-Muslim emailed me. He wrote; "Islam is the religion of terrorism and Muhammad was a terrorist." Why he wrote this? How he came to such a conclusion? First; he has neither studied Islam nor the life of the Prophet of Islam. Second he has read or seen the terrorist activities of some Muslim hard liners and extremists. Partly he is correct and partly he is incorrect. The Quran about mischief mongers and the enemies of peace candidly in Sura "The Cow"; "when it is said to them; 'make not mischief on the earth'. They say; 'we are only ones that put things right'. Of a surety, they are the ones who make mischief, but they realize it not" (2:11-12). The serious, objective and rational study of the Quran testifies this verity that Islam strongly condemns bloodshed and aggression. It is a religion of peace. The Meccans attacked Muhammad thrice. The battle of Badr; the battle of Uhad and the battle of Trench are solid proofs of the fact that the Muslims of Medina were assaulted by the idolaters of Mecca under the command of Abu Suffyan. When the Meccans breached the Treaty of Hudabiyya, then the Prophet of Islam moved to Mecca and without bloodshed conquered it. Had he been a terrorist or an aggressor he would have ruthlessly killed his enemies. The people who had tortured him and had turned him out from his native place would have also been wiped off. On the contrary what he did. He announced general amnesty. In the words of Quran he said; "Today No vengeance" – Pardon for all. Mercy for all. When his deadliest enemy Abu Suffyan accompanied by the uncle of the Prophet, Hazrat Abbas came and sought mercy and pardon, the Prophet forgave him. Besides it is on record that Prophet Muhammad (PBUH) never wielded sword or carried sword. He never killed anyone in his life. The Quran says about the Prophet: "we have not but sent you as a mercy for all the worlds". How such a man can be regarded as a terrorist? Here I must admit that some people are involved in terrorist activities. They are killing Muslims and non-Muslims in the name of religion. They are sectarian terrorists. They are suicide bombers. They have bean brainwashed. They believe in extremism. Such elements must be condemned. Jihad is not offensive. The Quran in Sura "The Cow" says; "Fight in the cause of God those who fight you, but do not transgress limits; for God loves not transgressors".(2:190). The Islamic concept of Jihad has some basic human modest rules. It is written in the books of Bukhari and Muslim that Prophet Muhammad had strictly prohibited the killing of non combatants, elderly persons, children, women, handicapped and ailing ones. Book of Sunan Abe Dawud and Book of Muwatta mention that Prophet strictly prohibited Khalid Walid not to kill women and civilians. The civilian life must not be disturbed. The holy places of prayers must not be attacked. Islam rejects terrorism. When the Quran in Sura "The Cow" announces; "There is no compulsion in religion", then how forcibly one can ask others for conversion? Jihad is a war against aggressors and transgressors. To fight for wealth, nationalism, territory, honor, race or class is not Jihad. The brief definition of terrorism is that it is a form of warfare in which innocent people are specifically targeted in order to instill fear in a society. Hence, terrorism is against Islamic principles. In Sura "The women" it is clearly mentioned that Jihad is only and only against terrorists and aggressors. It is not against peaceful civilians of any country, creed, clan or class. Let us all respect each other's ideas and ideologies. Let inter-faith dialogue be encouraged. The spirit of co-ordination and co-existence is the spirit of Islam. The extremists and terrorists must be either educated or eliminated. The coming centuries must see divinity through humanity. Humanity must be our message and mission. The monarchs, the dictators, the tyrants, the despots and the transgressor must be eliminated, not the innocent, docile and defenseless civilians of any faith. Nobody can be permitted to spill the blood of any human in the name of faith or crusade.

Islamic Concept of Knowledge

There are three theories of knowledge. First; the Idealistic notion. Second; the Materialistic notion. Third; the Islamic notion. The Idealists like Plato believe that the material world does not exist at all. Only the world of Ideas, Forms or consciousness exists. Plato believed that knowledge was a function of the recollection of previous information. He based his theory on his specific philosophy of the archetypes. He believed that the soul has a prior existence. He said all ideas and things are shadows and reflections of those archetypes and realities that are ever lasting in the world in which the soul had lived. It is also known as Plato's Theory of Ideas. According to the Materialists, the spiritual or immaterial world does not exist. The Materialists are also known as the realists, the empiricists or the Marxists. These empiricists believe in five senses. They consider sense perception as the source or means of knowledge. They have no faith in mind conceptions without sense perceptions. John Stuart Mill, David Hume and Berkeley were the exponents and proponents of the doctrine of sense perception. Knowledge is through experience and teaching. David Hume says that when a babe is born his/her mind is like a clean slate. With the passage of time it receives impressions and pictures. As we teach a small kid and show him different pictures, he starts learning from outside impressions. When we show the picture of a horse to a baby he/she starts recognizing horse. Then we tell the babies; it is a goat; it is an apple; it is an aero plane etc. The empiricists do not believe in the existence of soul and innate knowledge. But it can be said that the empiricists talk about external information. They have failed in differentiating between material information and intuitive inspirations or knowledge. Besides, the materialists we find the Rationalists like Aristotle, Rene Descartes and Immanuel Kant. They believed in Mind perception. Descartes, French philosopher (1596-1650), author of Discourse on Method; The Meditation; Principles of Philosophy; The Passions of the Soul; and Rules of the Directions of the Mind opined that God exists from the certainty of his knowledge of Himself. He believed in the duality of Soul and Body. His belief in the immortality of soul made him rationalist and intuitionist at a time. Kant, German philosopher (1724-1804) in his master piece entitled

"Critique of Pure Reason" writes that knowledge can be obtained apart from any sense experience.

Let us throw some more light on the notions of the empiricists to clearly understand the notion of the Rationalists. The advocates of Empiricists state that sense perception supplies the human mind with conceptions and ideas. According to this theory, the mind merely manages the conceptions of sensible ideas. John Locke, the eminent British philosopher propounded this theory. In his book titled, "Essay concerning Human Understanding", he rejected the Cartesian notions of Innate Ideas. He attributed all conceptions and ideas to the senses. The Marxists and the Behaviorists like Pavlov, Freud, Lenin and Mao reject the mental, subjective and theoretic notions of knowledge as on the other hand philosophers like Plato, Epicurus and Democritus reject the objective reality of knowledge. George Politzer, a renowned communist scholar and activist in his book titled "Elementary Principles of Philosophy" about knowledge writes; "it is sense perception". The great Chinese communist leader Mao Tse Tung writes; "The source of all knowledge lies hidden in the perception by the bodily human sense organs of the objective world which surrounds us." The empirical theory focuses on experimentation. This theory gave birth to materialism and atheism. It rejects the principle of causality and proclaims the habit of the association of ideas and necessary relations Syed Muhammad Baqir Al-Sadr in his famous book entitled "Our Philosophy" about the logical and scientific failure of the sense perceptions theory writes; "it is possible for us to show the failure of the empirical theory in its attempt to attribute all the human conceptual notions to the sense by investigating a number of the notions of the human mind, such as the following; 'cause and effect'; 'substance and accident'; 'possibility and necessity'; 'unity and multiplicity'; 'existence and non-existence'; as well as similar notions and conceptions." The ancient Greek philosophers used deductive method of inquiry instead of inductive method. According to the Rationalists the theoretical knowledge depends on necessary primary knowledge and it is called 'thought' or 'thinking'. As all knowledge is produced by previous knowledge, and so on, until the progressive series reaches the primary rational knowledge that does not arise from previous sense perceptional knowledge. The sense perceptional knowledge deals with the existence and non-existence of a thing. It is the field of physics. But the Rationalists deal with Metaphysics that deals with ideas, soul and thoughts. Aristotle, Avicenna and Averoes were the exponents of Rational doctrine. The former used deductive and latter use inductive method. The Existentialists like Yean Paul Sartre believe in existence and knowledge through the existence of ego. The natural sciences based on pure experimentation need rational principles that are prior to experimentation. The mind accepts the following directly; the principle of causality; the principle of harmony between cause and effect and the principle of non-contradiction that asserts that it is impossible for negation and affirmation to be true simultaneously. The Rationalists believe that mind has some fixed knowledge which is independent of sense perceptions. Islam rejects the notions of both, the idealists and the empiricists. Islam believes in the existence of matter as well as of soul. About senses and sense perceptions in Sura "The Bee" the Quran says; "it is He who brought you out of your mother's wombs when you did not know anything. He gave you hearing, sight and intelligence and affections in the hope that you will be grateful." (16:78). The material universe is a reality. The Quran in Sura Adoration says; "Allah is the one who created the heavens and the earth and all that is between them in six days." (32:4). Then the Quran testifies the creation and existence of soul in Sura "The Israelites" as such: "They ask you concerning the soul, say: Soul is the special command of my Lord. You have been given very little knowledge (about it)."(17:85). As man is the blend of matter and soul, hence he/she attains knowledge through two sources; material and spiritual. The Quran in Sura "The Prostration" says; "He who has made everything which He has created Most Good; He began the creation of man with clay. He made his offspring come into existence from an extract of insignificant fluid, then He gave it proper shape and blew His spirit in it.: (32: 7-8). God gave knowledge to Adam through inspiration; not through empiricism. In Sura "The Heifer" the Quran says: "And He taught Adam the nature (names) of all things."(2:31). About the advancement of knowledge the Quran in Sura "Ta Ha" says: "Be not in haste with the Quran before its revelation to you is completed, but say, "O my Lord! Advance me in knowledge." (20:114). According to the Law of Newton you see apple falling down but you can not see gravity. Hence Islam believes in matter and soul as the sources of knowledge. Our mystical experiences and dreams totally reject materialism and open the vista for the knowledge of revelation. Without revelation we can never discern between vice and virtue. William Shakespeare says; "Nothing is good or bad, it is our thinking that makes it so". By saying this he makes values as relative ones. On the other hand Immanuel Kant has said, "Good is good and bad is bad." By saying this he showed his faith in Absolute Values. Revelation is the supreme authority on good and bad. Dr. Ahmed K. Nazir in his book entitled, "In light of Al-Quran" writes; "A primary task of life for us is to learn and be able to differentiate between good and bad." Of course the real guide is God and the straight path is the path shown by God. This is true knowledge and one should strive to seek it and act on it.

ISLAMIC CONCEPT OF MARTYRDOM

The Arabic word mentioned in the Quran for martyrdom is "shahadah" which means witness. Witness about whom? Witness about God. When we recite the words of "shahadah" from our mouth, it is a verbal witness of the existence of God. But when a martyr spills his blood and sacrifices his life, solely for the noble cause of justice in the way of God, he is "shaheed". Such a person does not need a burial bath with water or a new white shroud. He has become pure by bathing in his own blood. In Sura The Heifer, the Holy Quran says, "And do not say of those who are slain in the way of Allah; they are dead. Nay, they are living, though you do not perceive (it)." (2:154). The martyrs attain eternity. They never die. At another place in the Quran it is said that the martyrs are given food. What sort of food (Rizq) it is, only God knows. The question of martyrdom is also mentioned in Suras Al-Imran; The Repentance; The Pilgrimage and The Prophet. The man who is an aggressor or transgressor or a terrorist is not a martyr. The Quran makes it clear that it is permissible for people to fight back against those who attack them. The Quran in Sura The Heifer says: "Fight in the cause of God those who fight you, but do not transgress limits: for God loves not transgressors." (2:190). In this verse it is clear that Jihad is defensive as opposed to offensive.

Fighting in the cause of God means upholding the principles of divine law and protecting oppressed people. In Islam, war is only permissible to maintain justice. Islam does not allow its followers to attack peace loving and docile nations. The Quran exhorts to fight for the weaker ones. In Sura The Women the Quran says: "And why should you not find in the cause of God and of those who being weak, are ill- treated (and oppressed)? Men, women and children whose cry is: our Lord! Rescue us from this town, whose people are oppressors, and raise for us from You one who will protect; and raise for us from You one who will help." (4:75). This verse also clearly shows that Islamic war is only against oppressors. It is not to kill or attack non-Muslims for the sake of territory, power, wealth or forced conversion. Once again in Sura The Heifer the Quran announces: "And fight them on until there is no more tumult or oppression and there prevail justice and faith in God. But if they cease, let there be no hostility except to those who practice oppression." (2:192). Islam does not permit the killing of women and children or the elderly, the handicapped and the sick. There are also passages of love, mercy, peace and compassion in The Torah, in the Bible and in the Quran.

We must avoid bloodshed in the name of religion. Some Muslim hardliners and extremists preach and practice terrorism in the name of holy war. It is highly tragic. It is tantamount to defacing and debasing the Islamic spirit. In some Muslim countries suicidal bombing is preached against non-Muslims. Some Muslim sects are killing each other in the name of religion. I am sorry to say that some Muslim fanatic clerics are brain-washing youth to kill the civilians and innocent, peaceful people in order to earn a ticket to heaven. Enlightened Muslim clerics and scholars must teach the Muslim public to differentiate between Jihad and terrorism. Martyrdom means to lay down the life to save the oppressed people and to maintain justice, peace and compassion. Martyrdom does not mean to kill civilians through terrorist activities. About the greatness of the martyr, the Prophet Muhammad (PBUH) says: "one noble deed is greater than another until a stage comes to martyrdom which is unsurpassed by any virtuous deed." In Muslim history we find that the Meccan pagans attacked Medina and Prophet of Islam responded in defense. His uncle Amir Hamza was martyred in the battle of

Ohud. Hind, the wife of Abu Suffyan, ripped open Amir Hamza's chest, chewed his liver, and mutilated his body. His grave is at the foot of the mountain where the battle occurred. I had the opportunity to visit Amir Hamza's grave and offer Fatiha.

The Prophet Muhammad's grandson, Imam Hussain, and all of his family were mercilessly martyred by Yazid bin Mawiyya bin Abu Suffyan on the Plain of Karbala. This was arguably the most tragic event of Muslim history. Yazid was the arch enemy of Islam, who hypocritically accepted Islam after the conquest of Mecca. According to Muslim historians, including Tabari and Ibu Hisham, when the Caliphate was turned into a monarchy by Amir Mawiyya and he nominated his drunkard, debauch, renegade and apostate son Yazid as ruler, Imam Hussain did not accept him as his leader or ruler. It was this that triggered the tragedy of Karbala.

Maulana Abu Ala Moududi, a great Muslim writer of present times, in his book, "Caliphate and Monarchy," praises the sacrifice of Imam Hussain and condemns the character and conduct of Yazid. Imam Hussain stood for Islamic principles of monotheism, freedom, justice and equality, while Yazid was an instrument of tyranny, monarchy, oppression and injustice. This was not a fight between two princes as stated by Mehmood Ahmed Abbasi in his blasphemous book entitled "Caliphate of Mawiyya and Yazid." The late principle of Deoband Islamic School, Qari Muhammad Tayyib, wrote a book rejecting the outrageous thesis of Mehmood Ahmed Abbasi. The Sunnis and the Shias had both respected Imam Hussain. Only a few Muslims, under the influence of Khawarij, had sided with Yazid. People like Al-Ghazali and Ibn Tamiyya desired to erase this battle between the truth and falsehood from the pages of Muslim history, but such people were never appreciated by the majority of Muslims.

On July 16, 2004 in the *Muslims Weekly* I read a letter of a school girl named Noor-Al-Maliky which is quoted by Dr. Jerald F. Dirks in his column "Letters to My Elders in Islam." Under the title "Erasing Life," Noor Al-Maliky writes: "one of the things I would erase would be the murder of Imam Hussain. Just think how Islamic history might be different if that one, single event could be forever blotted out. The differences between Shia and Sunni might never have evolved as they have. Without such differences might not there be a better, purer Islam today?" The whole letter expresses the very sincere desire of the writer for the Shia and Sunni unity, which must be praised. However, the fact of the matter is that the martyrdom of Imam Hussain was not the seed of discord between the Shias and the Sunnis. It was the right of Caliphate after the departure of Prophet Muhammad which created political divisions and discordance. Shias and Sunnis are not the only ones who differ on some non-important issues. The Wahibis and Ahl Hadeeth and many sub-sects differ with each other on different trivial jurisitic matters.

Ibn Majah, a book of Sunni collection of Hadeeth notes these sayings of the Prophet Muhammad (PBUH): "Hassan and Hussain are the leaders of the youth of heaven. Hussain is of me and I am of Hussain." Conversely, the character of Yazid is described by Jalal-ud-Deen Sayyuti in his book entitled "History of the Caliphs" in these words: "Yazid was addicted to wine. He abandoned prayers. He even had sex with this step mothers." Imam Hussain is the Chief of Martyrs. A few moments before his martyrdom he says: "O, God; I have left the whole world to seek thee. I accepted the orphanage of my children in thy memory. If in thy love my body is chopped in to pieces, my heart won't accept any one accept thee." Then he says: "If Islam can not be established without my murder, O, swords strike me and mangle me into pieces." I am happy to find Noor Al-Maliky in the quest of better and purer Islam. But without Hussain there is no Islam at all. It is all terrorism and tyranny.

Dr. Allama Iqbal in one of his Persian couplets says: "I have learnt the secret of Quran from Hussain." Great Indian saint Hazrat Moeen-ud-Deen Chishti Ajmiri says: "Hussain is the foundation of Islam." Maulana Mohammad Ali Johar had said; "The murder of Hussain is, in fact, the permanent death of Yazid. Islam is revived after every Karbala." Hence we find Hussain, the chief of Martyrs as the real Islam; as the foundation of Islam and as the revival of Islam. The Tyrant rulers of the Umayyed and the Abbasid with all their might could not erase the event of Karbala. We should shun such desires. Rather we should introduce Islam in the light of tragedy of Karbala, as Hussain not only belongs to the Shias and Sunnis but in the words of Josh Malih Abadi: "Let the humankind wake up. Every nation will claim Hussain belongs to us." Islam is the religion of martyrdom and Hussain is the chief of Martyrs. The imperial approach towards Islam has totally misrepresented the real spirit of Islam. We must differentiate between aggression and Islamic war. Yazid was an aggressor and a monarch, hence the martyrdom of Imam Hussain is quite Islamic and glorifies the Islamic concepts forever.

ISLAMIC CONCEPT OF MONOTHEISM

The Arabic word "Tawhid" means oneness of God. In English it is called Monotheism. Theism means belief in God and atheism means negation of God. Polytheism means belief in the plurality of God. When we ascribe partners with God it is "Shirk". Idolatry is also strictly prohibited in Islam. There were three hundred and sixty idols in the Kaabah when after the conquest of Makkah the Holy Prophet raised Hazrat Ali on his shoulders and asked to break all the icons, which he did. When we believe in Monotheism rejecting all other self-made gods actually we reject duality and plurality. The message of monotheism is one God and one humankind. Universe is one; hence its diverse scenes and signs manifest all inter links with unity and unison. The Muslims are Unitarians. They neither believe in the Christian concept of Trinity nor in the Hindu concept of polytheism. God is one with multifarious manifestations and tributes. The Muslim mystics are divided in to two main schools of thought in this respect. Wahda-tul-Wajood and Wahda-tul-Shahood. The former means pantheism. The philosophy was introduced in the Muslim world through the influence of Greek philosopher Plato. Sheikh Mohuyyudin Ibn Arabi is its pioneer in Muslim Sufism. Mulana Jala-ud-Deen Rumi was also its exponent and proponent. All is He is the simple elaboration of this intricate concept. The Hindu philosophy of re-carnation and idolatry are the results of pantheism. All is from Him, is known as apparentism signifying the palpable and manifest being in all objects of universe. God reflects his Being through his creatures. The difference between Pantheism and Manifestism can be described by an example. The Sun and its light. The Pantheists believe the Sun and light to be one. While the Illuminationists believe light to be the reflection of the sun, not the sun itself. According to the Pantheists God and universe are one. They are not separate. But according to the believers of illumination universe is the reflection of God; not the part of God. They mostly cite this verse of the Quran to support their thesis: "God is the light of the skies and the Earth." In a book entitled "The Mujaddid's Conception of Tawhid" by Dr. Burhan Ahmed Farooqi sheds much light on this subject. This book is about the beliefs of Seikh Mujaddid Alf-e-Thani known as Sheikh-e-Sirhind. He was charged to be an illuminationist, negating Pantheism. In the Quran, time and again the Oneness of God has been proclaimed. God is not divisible. No object is like God. The Quran explicitly stresses on the need of monotheism. Hazrat Ali in Nehjul Balagha in a detailed sermon on Tawhid expounds that God is a Necessary Existence. God, himself in the Quran in Sura The Heifer in verse no. 163 announces His Oneness likewise: "And your God is One God; there is no god but He, Most Gracious, Most Merciful". Only the men of sanity and logic can comprehend the usefulness of the concept of oneness of God. The Quran in Sura Al-e-Imran in verse no. 18 announces: "There is no god but He; that is the witness of Allah, His angels, and those endowed with knowledge, standing firm on justice".

In Sura Yusuf in verse no. 38 it is clearly mentioned through Joseph that all the prophets were the preachers of monotheism. The Quran says: "And I follow the ways of my fathers, Abraham, Isaac, and Jacob; and never could we attribute any partners whatever to Allah; that (comes) of the grace of Allah to us and to mankind; Yet most men are not grateful". The Quran regards polytheism as a doctrine of ignorance and transgression. The men of sagacity and knowledge can never be polytheists, atheists or skeptics. The Quran in Sura Israelites verse no. 39 announces: "Those are among the (precepts of) wisdom, which your lord has revealed to you. Do not take, with Allah, another object of worship, lest you should be thrown in to Hell, blameworthy and rejected."

The Quran in the 30th sura in Sura Al-Ikhlas (Purity of faith) presents the gist of the philosophy of Monotheism. It says; "Say: he is Allah, the One and the only Allah, The Eternal, Absolute. He begets not, nor is He begotten. And there is none like unto Him."

The Sura Al-Ikhlas rejects the Christian concept of Trinity and the Hinduistic concept of goddesses. God does not have sons, daughters or wives. Islam strongly rejects any kind of physical association with God. According to the Quranic philosophy 'Tawhid" (Monotheism) and "Adl" (justice) are identical. They are in concordance and in concurrence as far as the mission is concerned. Similarly "Shirk" (partnership with God) and "Zulm" (Transgression) are synonymous terminologies – In the opening sura of the Quran it is said: "Praise to Allah, the Cherisher and Sustainer of the worlds". Islamic concept of God is universal. It is not like Judaic concept of God. The Jews believe in Racism. Their God is the God of Jews only. It is a very dangerous and monopolizing concept of God. About the Prophet of Islam, the Quran says; "we have sent you as a mercy for all worlds." The prophet of Islam was sent to all humankind. The Quran is the book of all worlds. It says about itself; "Surly it is an advice for all worlds". Hence God, Prophet and Book of Islam are universal. The concept of oneness of God is the concept of oneness of humankind. This was the reason that Islam gave it the focal importance. Hazrat Usman, Hazrat Abada bin Samat and Hazrat Maaz bin Jabal unanimously narrate from the Holy Prophet that whoever believes in monotheism he will go to heaven. Let Allah grant us wisdom and faith to serve humankind through the Islamic concept of Monotheism.

ISLAMIC CONCEPT OF POETRY

In Greek language poet means a "seer" and Arabic word "shair" means the man of consciousness and wisdom. Hence it can be said that poets are the sensitive people with higher senses and sensibilities. William Wordsworth says that poetry is intermittent inspiration and overflow of powerful emotions expressed in tranquility. Matthew Arnold regards poetry as the criticism of life. Some critics consider poetry as creation of higher and nobler human ideals. God has created Prophets, poets and philosophers. No one can make them in factories, workshops and academies.

Poets are born poets. Then why there is a general consensus that the Quran has condemned poets and poetry is something to be despised or rejected. Many people ask me about poetry. They pose the same traditional question which the dry priests tell them. Poetry is prohibited in the Quran. Is it? Let us briefly shed light on this subject.

First of all we must understand that out of context we can never arrive at our destination. The Quran should be read and understood in totality of its message and spirit. Its verses are local and universal. Some verses are in local environments but leave universal and eternal message. Similar is the case with the Quranic verses revealed about poets. There are two main verses dealing with the subject of poets. In Sura Yasin in verse 69 the Quran says: "We have not instructed the (Prophet) in poetry, not is it meet for him; this is no less than a message and a Quran making things clear." Why this verse was revealed to the Prophet? Simply because the Quranic idiom, language and style are so unique that none can excel it. It is neither poetry nor prose. Its lucid, lyrical and mellifluous style is not less than any miracle. The heretics regarded this rhythmic and musical idiom of the Quran as poetry and magic. The infidels leveled three false charges against the Prophet (PBUH) of Islam. They said; he is a magician; he is a poet; he is a madman; he is an epileptic. God negates their accusations in Sura Najm by saying; "By the star when it goes down, your companion is neither astray nor being mislead. Nor does he say (anything) of (his own) desire. It is no less than inspiration sent down to him. He was taught by one Mighty in Power, endued with wisdom."

These verses of Sura Yasin and Sura Najm clearly exhibit the truth that God rejected the claim of the infidels who regarded the Quran as the book of poetry and Prophet Mohammad as a poet. The poets in general are not condemned in Sura Yasin. It is an apt reply to the infidels that the Quran is a message from God with a serious mission and motto. During the life time of the Prophet the Arabs were known for their poetic eloquence and excellence. They named all non-Arabs as "Ajamy" which means the dumb. The Arabs were much proud of their poetry and oratory. They used to challenge others in the matters of eloquence. IT is the way of God that He conferred special miraculous powers to different prophets as required by time. During the time of David the work of smithy was in boom. God gave the power of melting iron by hand to David. It was a miracle. The necromancy and sorcery were at height in the period of Moses. God gave him a staff which showed miracles. It devoured the snakes of the magicians and also parted the sea in to two making route for his men. In the time of Jesus Christ the people were expert in treating the patients through herbs and through spiritual incantations. God gave miraculous power to Jesus to spiritually treat the lepers and the blind. He even raised the dead in to life. Similarly during the period of Prophet Mohammad (PBUH) the poets used to paste or hang their writings on the walls of Kaaba and prove their excellence. "Saba Moalleqat" were very much popular writings hung on the walls of Kaaba. Each year there was a poetry contest at Mecca in which great poets from all over Arabia used to participate. Under such circumstances the Prophet also hung the Sura Al-Kausar on the wall of Kaaba. A man of letters after reading the Sura Al-Kausar wrote underneath: "This is not the word of man." This was the reason that the heretics out of shear jealousy, heresy and infidelity called the Prophet a poet which was defied by God. "The poets" is full chapter in the Quran. In it God says; "And the poets, - it is those straying in evil, who follow them; don't you see that they wander distracted in every valley? And that they say what they do not practise. Except those who believe, work righteousness, engage much in the remembrance of Allah, and defend themselves only after they are unjustly attacked." These verses divide poets in to two classes. The evil ones and the righteous ones. The poets who spread evil are condemned. The poets who preach nobility are praised. Here one question arises. Is it only for poets? Is it not for prose writers? Or is it not for all humans? If somebody preaches profanity in prose will he be appreciated? Sacrilegious ideas or deeds have to be condemned. When the Quran talks about the poets it is in local as well as in universal context. God told the people that Prophet Mohammad (PBUH) was not a day dreamer or idle claimer. Rather he is a Prophet, an activist and a dynamic soul with practical mission. Good and positive poetry is not condemned. The Holy Prophet used to ask people to recite the holy poetry of Hazrat Abu Talib. Hassan bin Sabit used to recite "Naat" in the presence of the Prophet. Hazrat Ali was a poet. In Muslim literature the spiritual and didactic poetry of Saadi, Rumi, Sanai, Attar, Amir Khusroo and Allama Iqbal has special place. In western literature the Paradise Lost and Paradise Regained of Milton; The Faerie Queen of Edmund Spenser and the Metaphysical Poems of John Donne have high place. These writers justified the ways of God to Man. They enhanced the divine mission of the prophets through their facile pen and noble spirit. Hence in the light of above brief dissertation we can profess that Islam does not oppose poetry if it is written on didactic and divine lines.

ISLAMIC CONCEPT OF PROPHETHOOD

The animals have instinct, no intellect. The herons learn wading themselves. Who teaches the birds how to fly? Ducklings swim naturally. The horse grazes grass but does not eat meat. The lion eats meat but does not graze grass. What is all this? Actually the instinct itself works as a guide. Man has also been given instincts. He needs bread. He needs sex. But he is above animals. He has been endowed with a special boon and that is intellect. Man is free to exercise his mind. Whether he selects right path or wrong path it is his own choice. But God sent prophets to all nations to guide them so that they are not strayed from the right path. Maulana Abul Ala Maududi in his book entitled, "Towards Understanding Islam" writes; "The Prophets distinguish themselves in human society by their special aptitudes, natural bents of mind and a pious and meaningful way of life, more or less in the same way as other geniuses in art and science distinguish themselves by their extraordinary capacities and natural attitudes."

When a man invents a machine, he also issues instructions manual how to operate it. A doctor gives instructions to his patient how to use the recipe. These are done for the benefit of people. Without instructions we can be misled. Similarly God created humankind and issued instructions in the form of divine scriptures guiding them about vice and virtue. About free choice between right and wrong and on the necessity of the Prophets, Yousuf N. Lalljee in his book entitled "Know your Islam" writes: "Mankind was created with freedom of choice, and since the beginning of the human race our creator has chosen certain excellent individuals to inform mankind of God's message and how to choose between right and wrong." Besides giving moral lessons the prophets present themselves as role models. They are not like preachers or philosophers who discuss and argue but do not practice. The Prophets first practice and then preach. They come to establish justice, moderation and balance. In Sura "Al-Hadid" the Quran says: "we sent afore time our messengers with clear signs and sent down with them the Book and the Balance (of right and wrong) that men may stand forth in Justice."(57:25) Besides the rejection of despots and tyrants the main purpose of the advent of the Prophets was to renounce and denounce idolatry. Idols represent demigods, the idols of wealth; the idols of power; the idols of beauty; the idols of arrogance; the idols of dictatorship and the idols of prides and prejudices. When the prophets gave the message of One God it meant oneness of humankind. Hence Monotheism is the core and crux of the divine message. In Sura "Nahl" the Quran says; "And verily we have raised in every nation a messenger, proclaiming serve God and shun false gods." (16:26). About the importance of this message one must borne this fact in mind that a true follower of the prophets is the one who rejects despotism, extremism, terrorism; injustice and tyranny. Every prophet did not bring Shariah (The Law). According to the Quran some prophets have been mentioned and some are not mentioned. Nearly twenty five Prophets are mentioned in the Quran.

But Noah, Abraham, Moses, Jesus and Muhammad (Peace be upon them) are the prophets given the Law and Books. So many other prophets have been also given Testaments but they were not given new "Shariah". Generally it is believed that one lac twenty four thousand apostles were sent by God to guide the human kind. It is mentioned in the Quran that the coming of the Last Prophet Harazt Muhammad (PBUH) with the Final Message was the result of the prayer of Abraham when he was erecting the walls of Kaaba at Mecca. In the words of the Quran he prayed to God; "Our Lord! Send amongst them a Messenger of their own, who shall rehearse your signs to them and instruct them in scripture and wisdom, and sanctify them: for you are the Exalted in Might, the Wise."

Hence according to the supplication of Abraham there were four duties of the last messenger. He had to recite the divine verses of God. He had to exhort them. He had to teach them wisdom. And he had to purify their souls. We see that Moses and Jesus Christ also performed the same prophetic mission and faced the tests and trails of the time. Here it seems imperative to mention that God chose the prophets from different classes and sections of society. Noah was carpenter and Moses was a shepherd. David and Solomon were the kings. But they all claimed oneness of God and maintenance of Justice. Indeed, humanity was groping in darkness of ignorance, injustice, and inequality and superstitions when these prophets lit the candle of faith, virtuosity, humility, brotherhood and rationality. When Prophet Muhammad appeared the Arabian Peninsula was steeped in ignominy and ignorance. It was an abyss of darkness like Ad and Thamud. But he turned those beasts in to excellent humans. To date we need good humans who can love humankind without creed, class, country and color prejudices. These prophets were the redeemers and saviors of humanity. If we are their followers we must follow the charter of humanity and divinity.

ISLAMIC PHILOSOPHY OF GENDER

We are standing at the cross road of gender philosophy. A few days ago I called on an American writer Elder George. He gifted me few flyers written by him. These are "Patriarchy"; 20th Century Decadence; Why Marriage? To my sons; and To my Daughters. Besides he gave me a book entitled "Dear Brothers And Sisters: Gender and its Responsibility". This book is a comprehensive study on the matters of gender. I have gone through it and found it a very philosophical attempt dealing with the nature of gender in the different spheres of universe. Under the title "Welcome" in each booklet he addresses the readers and writes:

"There are many issues affecting all of us, some of which are listed on our website at www.mensaction.net, and which we also list here;

Two million men in prison – One million youth in street gangs – Twenty million children being raised with out a father – Ten million women suffering from depression - The pollution of the environment - The toxification of our bodies -The desecration of mother earth and moral decadence."

I went through these booklets and deduced the wisdom. He believes in the philosophy of Gender and the importance of family so do I. Here I would like to add some more information, which I have got through my previous studies and Islamic philosophy. Nature has endowed some qualities to different species. The characteristics assigned to mango are different than the characteristics of apple. But it does not mean that one is inferior to the other. All fruits have different tastes, colors, shapes and effects. They are all useful and eatable. Similarly the wheat in corps has different functions and characteristics than the barley or rice. The qualities of lion are different from the qualities of elephant. The nature of sparrow is different from the nature of eagle. But we do not condemn these different species or goods. Man is man and woman is woman. Both differ in physique, psyche and nature. But their innate differences assign them different duties and responsibilities. When they act according to natural division they are happy, healthy, prosperous and progressive.

Elder George about the natural duties of women in his booklet entitled "To My Daughters" on page 8 writes: "Nevertheless, there are many ways in which your nurturing ability can be expressed much as in teaching, in the healing arts, in the core of animals, gardening, writing of children's stories, and in an almost infinite number of ways in which to care for the world in which you live".

It has been always my considered opinion that Men and Women have different natural duties to perform. There is no question of superiority or inferiority involved in the distribution of this natural division. They have different sex parts but it does not degrade, disgrace or debase anyone of them.

In my opinion we must promote the natural system of life. Masculine Gender and Feminine Gender are natural realities. In Mathematics we have one (1) and Negative one (-1). Even the figures have positive and negative impact. In physics we use the words matter and antimatter. In Botany we have masculine and feminine seeds and trees. And they have been assigned natural duties and by the law of nature they cannot shirk from their natural duties. Then, why humans are overlooking their natural duties and bringing chaos and disaster to human society. The modern Westernized ladies avoid breast-feeding to their kids. Hence they are becoming the victim of breast cancer. By sexual freedom people are becoming a pray to venereal diseases like AIDS, Gonorrhea and Syphilis. This is all because of unnatural practices.

To produce and nurture the babies is the natural duty of the womenfolk. But in our modern age the women are avoiding marriage. They want to enjoy life. They do not want to produce children. Homosexuality and lesbianism are being promoted. If it continues we are going to end human race. If this philosophy is accepted then we will be fashioning and furnishing unnatural system resulting in to total annihilation of humankind. Elder George in a booklet entitled "Patriarchy" - the natural way of Life, proves the whole universe patriarchal. He stresses on the need of marriage and discipline. In another booklet entitled "Why Marriage?" on page 10 he writes: "The entire universe is based upon marriage and what it produces. The marriage of the North Pole and South Pole produces magnetism. The marriage of the Sun and Moon produces light at night. The marriage of the anode and the cathode in a storage battery produces electrons". Mr. Elder George very philosophically proves that the Sun having masculine traits is polygamous and holds the planets together around it. About the culture he opines, " The culture that we are living in European is feminine and materialistic." About the cosmological, natural and religious connotation of polygamy he opines: " The purpose of polygamy is to make sure that no one is left out. There are few widows and orphans in the polygamous culture. Europe, having a monogamous culture, had people who were left out." Elder George is a naturalist. Islam, as well is a natural code of life. Islam stresses on the need of marriage and allows polygamy, though it is conditional and subject to special circumstances. It is a proven reality that Islam has presented a natural system of sex, which protects us from physical ailments, venereal diseases and psychic outbursts.

The Greek philosopher Plato and the German philosopher Karl Marx preached the philosophy of Free Sex. So many western thinkers also supported this idea. In our modern age British philosopher Bertrand Russell and French philosopher Yean Paul Sartre also preached the philosophy of Free Sex. In China Mao Tse Tung tried to practice Free Sex but soon he banned it concluding that not only it destroys family life but also makes the whole society morally crippled. When we break Family life we produce psychic deranged bastards. We act like animals. We deprive the children of their fathers. In old age we are the victim of loneliness, depression and desolation. The ladies in old age are duped and deserted. As there is no bond of sanctity between the couple, hence they have no social or moral responsibilities. This is the reason Judaism, Christianity and Islam strictly abhor adultery and command to marry to have a responsible, virtuous and chaste life through the custom of marriage.

ISLAMIC CONCEPT OF IJTEHAD

Islam has two fundamental principles, jihad and ijtehad. In strict Quranic terminology, Jihad means physical struggle or endeavor against suppression and aggression. It is a defensive war. It is not aggression. Ijtehad means intellectual endeavor to seek the solutions of day to day matters. Ijtehad has been much emphasized in Islam. It is a rational and analytical approach, based on the Quran and on the teachings of the Sunnah, for interpreting religious matters. Time and again the Quran says that its verses are for thinkers. It stresses the exercise of the rational mind. In Sura The Heifer the Quran says: "Do not treat Allah's signs as a jest, but solemnly rehearse Allah's favors to you, and the fact that He sent down to you the Book and wisdom, for your instruction." (2:231). This verse shows that Book and wisdom are prerequisites to keep society on track and a progressive and right path. God has put our brain in our skull not in our ankle. The place of the brain at the top of the human body signifies the value and importance of the mind. The Book has laid down the foundations, but we have to be wise in taking steps to build our lives upon it through the course of time.

The Quran has given us fundamentals but we must interpret these fundamentals wisely in accordance with the spirit of the time in which we live. Suppose a man asks a Muslim Jurist, "can a lady drive a car or fly an airplane"? If the Jurist is retrogressive he will say: No- because in the time of prophet of Islam ladies did not drive a car or fly an airplane. But if the jurist is modern and progressive he will respond: Yes – a lady can do both of these because at the time of prophet these means of transportation were not invented. It is narrated that when the telephone was invented the great jurist of Saudi Arabia said: "we should not use it because it is the voice of Satan." Here one thing must be mentioned that "Ijtehad" or rational enquiry is not permissible in the clear injunctions. It is only permissible in their relative interpretation. For instance, the five daily prayer times are obligatory in Islam. This means that even all the Muslim clerics and then entire Umma decided through consensus to say prayers only twice a day, this would be regarded as blasphemy. However, itejihad could be used to discuss the method of offering these prayers in differing situations as well as the method of performing other rituals. This is the reason the Quuran lays much stress on the need for rational analysis.

In Sura Al-Imran the Quran says: "And Allah will teach him the Book and wisdom, the Law and the Gospel." (3:48) This verse is about Jesus Christ. It also shows that not only the Quran but the Bible is also the book of wisdom. Hence wisdom is the foundation stone of the divine building. The Quran in Suras the Women, the Table Spread, Yunus, Yusuf, the Bee, the Israelites, Maryam, the Narration, the Confederates, Saad, the Believer, Gold Adornments, the Iron and the Friday Prayers mentions about the importance of wisdom. Besides the Quran there are so many sayings of the Holy Prophet (PBUH) which stress the need for wisdom and Ijtehad. Once the Holy Prophet (PBUH) said: "The first thing that God created is Intellect." Once he said that the man who does research in religious matters will be rewarded, but if he reaches the wrong conclusion, he will only have half the reward. When asked by the companions how a man with wrong conclusion can be rewarded, the Prophet responded, he will be rewarded for the effort he made in reaching a conclusion through analytical pursuits. At another occasion, when Harzat Maaz bin Jabal was assigned the duty to go to Yemen to preach Islam, he was instructed to use his mind to resolve the matters after consulting the Quran and the Sunnah. Dr. Allama Iqbal, in his book entitled "The Reconstruction of Religious Thought in Islam," stresses the need for rational analysis through Ijtehad as well as the need for those called upon to do this analysis to be men of piety, knowledge and truth.

It is very tragic that the doors of Ijtehad have been closed for centuries. Among the Shiites we have Mujtahids (The Jurists) and in the Sunnites we have Muftid (The Jurists) but mostly they are traditionalists who avoid considering modern or new interpretations. On the other hand, some Westernized Muslim scholars having little knowledge of Islam, are totally misinterpreting or misrepresenting Islam in the name of liberalism or modernism. Such unfounded innovation (Bidah) is a serious danger to the purity and integrity of Islam. Islam as a whole is never stale, static or stagnant. It needs neither retrogressive nor so called progressive interpretation. It needs original, real and wise interpretation. There is a saying of the Holy Prophet (PBUH): "All innovation in matters of religion leads to straying, and all straying leads to hell fire." Here we must bear in mind that derivation and innovation are totally contrary even to any rational or scientific discoveries or deductions. Fundamental Divine principles simply cannot be altered. For instance, the sanctity of the covenant of marriage is what protects the unit of the family and thus the entire fabric of society. This cannot be altered. We can discuss different forms or conditions relating to this sacred covenant can be discussed, but we cannot abandon or dilute this foundational spiritual truth. In America I see so many writers who, in the name of modernity are creating confusion about basic laws and norms of Islam. But some writers are doing service to Islam by raising radical questions and inviting Ijtehad.

The other day I had an opportunity to see Dr. Saleem Ahmed of Honolulu, Hawaii, USA. He has written a book entitled: "Beyond Veil and Holy War". In this book he has raised many questions and has answered some of them. He has given a clarion call for Ijtehad. The book deals with the basic Islamic concepts and throws light on practical and rational aspects of Islam. It is a remarkable and marvelous scholarly effort. The man is basically a Geologist but his study of religion places him in the company of researchers. On page 17 of the book he writes: "Being troubled by the actions of some Muslims which I feel may run contrary to the spirit of Islam, I have, in many places, called for Ijtehad, or objective soul-searching by Muslims, to help us differentiate between behaviors that Islam preaches and the practices some Muslims follow. In all such cases, a plea is made for us to "go back to the drawing board" and rethink these practices vis-à-vis the blueprint provided by God Almighty in the Quran."

Dr. Saleem Ahmed writes that the Quran and Sunnah are the basic sources of Islam. In chapter 3 entitled "Hadeeth – Strengths and Shortcomings" he states that as some of the Hadeeth do not tally with Quran or the practice of the Prophet, they should not be accepted. He does not refute Hadith, rather he points out that although we can find light and guidance in Hadith, we have fragmented into sects who fight each other over our differences in interpretation. It is not the Quran that divides us, but interpretations of Hadith. In this regard, on page 55 he writes: "while the Quran was revealed to Muhammad through Divine inspiration, written during his life, and confirmed by him, Hadeeth are human compilations of Muhammad's reported sayings and actions, complied some eight to ten generations after he had died and was no longer available to confirm them."

In Pakistan a rationalist, Ghulam Ahmed Pervaiz, has also written a book discussing the controversies in Hadeeth. Dr. Saleem Ahmed only rejects controversial Hadeeth which cause discords and divisions. Hence he writes: "Thus all kinds of inaccuracies, accidental or intentional, could have occurred." He rejects the theory of Professor Huntington and writes: "My intent is not to hurt anyone's feelings but for all of us to move forward collectively as we grope for ways to turn around the foreboding of clash of civilizations in to a congruence of civilizations." Dr. Saleem Ahmed preaches peace and moderation, and rejects extremism and terrorism. He lays much stress on human rights. In social and matrimonial matters he has given his opinion and has asked the Muslim Jurists to resolve these issues from the Quranic perspective. Besides pure religious matters Dr. Saleem Ahmed discusses International issues such as the politics of Israel and Palestine in a rational way. In my opinion, we need analytical and rational modes and methods to seek and search the real truth of Islam. Both the traditionalist and modernist must be abandoned. We need rationalists and realists for Ijtehad.

ISLAMIZATION OF KNOWLEDGE

The other day Dr. Shahid Sheikh phoned me and asked: "What Islamization of Knowledge means?" I said: "why are you asking me about it?" He responded: "Nowadays this phrase is becoming very popular in Muslim circles in America. The Muslim clerics and scholars desire to Islamize knowledge. How can we Islamize Mathematics?" On hearing this I burst out in to laughter and said: "Some Muslim clerics want Mathematics to become Muslim. But can we do that?" Never- The figures are neither Muslim nor non-Muslim. What we can do is to use knowledge according to the instructions of Islam and this means the Islamization of Knowledge.

A few months back I attended a conference at Hotel Marriott Washington D.C. Eminent Muslim scholar Dr. Hossain Nasr also used the term Islamization of English language. By it he meant to write more about Islam in English so that there should be no dearth of Islamic literature in English language. It is, of course, a good suggestion. In America and Europe mostly the non-Muslims are professors or heads of the department of religion. They look at Islam with Jaundiced eyes. Some of modern Muslim researchers under the influence of these orientalists in the name of so called modernity are misrepresenting Islam. Recently I have gone through a book of Asma Gull Hasan entitled "Why I am a Muslim". It is an excellent attempt of a young girl born in America writing on Islam. Her publisher at a place writes: "She has become recognized as an articulate and persuasive Islamic voice." When I was reading her book I was much inspired and admired her passion. But there are many points of differences which need a separate dissertation. At a place about Iblis (Satan) she writes that it is not mentioned in the Quran whether Satan was a jinn or an angle. It struck me as there is a clear cut verse in the Holy Quran that Iblis (Satan) was a jinn (genni). The Quran in Sura "The Cave says; "Behold! we said to the angels, "Bow down to Adam:" they bowed down except Iblis. He was on of the jinns, and he broke the command of his Lord." (18:50) The Genni are made of fire,.. In the 34th verse of the Sura Heifer it is mentioned that Iblis did not bow before Adam. He refused and was haughty. The Quran in Sura The Heights about Iblis says: "(Allah) said: what prevented you from bowing down when I commanded you?" He said: "I am better than he, you created me from fire, and him from clay." (&:12). What I intend to prove and propound is that in the quest of modernization and westernization we should not advertently or inadvertently mislead or be mislead. Islam is not a stale religion. It is ever fresh ideology for it provides basics for our concepts and conduct. We need to seek the solution of our day to day problems in the light of the Quran and Sunnah. We need not to be apologetic and should not turn a mosque in to a club or a swimming pool. Mosque is mosque and casino is casino. Club is club. Pool is pool. Islam is Islam. It needs not to be modulated or modernized according to the wish of the west. As I mostly write we need Ijtehad (Intellectual exercise) on modern issues. By Islamization of knowledge what I mean is the use of science and technology according to Islamic instructions. Islam ordains us to master the forces of the universe. The Quran in Sura Luqman says: "Do ye not see that Allah has subjected to your (use) all things in the heavens and on earth." (31:20) In Sura Dominion the Quran says: "it is He who has made the earth manageable for you." (67:15) Then in Sura Rehman (The Most Gracious) the Quran announces: "O you assembly of jinns and men! If it be you can pass beyond the zones of the heavens and the earth, you pass! Not without authority shall you be able to pass." (55:33).

The Quran does not believe in the adoration of the universe or material objects, it rather instructs to control the natural forces. Dr. Shabbir Ahmed, an eminent Muslim rationalist in his book entitled "Islam As I understand" on page 6 writes: "The status of the true believer (Mumin), however, is even more glorious i.e. harnessing the forces of nature by mastering physical laws and using forces for the benefit of not one nation, race or color, but all mankind." Allama Inayattullah Mashriqi the leader of Khaksar Tehrik in the sub-continent who is famous for his two books "Tazkirah" and "Hadith-ul-Quran" at a place has written that a scientist is a real Muslim for the seeks and searches the mysteries of the creator through His creation. Islamization of science and technology means the constructive use of these skills. Suppose a man carries a sword or gun in his hand. Either he will use them defensively to protect himself or the oppressed ones or he will misuse them or kill the docile and defenseless innocent people. The destructive use of science and technology is inhuman and un-Islamic. I know a person who was in trouble. He prayed to God and sought help in patience. The Quran in Sura "The Heifer" says: "O ye, who believe; seek help with patience and prayer :.(2:153) It is Islamization of Knowledge in psychology. Some people start using drugs and alcohol to allay their sorrows. They use un-Islamic methods and are destroyed. In politics the Quran ordains its followers to be clean, honest, just and righteous rulers. The oppressors, the fascists and the monarchs are condemned in Islam. This is Islamization of politics. Islam strictly orders to maintain social and economic justice and eliminate injustice. Islam believes in parity, equality and equity. It is Islamization in Economics and Sociology. Islam believes in parity, equality and equity. It is Islamization in

Economics and sociology. Islam prohibits pornography, nudity, immorality and obscenity. It is the Islamization of culture and literature. In my opinion to promote noble, peaceful and righteous human values means the Islamization of Knowledge?

MODERATION AND MODERNIZATION

The present world needs moderation and modernization. The religious people are mostly hardliners and extremists. They are also called prejudiced, bigoted and narrow minded leaches and wimps sucking the blood of humankind in the name of their cults. Each society is divided into three groups. They may belong to any country or creed; three groups exert their influence on society. First; there are atheists. These people are materialists. They claim to be scientific rejecting supernatural or spiritual doctrines. Philosophers like Hume and Nietzsche were the stalwarts of this ideology. Karl Marx and Darwin also preached atheism. Secondly; there are the believers who are moderate in their views and attitudes. They are in minority. They believe in the Cosmopolitic spirit of all religions. They are modern and moderate. They respect all ideologies. Their motto is inter-faith dialogue and are the pioneers of religious co-existence and religious tolerance. They do not believe in bloodshed or holy wars in the name of religion. They believe in serving humankind. Their slogan is "Live and let Live". They say: "God is love, let us love his all humans". Thirdly; there is a group of hard liners. These dye hard claimants of faith regard themselves to be the special creation of God. They think they are superior and nobler and sacred as well. They are terrorists and issue the tickets of heaven to their adherents and associates. They are negative people harming the civilized society. They are bringing bad name to religion. These are the people who brain wash the emotional younger generation to kill the followers of other faiths. They name it Jihad or holy war. Such people fight on two fronts. Internal Front and External Front. On internal front they wage holy war with their own co-religionists. On the historical differences or scriptural interpretation they issue the decree of mayhem and murders. They declare war on the brethren of their own faith. In history we find the Catholics and Protestants mercilessly shedding the blood of each other. The hardliners of three main Muslims sects viz; the Shias, the Sunnis and the Wahabis ruthlessly kill each other on minor ideological issues. Besides we see these hard liners fighting on External Front. They deem it their religious duty to eliminate the followers of other religions. Harold Lamb, an American historian, in his book entitled "The Crusades" has sketched the portrait of bloodshed between the Christians and the Muslims. For two centuries they had been fighting in the name of religion. Whether the Christians or the Muslims; the blood of every human being is sacred and needs protection. Once the emperor of England Richard and the Muslim Sultan Salahuddin Ayubi were about to make a peace truce and stop bloodshed and resolve the matters peacefully but the hardliners from either side failed their scheme. History mirrors the sagas of sorrow and sadness. I am a humanist. I cannot appreciate or justify bloodshed of humankind. Religions have been revealed to serve humans and show them the path of nobility, peace, prosperity, happiness and justice. Religions were not revealed to kill each other in the name of God. I am a Muslim, but I cannot tolerate injustice done to any non-Muslim. I can never be happy by shedding the blood of any non-Muslim. Religion teaches us tolerance and toleration. Bertrand Russell in one of his articles writes that tolerance is the basic requirement for education and civilization. The intolerant, irrational and illogical people have created havoc in the domain of world polity and culture. When I was reading the book of Harold Lamb I could not control my tears trickling out of my eyes. It was on the sad demise of a young Christian poet who wrote a plaintive poem to his mistress from the battlefield. About him on page 233 of the book The Crusade, Harold Lamb writes: "one of them, the young Castellan of Coucy, passed the time in his quarters composing a song. Humming under his breath, he traced words carefully upon stiff parchment for this was an important love song, to his wife:

Beau sire Dien, how may I endure
To leave the comfort and the courtesy
Of my lady, whose sweet allure,
Made her my delight and belleamire."

To date the Jews, the Christians, the Muslims and the Hindus are all out to kill each other. So many countries have become the hubs and harbors of terrorism. The peace of the world is at stake. In my opinion let us educate people and prepare them for tolerant and moderate attitudes. Private religious education, which is sowing the seeds of discord and destruction, be banned all over the world. Let us educate our posterities on modern scientific lines and teach them to love all humankind. Let the religious curricula be introduced in schools, colleges and universities with modern techniques to end religious biases, extremism and terrorism. Let the terrorists be dealt with iron hand and no sympathy or mercy be shown to them. By casual and traditional legal system, these religious terrorists cannot be eliminated. Special measures should be taken to eradicate them. Besides the policy of Moderation and Modernization can be highly productive and fruitful in enhancing the spirit of religious tolerance.

ON THE CHARACTER OF
PROPHET MUHAMMAD (PBUH)

Before announcing Prophet-hood, the Prophet of Islam Hazrat Muhammad (PBUH) lived the life of a pure and pious man. In his childhood he acted as a herdsman. In his adolescence he joined his uncle Abu Talib as a tradesman. He spent most of his time in the cave of Hira worshiping. He helped the poor and the needy. He married at the age of twenty five. His youth was crystal like morning dew. No blot or blemish on his character can be found. Youth is the period of strain and stress. Young people are easily trapped in the meshes of sexual corruption, adultery or fornication. History testifies the piety and chastity of Prophet Muhammad (PBUH) before his marriage and after his marriage. Even his sworn enemies called him the Honest, the Pious, the Truthful and the Trustworthy. When he was twenty five he married a great and pious lady of forty years named Khadijah. He loved her, respected her and lived happily with her. No body blamed or charged him. But when at the age of forty on divine will he announced the mission of God, the influential chieftains of Mecca turned against him. What was his mission? He announced to reject idolatry and accept monotheism. He condemned fascism and supported human freedom. He abhorred imperialism and capitalism and stood for justice, humanity, peace, equality and love. What was wrong in his mission? The anti-human forces opposed him. He was teased, tortured and troubled. He was exiled. He was attacked. The battles were imposed on him. His near and dear ones were killed. Once he said: "No prophet was teased as much as I am teased." Such a pious and kind man who gave a universal message was attacked and unfortunately is still being attacked by vicious minds. The cause of writing this article is the statements of some of evil minded people of our times. Last year, Jerry Vines, the former president of Southern Baptist Convention, the nation's largest Protestant denomination with 15 million members, described the Prophet Muhammad (PBUH) as a "demon-possessed pedophile." Televangelist Jimmy Swaggard referred to the Prophet Muhammad (PBUH) as a "sex deviant", "pervert" and "pedophile". Franklin Graham appeared on the NBC Nightly News, commenting on Islam he said: "we are not attacking Islam but Islam has attacked us. The God of Islam is not the same God. He is not the son of God of the Christians or Judeo-Christian faith. It is a different God, and I believe Islam is a very evil and wicked religion." Briefly commenting on these views one can say that if Prophet Muhammad was a "demon possessed", then how he preached and propounded godly wisdom? He should have given the message of Demon not of God. The Quran time and again condemns demon. The Quran is a message of noble, divine and virtuous values.

The Islamic teachings mirror generosity, virtuosity, fairness, wisdom and monotheism. How a Demon can speak against himself? It is not Demon but God speaking against Demon and his allies and associates. Sulayman Rushdie in his vile and notorious book titled "The Satanic Verses" has also expressed such unfounded malicious ideas. The heretics of Mecca said the same about the Quran what these modern so called intellectuals and politicians are saying. The honest intellectual giants of the west like Thomas Carlyle and Goethe paid immense tributes to the Prophet of Islam whom Jerry Vines and Jimmy Swaggart are calling "demon-possessed" and "pervert". On the sexual life of the Prophet much has been written. His supporters regard him sexually potent and balanced. His opponents call him over-sexed and pervert. In the history of Prophets we find Prophet Solomon having many wives. On the contrary we find Jesus Christ a bachelor. At the age of 33 he was taken to the heavens alive through the apparent crucifixion process. Polygamy was the order of the day. No body took it as something bad. The Arabs practised pologamy. In the wake of custom the Prophet Muhammad married some ladies. Hazrat Khadijah was fifteen years older to him at the time of marriage. Most of them were his age sake. In his fifties he married Harzat Aiysha, the daughter of Hazrat Abu Bakr when she was just bloomed to youth. Hinting this marriage some of the orientalists charge Prophet Muhammad as a "pedophile". It was not only the Prophet Muhammad who had married a young girl even the father of Harzat Aiysha, Hazrat Abu Bakr had also married a young girl in his sixties. It was the part of the prevalent Arab culture and custom. Hence not to be taken seriously. It is not objectionable either from religious or from social point of view. So far as the comments of Franklin Graham about Islam are concerned they are quite funny and ridiculous. He seems to be entirely unaware of history. Islam has never attacked anyone. It is a religion of peace and moderation. In the earlier days of Islam, it was the Meccans who thrice under the command of Abu Suffyan assaulted on the Muslims of Madina. The Quran shows full respect to Moses and Jesus. The Quran claims that Jesus like other Prophets was a Prophet. He was not the Son of God. In Islam no one is the son or the daughter of God. Time and again the Quran declares that God neither begets nor is begotten. The Bible also at different places pronounced Christ as the Son of Man and the Messenger of God. The Gospel of Matthew says: "one of them, an expert in the law, tested with this question: Teacher, which is the greatest commandment in the Law/ - Jesus replied: Love the Lord your God with all your heart and with all your soul and with your entire mind. This is the first and greatest commandment."(22:35-38).

The God of Jesus is the God of Moses and Muhammad. When Franklin Graham says that the God of Islam is not the God of Christians he is sadly mistaken. The Arabic word Allah means God. When Jesus was taken to gallows he said Eli, Eli – Which means Allah in Arabic and God in English. God is God. IT is the God of all humans. So far as the remarks of Franklin Graham about Islam as its being an evil and wicked religion are concerned I leave unto all honest and impartial sages and scholars to comment on it. What an academic dishonesty! Alas; what is wrong with such jaundiced and prejudiced minds. The Quran is the book which is the basic source of Islamic ideology. The balanced and neutral non-Muslim scholars have paid tremendous tributes to this original source of divine values. Sir E. Dennison Ross, Rodwell A. Sale, Palmer, Sarojini Naidu, Dr. A. Bertherand and De Lay O' Leary have paid great tributes to the Quranic wisdom. Only to quote an eminent English statement and orator Edmund Burke may prove our claim. He writes: "The Muhammadan Law which is binding on all from the crowned head to the meanest subject, is a law interwoven with the system of the wisest, the most learned and the most enlightened jurisprudence that ever existed in the world." What a difference between two opinions. Both the opinions hail down from non-Muslims. The Islam whom Franklin Graham regards "wicked and evil" is regarded "the wisest" by Edmund Berke. Let Allah show the right path to the detractors. The demand of interfaith dialog is to respect the religions of all human kind. The standing universal principal should be love your religion but learn to respect the religions of others as well. The demand of decency is to logically differ on principals in an educated and cultured manner. The way the above three mentioned persons have used slanderous language about the highly esteemed and divined personality can in no way be admired or accepted.

POLITICAL THOUGHT OF ISLAM

The political system advocated by Islam needs to be clarified. The modern Muslim scholars say that Islam is a democratic religion, yet many Muslim clerics today do not believe in democracy. I would like to discuss briefly what I feel is meant by Islamic democracy.

A few verses of the Holy Quran are presented here which give us the basics for Islamic political thought. In Sura Baqara (The Heifer) the Quran says: "And remember when your Lord said to the angels, I am going to place a successor (Khalifa) on Earth" (2:30). This verse is about the vice-regency of Adam. Then again in the chapter The Heifer about Abraham the Quran says: "And remember when the Lord of Abraham tried him with certain commands which he fulfilled. Allah said to him, verily, I am going to make you a leader (Imam) of mankind. Abraham said, 'And my offspring? Allah said, 'my providence includes not the wrong-doers (oppressors)'" (2:124). This verse shows that divine leadership is not for transgressors and tyrants. It is for righteous and just people.

In Sura Saad the Quran says: "O, David! Verily we have placed you as a successor (Khalifa) on the earth, so judge between men with truth and justice." (38:26). David was not only a leader or caliph or prophet but he was ruler as well. Hence according to the Quran a ruler must be truthful and just. It is the religious obligation of a ruler to provide justice to everyone irrespective of color, cult, class, country and creed. In Sura The Adoration while talking about the children of Israel the Quran says: "And we appointed from among them, leaders (Imams), giving guidance under our command, so long as they preserved with patience and continue to have faith in our signs" (32:24). Hence we see that patience and faith are the basic requirements for divine leadership.

In Sura Al-Qasas the Quran says: "And we wished to be gracious to those who were being depressed in the land, to make them (Imams) leaders and make them heirs. (28:5). This verse shows that Allah condemns transgressors and oppressors and divinely helps the oppressed ones making them leaders and heirs on the basis of justice and piety. Then at another place the Quran alludes about divine rulers as a man of physical fitness and of knowledge. According to Sura The Heifer in verse 247 the Quran tells us about Jalut appointed as king because of his knowledge and physical prowess. The Shias consider Imam Ali fit for these merits.

In Sura Al-Nisa (The Women) The Quran says: "O you who believe! Obey Allah, and obey the Messenger, and those charged with authority among you" (4:59). The above cited verses give us the basics of Islamic political morality. These verses tell us that a leader or a ruler in Islamic state must be a man of certain qualities. Muslim political thinkers like Al-Mawardi and Ibu Katiba also write that a Muslim ruler must be a pious, knowledgeable and just man with administrative qualities. There are numerous sayings of the Holy Prophet that instruct us to obey the men of piety and virtuosity. The tyrants and evil-doers must not be accepted as leaders or rulers.

These passages leave unanswered the question of how a ruler is to be chosen. Is it through nomination or through elections?

On this point we find Muslims divided. The Sunni sect believes that the Holy Prophet did not appoint his successor. He totally left it up to the Ummah (community). The Sunnis believe in "Ijmah"(consensus), which, of course bears some similarity to democracy. They say that when the Holy Prophet was on death-bed, he asked Hazrat Abu Bakr to lead the prayers. To their way of thinking this request indicates the superiority of Hazrat Abu Bakr.

After the Holy Prophet of Islam died, the Helpers of Medina and the Immigrants of Mecca had a heated discussion on the right of caliphate. Both the groups exchanged hot words. According to Tabari ultimately Hazrat Omar presented the name of Hazrat Abu Bakr and he was elected in Saqifa Bani Saada. Then Hazrat Abu Bakr, on his deathbed, nominated Hazrat Omar as his heir, who in turn nominated six people and asked for elections amongst them. They were Abdur Rehman, Uthman, Ali, Talah, Zubair and Saad bin Waqas. Hazrat Uthman was elected. Ali did not participate in the competition. When Hazrat Uthman was assassinated the majority of people openly elected Hazrat Ali as their Caliph. The Sunnis maintain that, after these four guided caliphs, the Mawiyya turned the caliphate into a monarchy.

The book of Abu Aula Mududi, entitled "Caliphate And Monarchy" sheds ample light on this issue. Now, the Sunni clerics say that Mushawart (consensus and counseling) must be adopted for Islamic concept of Caliphate. By Islamic democracy they mean the election of pious, honest and just people.

By contrast, Western democracy can change the basic moral and divine laws and regulations. The Western parliaments have passed rules favoring and allowing homosexuality, which is not permitted in divine scriptures. In an Islamic democratic state, the basic rules are the divine rules and cannot be changed by the decision of majority. Sovereignty lies with God. We can make laws and rules that deal with day-to- day matters of life, but these laws should not be contrary to the basics of Islam. Hence we see that the Sunni modern thinkers support parliaments and democratic system.

On the other hand, the Shias say that the Holy Prophet (PBUH) had nominated Hazrat Ali as his successor. They believe in the concept of Immah, which means that the door of

Prophethood was closed after the Holy Prophet Muhammad, and divine leadership (Immah) was prescribed by the Quran and the Prophet. They mostly quote from the Sura The Israelites the following verse: "On the Day when we will summon every people with their Imam (leader)." (17:71) By this verse the Shias mean that Hazrat Ali is their Imam and under his banner they will resurrect on the Day of Judgment. They say that when the Holy Prophet invited his near relatives to dinner and asked them to support Islam, none declared support except Hazrat Ali. On that occasion, the Prophet said; "O, Ali you are my brother, my minister and my successor." The famous Western historian, Gibbon, in his book, "The Rise and Fall of the Roman Empire" also mentions this event. They also say that in Hadith-e-Thaqalan, quoted by Muslims, Tirmidli, Ahmed ibn Hanbal, Tibrani and Mustadrak Al-Hakim, the vicegerency of Hazrat Ali is proved. The Prophet's pronouncement at Ghadeer-e-Khum, "whoever's Master I am, then this Ali is his master" shows that Hazrat Ali was nominated as the heir by the Prophet of Islam.

The Shias also cite from the Sura the Consultation:" "No reward do I ask of you for this except the love of those near to (my) kin." (42:23) By this verse they infer that the Household of the Holy Prophet on divine merits had the right of Caliphate (Khalafah) and leadership (Imamah). According to the Shia sect, it was Hazrat Ali who was the legal and divine heir of the Prophet.

But let us draw a conclusion out of this controversy. In my opinion, both the sects, the Sunnis and the Shias, believe in the divine merits of the status of caliphate and leadership. The Sunnis also believe in the Immah and Velayah of Hazrat Ali. Practically speaking, we have no other way but to go for elections and select pious and just people as our caliphs and leaders. Iran is a Shia state. They have a parliament, and they have a system of checks on the programs and policies created by the parliament. They have a council of guides. In Pakistan they have Islamic ideological council which deals with the laws. If there is any doubt about a law, it is referred to Islamic council for approval. This means that we have to adopt democracy to run the state. The Shia concept of Imamah also implies that the character of the leadership must be noble, just and righteous. If we regard these practices neutrally and impartially, we see that there is little basic difference in political thought between the Sunnis and the Shias. Both believe in the vicegerency of righteous individuals. The only way to see to it that such righteous people do indeed become leaders is Islamic democracy based in justice, peace and piety.

Finally, it is essential to mention that the Shias are known as "The Twelvers" because they believe in the spiritual and worldly leadership of the twelve Imamss from Imam Ali to Imam Mehdi. Some Shia clerics believe that as they were the pious and just personalities and also belonged to the Household of the Prophet. Hence, on merits, they had the right to be our caliphs (Khalifa) as well. However, after the disappearance from view of Imam Mehdi, we find some jurists (Faqaha) claiming to be his heirs, assistants, or the lieutenants. They are simply religious people. The majority of them refused to participate in politics.

Imam Khomeini, in his book entitled "Islamic Statem" has given the idea of the government of clerics. Another great Shia cleric, Ayatollah Shariat Madari, who was Imam Khomeini's contemporary, did not agree with his political ideas and deeds. Even Imam Khomeini did not reject the modern method of democratic elections. This shows that practically we have to reject nomination and go for elections. In Sura Shura we find that even the Prophet is asked to council with people in day-to-day social and political matters. The concept of Imamah in the Ismailis and Bohras is a spiritual monarchy having no Islamic sanction. Hence it can be said that the Sunnis and the Shias have no other way but to act upon the Islamic democracy, which is based on freedom, equality, peace, progress, justice and piety and is enacted through general elections. Here we all unite and reject monarchy, militarism and fascism.

RELIGION ON SEX

Hindu philosophy in "Koak Shastar" discusses the kinds of women and their emotional and sexual propensities. A lady of small stature has different sexual inclinations than a lady of tall stature. A lady with heavy bums differs from a lady of thin buttocks. Hindu literature is quite rich as far as sexology is concerned. But here I do not intend to discuss sexual relations or propensities of feminine folk. I am concerned about sex-discipline. To attain sexual pleasure there are five methods; Masturbation; Fingering; Homosexuality; Lesbianism and Marriage. Islam rejects first four methods, regarding them unnatural and uncivilized methods. In Islam marriage is prescribed for three reasons. First; the marriage between man and woman is the only natural way of seeking physical and mental pleasure. Second; for the procreation of lineage you have to marry. Third; to avoid venereal diseases you should avoid all other unnatural sexual methods except marriage. Let it be elaborated to have clear comprehension of the issue. Some people do not marry and masturbate. It effects their health badly. They become deranged and are constantly disturbed. Some young girls in traditional tribal or religious cultures satiate their sexual desire by fingering. It is also unnatural and non-procreative practice. It germinates hysteric ailments. Homosexuality has been condemned in the Quran. The nation of Prophet Hazrat Lot was involved in this heinous deed. Hazrat Lot admonished his people and asked them to refrain from it and marry the daughters of his nation. But his community was sunk deep in to the quagmire of this sexual perversion. God punished them and they were destroyed. The account of Sodom mentioned in the Bible and in the Quran speaks volumes of warnings and admonitions. The word sodomy has been derived from Sodom. The Lake of Dead Sea in the heart of Israel is a living example of this obnoxious human behaviour. Lesbianism is also un-natural and non-procreative. It we adopt the above-mentioned four methods to procure sexual pleasure then we will stop the process of procreation. That will be the end of humankind on the globe of the Earth. The only natural way to attain sexual pleasure keeping us away from psychic and physical diseases and providing us racial procreation is the marriage between man and woman.

The practice of "Gay Marriage" has become quite popular and rampant in western society. Some of the European parliaments have passed the bills in favor of "Gay Marriage". In December 2003 an American court in Massachusetts has declared Gay Marriage legal. This ruling sets the precedent that same-sex couples have the right to be married incontrovertibly. President of America George W. Bush has also criticized the decision of the court and announced to get a bill passed in the congress against such decisions. Vatican has also condemned Gayism.

Judaism, Hinduism, Christianity and Islam condemn adultery and all unnatural methods of sexual appeasement. According to the philosophy of Gender no two similar genders are involved in sexual cohabitation. A dog does sex with a bitch; not with a dog. A cock does sex with a hen; not with a cock. A horse does sex with a mare; not with a horse. An ox does sex with a cow; not with an ox. A bull does sex with a buffalo; not with a bull. A lion does sex with a lioness; not with a lion. It is vice versa as well. No bitch does sex with a bitch. No hen does sex with a hen and like wise. Even animals do not practice the unnatural method of sex. There is a book entitled ID, Ego and super Ego by Sigmund Freud. Ed is animal sex element. Modern perverted people believing in unnatural methods want to rank us in animal fold. Then how humankind can be permitted to be involved in unnatural methods of sex such as homosexuality and lesbianism. The Christians opt for court marriage instead of church marriage because then they cannot divorce. The religious instructions are hard and sever. The Christian clergy can think over it in the need of modern needs how to bring social reformation in the matters of divorce to facilitate the Christian community.

Free sex is also a hoax. The concept of partner with out marriage is strongly condemned by The Torah, The Bible and The Quran. Fornication and adultery are prohibited in the scriptures. Reason being "Free Sex" creates social problems and sexual diseases. It is medically proved that once a woman cohabits with more than one man she breeds bacteria, which causes gonorrhea, syphilis and AIDS. Besides sexual diseases, Free Sex breeds permanent social perturbance and psychic perplexity. When a lady practices Free Sex she becomes habitual of different males and their sexual strength. According to the experts on sex such a lady can never have sexual satisfaction. When once she enjoys a sexually over strong man if she misses that man then she can never be satisfied by average man. There are certain reasons religions have strongly prohibited Free Sex and illegal Sex. The Torah says" "You shalt not commit adultery" (Exodus – The Ten Commandments)- The Bible says: "You have heard that it was said, do not commit adultery. But I tell you that anyone who looks at a woman lustfully has already committed adultery with her in his heart". (Matthew 5:27). The Quran says: "Nor come nigh to adultery. For it is an indecent deed and an evil way". (Al-Isra- 17:32).

In sum it can be said that all sacrilegious sexual practices have been condemned by all religions. We must act upon the divine commandments to avoid physical, psychic and social diseases and problems. Extra-marital relations are also strictly prohibited in religions. Instead of producing bastards and half parent children let us produce legitimate kids. Spouse should not replace wife and sibling should not replace kid. Let us come back to natural system.

RELIGION REJECTS TERRORISM

It is a general impression that religious people are hard liners, extremists, fundamentalists and terrorists. History has also proved that in the name of religion blood of innocent people has been mercilessly shed. A few days ago I borrowed a book from the municipal library of Valley Stream, New York. Its title is "The Crusade" written by Harold Lamb. The way for two centuries the Christians and the Muslims had been fighting and shedding each other's blood it is very sorrowful. Once the king of Britain Richard and Al-Adil, the younger brother of Muslim ruler Salahuddin Ayubi in a meeting decided to resolve the matter amicably and peacefully. Richard offered her sister for wedding to Al-Adil but she refused. Besides some hard-liners from both sides never let them decide the issues peacefully. I admire the intent and proposal of Richard for peaceful negotiations to resolve the issue and to end the Holy war. Similarly in 1229 through a truce between emperor Frederick and emperor of Egypt Al-Kamil Palestine was divided. The holy places of Muslims like Al-Aksa Mosque was decided to remain in the control of the Muslims and the holy places of the Christians like the Sepulcher remain in the custody of the Christians. But hard linders from both sides opposed the truce and once again created big problems leading to turmoil and chaos. Gregory, the Pope in Rome and other priests accused King Frederick believing more in Muhammad than in Jesus Christ. The papal forces turned against him for making peace truce with the Muslims and even doubted his faith. In my opinion the attempts of Richard and Frederick to resolve the issues peacefully are the golden chapters of the human history. The hard-liners from both sides had marred the situation and in the name of religion created unprecedented crisis. The blood of mankind is holier than anything. We must understand the spirit of all divine messages and that is nothing but maintenance of justice and love of mankind. The Holy Bible says: "God is Love". We have been time and again exhorted by Jesus Christ to love the neighbor, the needy, the patient and the weaker ones. Jesus never preached bloodshed. Once he said if someone slapped on cheek you offer the other cheek to him as well. It is a great message of peace and sacrifice. Moses faced the tyranny of Pharaoh and stood for the oppressed and repressed people of his time. Prophet Muhammad (P.B.U.H) condemned oppression and terrorism. Even after conquering Mecca when he had all power and authority to crush his enemies, he did not deal with them harshly. He was all mercy and showed deep love and sympathy for all mankind. He never pressed anybody to accept Islam. He never got anyone killed overtly or covertly. He condemned bloodshed and cruelty. Actually, he promulgated and propagated the cult of Abraham. He endorsed the moral and human values preached in the Gospel. The Old Testament candidly rejects bloodshed. In Exodus it is ordained "you shall not murder". Out of the Ten Commandments given in the Torah it is a clear injunction of God, which condemns aggression. The New Testament also exhorts: "you have heard that it was said to the people long ago, 'Do not murder, and anyone who murders will be subject to judgment'. But I tell you that anyone who is angry with his brother will be subject to judgment". (Matthew 5:21). The Holy Bible has preached love to the extent that a man feels impelled to name Christianity as a religion of love. The Quran is also very antagonistic to terrorism. The Islamic concept of crusade is not offensive. It is purely defensive. Islamic Jihad means to struggle against aggression, oppression, repression, transgression and terrorism. In Islam holy war means to fight the aggressive forces and to help the oppressed people. The history of Muslim emperors is full of bloodshed. They had been fighting each other for thrown and crown. They had been attacking the non-Muslims for expansion of their governance and territory. It is history of Muslim imperialists. It is not the history of Islam. When the Umayyads ruled over the Muslims, they claimed to be the successors of the Holy Prophet Muhammad (P.B.U.H) and carried the standards of Islam. The Abbasids defeated them.

They also fought in the name of Islam and snatched the power from the Umayyads. The Muslims had been killing each other in the name of Islam. They had no democratic spirit or system. They established monarchy instead of establishing a democratic system. According to the message of Sura-e-shoora (The Counsel) of the Quran it is the political duty of the Muslims to establish a democratic state.

The Quran classifies mankind into three categories. First, the Quran says: "surely the believers are brethren". It means no Muslim should harm any Muslim. They ought to live like real brothers with peace, trust, patience and affection. But are the Muslims living like the brothers? They are divided into so many sects. Religiously for centuries they are killing each other. Even today in some Muslim countries the hard-liners of one sect are preaching the younger generation to kill the people of other sects if they want to attain the Heaven. Sectarian terrorism is outrageously creating immense fear and fright in the Muslim world.

Second, the Quran instructs us to deal with the Jews and the Christians honorably, humanely, peacefully and justly. They are named as "Ahl-ul-Kitab", the People of the Book. Repeatedly the Quran invites the People of the Book to be united on common factors of religion and respect the religion of each other. At a place the Quran exhorts the Muslims not to abjure the false Gods of the unbelievers lest they should abuse or abjure your true God In the Sura "The Family of Imran" in verse number 3, the Quran says: "He has revealed to you the Book with truth, verifying that which is before it, and He revealed the Torah and the Gospel aforetime, a guidance for the people and He sent the Quran". This verse verifies the sanctity, glory and sacredness of the Torah and the Bible, regarding them as the Books of Guidance. It is the universal spirit of Quran. Further, in the 20th verse of The Family of Imran, God asked the Prophet Muhammad (P.B.U.H) to present the message of Islam with wisdom and politeness, whether they accept it or reject it. In the same Sura in verse number 64 it has been announced: "Say: O followers of the Book! Come to an equitable proposition between us and you that we shall not serve any but God". This verse also gives the message of co-existence and cordiality between the Muslims and the non-Muslims. Prophet Muhammad (P.B.U.H) wrote letters and sent emissaries to neighboring rulers explaining to them the message of God and invited them to the fold of Islam through reasoning. He did not spread Islam through sword. It is on the record that Prophet Muhammad (P.B.U.H) never initiated war or carried sword, lance, spear, arrow or axe in his hand. He was the Prophet of peace. The truce of Medina with the Jews is an example of his peaceful policy with the non-Muslims. If today any Muslim kills any non-Muslim in the name of religion he is to be condemned in the light of Islamic teachings.

Third, the Quran also deals with the Pagans on human level. It nowhere instructs his followers to kill non-Muslims. The Quran gives a friendly and peaceful message to the non-Muslims. It says: "Even as we sent among you an Apostle from among you who recites to you our signs and purifies you and teaches you the Book and the wisdom and teaches you that which you did not know". (2:151) According to the Quran the Prophets were sent to maintain peace and justice. They were not dictators. They were teachers and preachers presenting their own image as concept and precept. In Sura entitle "The un-believers" the Quran says:

"Say: O unbelievers!
I do not serve that, which you serve,
Nor do you serve Him, whom I serve,
Nor am I going to serve that, which you serve,
Nor are you going to serve Him whom I serve.
You shall have your religion and I shall have my religion."

The above verse is about non-Muslims. Even they are not supposed to be killed in the name of God. In an Islamic state they can live independently and practice their religion without any fear or pressure. Their life, property and honor are safe in a Muslim state. Islam grants full human rights to the non-Muslims as well. Islam is anti terrorism. The religious hard-liners who invoke or incite their adherents to shed the blood of humans to achieve redemption or salvation are badly mistaken. They are the brothers of Satan. They are predators and transgressors. They are condemned in the Holy Quran. In Sura the Cow when Abraham beseeched God for the leadership of the mankind for his progeny, God responded: "My covenant does not include the oppressors." It means God condemns oppression. The God chosen people (Prophets) never shed the blood of mankind. They are the preachers of peace and brotherhood. It is the political religion, which has brought misery to mankind. If we seriously desire to save religion we will have to save mankind. No mankind, no religion. When God expressed his plan to create Adam, the angels opined that Adam would shed blood on earth. They meant that the son of Adam would create mischief and tyranny. God said: " Assuredly I know what you do not know". (The Cow verse number 30). It actually meant the vicegerency of Adam. It was divine authority entrusted to man. It was human potential to be co-worker and friend of God. Man has to prove his worth by being the messenger of peace and love.

It can be safely said that no religion preaches bloodshed. The wars, which had been fought in the name of religion, were political oriented and temporal ridden. Let us learn a lesson from our history and avoid wars in the name of religion. We must understand the spirit of all religions and that is nothing but the service of God and the service of mankind. The human who does not love other humans cannot love God. The negative and destructive use of religion is like a lethal weapon in the hand of a mad man. We should act sanely and humanly. This is the only message of God, which is eternal and all - embracing. Let us try to follow it if we want to save the humans from disaster, desolation and destruction.

THE ABRAHAMIC RELIGIONS

All the Abrahamic religions (Judaism, Christianity and Islam) are in search of a congenial society and provide a series of commandments, to be followed by the people. Accordingly the Torah, the Bible, and the Quran variously affirm these injunctions. Principal commandments of Islam and how they ensure the advancement of human society and social justice particularly in terms of the social, economic and political institution are briefly discussed in this article. As Abraham mentioned Abram in the early text of The Torah is the father of all prophets and source of all faiths we find his mention in the books of all Abrahamic religions. Hence we can say that all believers can unit in the name of Abraham and the interfaith dialogue can lead us towards the dale of dalliance. Let us see how we can promote the culture of the religious tolerance and universal fraternity.

The Torah

1.   The mention of Abraham in Torah.
In the Holy Torah in Genesis it is written: The call of Abram "The Lord had said to Abram, "Leave your country, your people and your father's household and go to the land I will show you." "I will make you in to a great nation and I will bless you; I will make your name great, and you will be a blessing. I will bless those who bless you, and whoever curses you I will curse; and all peoples on earth will be blessed through you." (12: 1-3).

Verses from 12 to 25 of Genesis deal with Abram.

2.   In Exodus of The Torah (chapter 20) and Deuteronomy (chapter 5), the Ten Commandments are recorded, which provide bases for social, moral, economic and religious codes of living.
3.   The chapters 21, 22, 23 under the titles personal injuries, protection of property, social responsibility and laws of Justice and Mercy shed light on social laws.
4.   In Leviticus, in The Torah from chapter 11 to 19, also deal with religious laws which have influence on the social, economic and moral life of the people.
5.   In psalm 26, Prophet David says: "I do not sit with deceitful men, nor do I consort with hypocrites; I abhor the assembly of evil doers and refuse to sit with the wicked. Do not take away my soul along with sinners or my life with bloodthirsty men, in whose hands are wicked schemes, whose right hands are full of bribes. But I lead a blameless life; redeem me and be merciful to me."

Only this one Psalm is sufficient from the Psalms of David, mirroring the social, moral, economic and political divine systems. The terms like "Deceitful men" and "hypocrites" portray moral system. "The wicked" and "bloodthirsty" are the terrorists and tyrants. The people who receive "bribes" reflect the corrupt economic system of a society and the state. This Psalm excellently covers the divine codes and laws for all societies until the Doomsday.

The righteous, the truthful and the men of upright character have been praised in the Psalms of David. The sinners, the wicked and oppressors are cursed in these Psalms. There are 150 Psalms of David and they all are full of wisdom and exhortation and leading humans to the right path. These Psalms lay down the basics of morality, polity and economy. Justice is the core message of these Psalms. And the fabric of Justice stands on the strong pillar of love of God, in testimony of which the test and trial of Abraham's sacrifice is also exalted.

6. The proverbs of Solomon, son of David and king of Israel, are the best examples of divine wisdom and exhortations. They shed light on peace, discipline, guidance, insight, social justice and love of God. In these proverbs, bloodshed, ignorance, foolishness, cruelty and evil deeds have been condemned.

The Bible
1. In the Gospel of Matthew from Chapter 5 to 7, there are basic instructions and injunctions which deal with human life as well as social and moral laws.
2. "Give to Caesar what is Caesars', and to God what is Gods'". Matthew (22:21). This saying of Jesus Christ throws light on the stately and religious matters.
3. About Abraham Jesus says in Matthew: "And do not think you can say to yourselves, 'we have Abraham as our father'. I tell you that out of these stones God can raise up children for Abraham (3:9).
4. Jesus announced the fulfillment of Law. He was the supporter of Abrahamic faith and Mosaic Laws.
5. The Gospel of Matthew records the words of Jesus as such: "Do not think that I have come to abolish the Law or the Prophets; I have not come to abolish them but to fulfill them. I tell you the truth, until heaven and earth disappear, not the smallest letter, not the least stroke of pen; will by any means disappear from the law until everything is accomplished. (4:17).
6. On the whole, the Holy Bible aspires for the establishment of the Kingdom of God on Earth.

The Quran

Islam, like Judaism and Christianity, claims to emanate from the spiritual fountain of Abraham. There is a full Sura (chapter) in the Quran ascribed to the name of Abraham. He has been paid much homage and respect in the Quran. The Quran describes Abraham as the sincere servant of God. In Sura Abraham the Quran says: "Remember Abraham said: 'O my Lord! Make this city one of peace and security; and preserve me and my sons from worshipping idols. O my Lord! they have indeed led astray many among mankind; he who follows my ways is of me, and he that disobeys me – but you are indeed oft-forgiving, most merciful."(14:35-36) These verses are of great importance and give us the gist of the Abrahamic mission and message. Peace and security was the cherished goal and desire of Abraham. He abhorred bloodshed, extremism and terrorism. Then he condemned idol worship. It means that he invited to monotheism. Again, he announces his way, which is the way of God. The way of God is essentially the kingdom of God on Earth. Actually, this concept provides a system, based on the glorious principles of Justice. The Quran announces Abraham as the leader of all nations. The Holy Quran, like Torah, has mentioned the test and trial of sacrifice of Abraham. Abraham is ascribed as the leader, whose ways are to be followed. This is an invitation for interfaith dialogue. It is a call for unity and peace to live with the spirit of co-existence and avoid bloodshed in the name of religion. About Abraham, the Quran says: "And remember that Abraham was tried by his Lord with certain commands, which he fulfilled: He said: "I will make you the leader of nations." He pleaded: "And also Imams (leaders) from my offspring." He answered: "But my promise is not within the reach of evil-doers." (2:124) This verse deals with the leadership of humankind. The Quran warns that the transgressors and tyrants do not represent God, such evil doers represent Satan. Hence through Abraham, the concept of divine political leadership is obtained. The righteous and just people can only represent God. Then, the Quran announces the religion of Abraham as the basis for all religions. The Quran says in Sura The Heifer: "And who turns away from the religion of Abraham but such as debase their soul with folly? Him we chose and rendered pure in this world, and he will be in the Hereafter in the ranks of the Righteous."(2:130)

Principal Commandments of Islam

Islam is a scientific religion. It is a complete code of life. It provides basic principles to keep balance and equilibrium in human society. Being a natural religion it does not go against human nature. Accordingly, with this background, the following can be regarded as the principal commandments of Islam.
1. Monotheism
2. Prophethood
3. Day of Judgment
4. Justice (social, economic and political)
5. Ethics
6. Laws
7. Rituals (Salat, Saum, Zakat, Hajj).

1. Monotheism: Islamic concept of Tawhid encompasses the whole of human activities. Islam rejects atheism and polytheism on rational grounds. Idolatry is prohibited in Islam, as it geminates tribalism and nationalism. The idols in Kaaba represented different tribes. Monotheism invited the One God and oneness of humankind. Monotheism rejects monarchy, tyranny and dictatorship. The Quran offers reasons for monotheism. The Quran says: "He has neither a colleague nor a partner. He begets not, nor is He begotten, there is none like Him" (112:1-4). The concept of "Tawhid" (monotheism) casts immense impressions on social, economic and political life of mankind.

2. Prophethood: The Quran mentions 24 prophets. Each prophet brought the fundamental message to peoples. Adam was the first and prophet Mohammad (PBUH) the last prophet. Man is given free choice. The prophets were sent to show the right path by precept and example. Prophet Mohammad (PBUH) is the seal of prophets. He is mercy for all the worlds. He brought the Quran, the last word and message of God. About the prophets, the Quran says: "For each nation, there is a guide." The prophet hood has indeed left indelible prints on the path of humanity. Professor Malcolm Clark in his book entitled "Islam for Dummies" about Prophethood writes: "Most of these prophets

bring the same message: an exhortation to justice in dealing with others and a call to return to worshipping only God." Prophets were the guides, the messengers, the reformers, the revolutionaries and the leaders.

3. Day of Judgment: The concept of "Qayamah" is very important to avoiding sinful and brutal existence. The life style of the believers who have been promised and abode in Paradise with pleasure and comfort is different from the life style of unbelievers, who have been condemned to the fire of Hell with pain and torment. Hinduism and Buddhism share a concept of Karma: "as you sow, so shall you reap". The Quran also in this context announces: "There is nothing from man but what he strives for." It means man must do good deeds to win this world and world hereafter. On the Day of Reckoning the account of each one's deed will be opened and his limbs will provide witness and he will be judged accordingly. The right doers will get their account in right hand and the wrong doers in left hand. This concept creates much impact on the social life of each one of us.

4. Justice: Justice or Adl is one of the principal commandments of Islam. Nearly about 44 times, the Quran has emphasized on rendering justice. Islam deals with social, economic and political justice. Social Justice is Islamic sociology. It is based on human fraternity, unity and dignity in righteous association. Economic justice deals with fair and equitable distribution of God's bounties for the general good. Islamic economy is neither capitalism nor socialism. It is a mixed economy. The Quran, the Ahadith and Muslims thinkers, such as Shah Wali ullah Delhavi, Dr. Mohammed Iqbal, and Imam Baqir-us-Sadr have written on this subject in detail, as against capitalistic thinkers (e.g. Adam Smith, Dr. Alfred Marshall, Canon and Pegu) and socialist advocates (e.g. Plato, Karl Marx, Angels, Lenin and Mao). And Political justice deals with Islamic political thought. Islam is neither western democracy and liberalism nor socialist regimentation and totalitarianism. It is a social-cum-spiritual democracy known as "Khalafat". The Quran in Sur Al-e-Imran and the Sura (The Council) endorses the concept of consensus which is known as "Ijmah." Monarchy is rejected in Islam. The treatise of Muwlana Abu Aula Mududi entitled "Khalafat-o-Malookiyat (The Caliphate and Monarchy) throws much light on this mat-

ter. Muslim political thinkers such as Al-Mawardi and Ibn-e-Qutaiba have also discussed Islamic political thought in detail. Islamic notions of Governance and leadership are the key prescriptions, laying down the foundations of Islamic society and state.

5. Ethics: Like the Torah and the Bible, emphasize on social and moral commandments, covering all aspects of life, Islam stands on the pillars of moral values and believes in virtue and vice. Unlike some other systems, Islamic values are not relative values but are absolute values. The attributive names of Allah themselves represent values. Peace, patience, sacrifice, perseverance, piety, charity, righteousness, honesty and truthfulness' are positive values, while falsehood, hypocrisy, gambling, theft, adultery, adulteration, drinking, bribery, murder and back biting etc are negative values. Some Westerner thinkers (e.g. Socrates, Bergson, Lord Snell and Dr. De Brgbe) equally condemn immoral societies. However, the Islamic system of values distinctly and greatly influences the mode of thinking and behavior of a society.

6. Laws: Islamic personal, judicial, fiscal and criminal laws are natural, effective, ideal and excellent. Divinely ordained, in essence, they are impartial and equal in their operation for every one, high or low. They encourage a pious and noble society, while discouraging a vicious and ignoble one, thereby emphasizing ducness in the administration of justice. On the one hand, they reward good behavior, to be exemplary. On the other hand, they punish malevolent conduct, to provide deterrence. The Quran, Hadith, the tradition and the Muslim Jurists have, in detail, discussed Islamic jurisprudence. Once operative, these injunctions have self-purifying effects on the life of individuals, groups, and the society as a whole.

7. Rituals: Islamic rituals and practices such as Salat, Saum, Zakat, and Hajj have deep meanings and influence. These practices elevate man spiritually, socially, morally, physically and psychologically. They are spiritual and innately mundane systems, satisfying inner and outer needs of soul and body. They train believers, individually and collectively for practical life in all circumstances. The Quran has time and again laid much stress on the needs of prayers and religious rituals. The Muslim clerics and scholars have written much on the need of such rites.

These rituals imbibe and infuse the spirit of nobility, sublimity, moderation and humanity, in to human perfection and elevation.

Conclusion

Hence, commandments of Islam furnish and burnish the rusty souls, societies and states. They develop social, economic and political institutions in the service of mankind. They promise blessings for the entirety of all human beings, without distinction of race, color, nationality, culture, or creed. However, their functional quintessence lies in the establishment of the Islamic state, which can guarantee a just environment. Yet, in a broader context, as all the Semitic religions (Judaism, Christianity and Islam) derived from the Abrahamic source lay stress on the need of virtuous life with justice (social, economic, political), they ought to unite their aspirations on common grounds for the betterment of the much divided, precarious, and disillusioned world. As no divine religion harbors on hatred, vice, and injustice, all believers of God must come together in the spirit of tolerance, moderation, and wisdom to usher in an era of peace and harmony on the earth.

THE CONCEPT OF ZAKAH

Shamim A. Siddiqi in an article published in weekly "Muslims" New York on November 28, 2003 under the title Zakah And Its Future - Some Fundamental Questions has expressed his concern about the future concept and implementation of Zakah. He has posed five questions, which need to be accurately, and promptly answered. Zakah represents the economic system of Islam. In the Holy Quran time and again the payment of Zakah has been emphatically ordained. In the very beginning of the Sura The Cow All Almighty ordains; "Those who believe in the unseen and keep up prayer and spend out of what we have given them". Here the word "Yunfiqun" has been used. In Arabic language the word "Nafaq" means, "Tunnel". The water passing through the tunnel does not stop. It keeps on moving. This gives the idea of the circulation of money. Dr. Kenze, an authority on modern economy condemned hoarding.

The Islamic economic thought also condemns hoarding. A Muslim thinker Ibn Hazm is of the view that besides Zakah the Islamic regime can levy other religious taxes upon the people whenever the need arises. The Quranic verse: "They ask you what to spend: say; more than need" signifies the fact that besides Zakah, Khums and Sadaqat more than need must be surrendered voluntarily for the welfare of the needy ones. The Muslim socialists interpret this verse as the basic verse of Islamic Economic System. According to them no one can possess more than the basic human needs, which includes housing, health, bread, marriage and education. These basic needs must be provided to each and every citizen in an Islamic welfare State. After this brief introduction I find easier to answer the questions raised by Shahim A. Siddiqi.

Question number one deals with the existing rate of Zakah which is 2 ½ percent. It be revised to some higher denomination to get greater yield to meet the needs of the society. Its simple answer is that nowhere in the Quran the rate of Zakah has been fixed or prescribed. A great Muslim scholar of the Sub-Continent Shah Waliullah Delhavi was of the opinion that under special or urgent need an Islamic state can charge forty percent of the annual savings as Zakah. The modern Muslim Economists seem more inclined to raise the rate of Zakah according to the need of time and country. The second question deals with the Nisab of 7½ tola of gold and 52 ½ tola of silver as fixed quantity for Zakah. Is it fixed or it can be revised in the modern age? In my opinion we should solve these issues in the light of Ijtehad. There is nothing final, fixed or ultimate in Islamic jurisprudence accept the "Mohkamat" (The fundamentals) of the Quran. This can be raised according to the need and situation. Third question is about the scope of Zakah. In Shariah, Zakah is levied on nine commodities. Besides gold and silver it is on cattle, crops, and fruits. But here we should introduce an innovative technique to broaden the scope of Zakah. The cattle, crops and fruits have been used as local Arabian symbols with a universal connotation. Suppose in crops there is Zakah on wheat and barley. The people who grow rice do not pay Zakah on it. Similarly there is Zakah on dates but it does not mean that the people who grow oranges, mangoes or apples are exempted from paying annual Zakah. These crops and fruits are representatives of all kind of other seeds, crops and fruits. If there is Zakah for camels in modern age it must be on cars and aeroplanes belonging to individuals. Hence we need advancement and expansion in the light of Islamic principle of enquiry. The fourth question deals with the fixation of minimum standard of living as each society varies in level of progress. What should be the barometer deciding who is entitled to get Zakah. In my opinion it is not the question of level of progress. It is the question of basic human needs. Basic human needs are universal. The people who are deprived of food, health, housing and education facilities they ought to be given Zakah. It is like a stipend and Islamic government owes it to all needy and poor people. The fifth question deals with the spending of Zakah. According to Islam under the account of eight heads Zakah can be expended at individual and collective levels. In my opinion, that these eight heads approximately cover all the important aspects of human life and society. Shamim A. Siddiqi specially enquires about the seventh head "Fi-Sabeelillah" which means for the cause of Allah. Actually when we serve the have-nots and the down trodden we serve the cause of Allah. The concept of "Qarz-e-Hasana" (The Benevolent Debt) in the Quran means to give free loan to the needy to attain the favors and blessings of God. The modern jurist can interpret the term cause of Allah to spend the money of Zakah for the projection and publicity of the divine mission and message of religion.

In nutshell, in conclusion, it can be said that we can bring changes in the system of Zakah per need and time. Here I want to make it clear that in Muslim countries both systems are in practice, which is against the principle of justice and spirit of Islam. The government charges house tax, property tax, wealth tax and health tax and also charges Zakah. This is a double system, which is a burden and is unwanted. Duality of system is not allowed in Islam. Let there be one system, which should meet the requirements of the state and society at a time. I float this idea for the Muslim jurists and scholars to comment on it and guide us.

THE DAY OF JUDGMENT IN ISLAM

As justice is the main concern of Islam it is necessary that people should get justice in this world and the world hereafter. It sounds natural and logical that everyone should reap what he has sown. One should receive the fruit of his deeds. If one has sown flowers he should pluck flowers. If one has sown thorns he should pick thorns. Virtues breed virtues and vices breed vices. The Day of Judgment in the Quran has been also named as the Day of Reckoning, the Day of Resurrection, the Dooms day or the Day of Accountability. The account of the deeds of everyone is being maintained. Islamic concept of two angels maintaining the record of ever word and movement is scientific. The video has solved this mystery. The alpha and beta rays have special role in photographic process. The Gamma rays play their own part. It is a great lesson. If through material rays we can preserve activities there should be no doubt about our record preserved by the special divine agencies. The Quran in Sura "The Friday Prayers" announces: "The death from which you flee will truly overtake you; then will you be sent back to the knower of the things secret and open; and He will tell you (the truth) of the things you did."(62:8)

Everybody's record is being maintained during his life period. It is very accurate record. The day of judgement is the day of justice. No body will be wronged. His limbs will be his witness. He will see his record and his video film will be shown to him. Everyone will be rewarded or punished according to his deeds. The Quran in Sura "The Israelite" says; "Everyman's fate we have fastened on his own neck. On the Day of Judgment we shall bring out for him a scroll, which he will see spread open. Read thine record sufficient is thy soul this day to make out an account against thee". (17:13-14).

As the literal meaning of Arabic word used for the Day of Judgment "Qayamah" is to raise up, hence the question arise as to why they should be raised up after demise. There are three reasons for "Qayamah". (a) It is the demand of natural and divine justice that everyone should get the result of his life examination. As in academies one is given result of his tests, similarly everyone must get the result whether he passes or fails. About the examination of Life in Sura "The Bee" the Quran says: "Whoever works righteousness, man or woman, and has Faith, verily to him we will give a new life, a life that is good and pure, and we will bestow on such their reward according to the best of their actions." (16:97). (b) Had there been no concept of the Day of Judgment there would have been no human morality. Might is right would have become the law of the day. Atheists are of two types. The ideological atheist and the practical atheist. The practical atheist is the one who claims to have a religious faith but in practical life he acts otherwise. It is my considered opinion that the man who believes in God and fears God can never be a sinner or a transgressor. Hence to maintain the supremacy of Right over Might we must believe in the concept of the Day of Judgment. The concepts of Hell and Heaven are very essential to keep balance in human conduct. The tyrants, the oppressors, the murderers and the aggressors must be punished. If they escape in this world because of their power, pelf and influence they must be punished on Doomsday. Abraham must be rewarded and Nimrod must be chastised. Moses must be rewarded and Pharaoh be punished. Hussain be rewarded and Yazid be punished. It is divine justice and God promises that. In the Quran in Sura "Abraham" about the virtuous and righteous people God says; "But those who believe and work righteousness be admitted to gardens beneath which rivers flow. To dwell therein for aye with the permission of their lord."(14:23). (c) All the prophets have promised this day. They were sooth – sayers. They were divinely appointed. They were not liars. They were the messengers and warners sent from God. We must believe in their words and vows. We have no reason to reject or refute them. They valiantly, patiently and boldly bore the inflictions and excesses. They were tortured. They were persecuted. They were executed. But they never bowed before tyrants and vicious forces. Their steadfastness and perseverance testifies the truth of their mission when such truthful people believed in the Doomsday, we have no reason to disbelieve in which they believed. Now let us briefly discuss the Quranic logic about the Day of Judgment. The Quran refutes the plea of the unbelievers who say that how it can happen. After death when we will be turned into dust, then how can we resurrect? The Quran in Sura "Yasin" announces; "Does not man realize that we created him from a seed of fluid? Yet he does not believe and forgets even his own creation. He says as to who could revive the decayed bones back to life from nonentity." (36:79). After giving the argument of first birth the Quran gives the second argument. It says: "one of the clear divine signs is that you see the earth dead and motionless, but as soon as Allah pours rain on it, it comes to life and becomes fertile and green. Allah who revives the dead earth to life will also revive the dead man to life. Allah is able to do all things: (41:39). Then in Sura "Saad" the Quran gives third argument on the basis of Justice. It is related to the Islamic concept of Good and Bad. The Quran says: "We have not created the heavens and the earth and all that is between them in vain, though this is the belief of the infidels. Woe to the disbelievers; they will suffer the torment of the Hellfire. Do we consider the righteously striving believers equal to the evil doers in the earth? Are the pious ones equal to those who openly commit sins?" (38:27-28).

These are the Quranic arguments about the Day of Judgment which no same person can reject. In verse 20 of Sura "The Iron", in verse 20 of Sura Winding Sand Tracts and in verse 200 of Sura The Heifer the necessity of the Day of Judgement is mentioned. In Sura Mominun in verse 100 about 'Barzakh' (purgatory) the Quran says: "After death people will be behind Barzakh until the day of their resurrection. (23:100). According to the Quran it will be a great blast and earthquake. On the Day of Judgment people will emerge from their graves and congregate. The unbelievers will be raised with black faces and the righteous one with bright faces. The virtuous will be given the book, result sheet in to their right hands and the evil doers will be given in to their left hands. It will be an eternal life. May Allah grant us guidance to do good deeds and abstain from evil deeds!

THE HAZARDS OF RELIGIOUS INTOLERANCE

People are scared of snakes. There are so many kinds of snakes. Some are poisonous and some are not. But people often consider all snakes are dangerous and despicable. Why is this? The reason is that some of them pose a threat to life. When some people see a snake, they fear death and feel that either they must kill the snake or be killed by it. A Pakistani journalist and scholar Niaz Fatehepuri once wrote: "all snakes are not poisonous but all clerics are poisonous." He was diametrically apposed to priest-hood. When I read his views I could not understand why he was full of spite against clerics. Rather I took his opinion a bit sarcas-tic and poisonous. But these days, when so many people are killed in the name of religion and religious extremism is rampant, it would seem that perhaps the epithet of poisonous snake does indeed apply to many clerics.

In India, the Hindu Pundits preach hatred. They glorify their own religious rituals and condemn those of others, and murder Muslims, Christians and Sikhs. The Israelis and the Palestinians are killing each other. The Russian communists persecute the Chechen Muslims. The Jews were massacred by the Nazis. In Pakistan there is sectarian extremism. Some clerics are all out to preach religious fanaticism, extremism, suicide bombing and terrorism. So many Shia, Sunni and Wahabi "ulema" and per-sonalities have been killed. The invisible hand of Indian intelli-gence agency cannot be ignored in all such tragic incidents. In some of our religious schools our clerics are preaching extrem-ism, hatred and bloodshed. They must be contained. Pakistani intelligence agencies should infiltrate their agents into such schools. The students and teachers should be paid to inform on such reprehensible behavior. Recently, nearly thirty-five Shias were massacred while offering Jummah prayers in the Zainabia Mosque of Sialkot. A week later, forty Sunnis were murdered while holding a religious meeting in Multan.

Daily one or another political personality is targeted. It is a great challenge for the government. No government wishes dis-turbance. No government can afford terrorism. Law and order are the first priority of every government. It seems a big prob-lem for the government to deal with this horrendous situation. Every serious and sincere Pakistani is worried about the pre-carious state of affairs. India blames Pakistan for insurgency in Indian occupied Kashmir. Whenever there is any explosion or killing we say India is involved in it. But the question arises as to who these terrorists are. They are not Indians. They are Paki-stanis. They are purchased commodities. They must be brought to justice. As we have failed to maintain justice, the result is obvious. The responsibility of these deplorable situations be-longs to our rulers who care more about amassing wealth than carrying out their responsibilities.

A country devoid of justice cannot have peace. A world wherein injustice prevails will remain drenched in blood. The Torah says: "You shall not murder" (20:13). The Bible says: "you have heard that it was said to the people long ago, 'Do not murder' and anyone who murders will be subject o judgment'. But I tell you that anyone who is angry with his brother will be subject to judgment." (5:21). The Quran announces in Sura Nisa: "If a man kills a believer intentionally, his recompense is Hell, to abide therein (for ever): and the wrath and the curse of Allah are upon him, and a dreadful penalty is prepared for him". (4:93). All divine books condemn murder and bloodshed. Then in Sura The Table Spread the Quran says: "on that account: we ordained for the children of Israel that if anyone slew a person – unless it be for murder or for spreading mischief in the land – it would be as if he slew the whole people; and if anyone saved a life, it would be as if he saved the life of the whole people". (5:32). When I talk of the snakes I mean those humans who kill each other. They are filled with the poison of prejudices and hatred. In the name of faiths they feel satisfied by killing each other. God has condemned bloodshed but some of the so-called custodians of religions seek different justifications to behead each other. In Iraq the situation is quite horrible. The combating forces are killing each other. Peace and democracy are imminent prerequisites. But the way some innocent civilians of different nationalities are kidnapped and beheaded, no code of morality, humanity and religion permits such odious acts.

The question arises how to end extremism and terrorism. In my opinion there are two types of terrorism; Political Terrorism and Religious Terrorism. Both need different approaches. Political terrorism can only be ended if we provide justice to the oppressed nations. We should resolve the issues of Palestine, Kashmir and Chechnya in the light of the UN resolutions and by democratic means. We should not suppress any nation. The root causes must be eliminated. The aggressors must be brought to justice. For uprooting religious terrorism we must introduce modern sciences in our religious centers. In some seminaries in Pakistan we are teaching them Shiaism, Sunnism and Wahabism. We are not teaching them Islam on modern and scientific requirements. The Ministry of Religious Affairs should introduce modern and moderate curriculum. The Islamic private schools (madrassas) that do not co-operate with the policies of Religious Ministry must be closed. With the consent of religious scholars and ulama from all sects a unanimous syllabus should be introduced. If sectarianism is not contained now Pakistan will become a volcano. Foreign aid to all those Islamic centers must be banned. On television, Radio and in Press eminent religious scholars and clerics should preach moderation and patience. Positive brain washing is a must. Our youth in some of the seminaries is being negatively brain washed. Suicide bombing is a hazardous policy. Without education we can never achieve our national goals. Besides we must take other stern and strict measures. The traditional police, agencies and courts of Pakistan have completely failed in controlling religious extremists. They are neither arrested nor punished. By traditional methods they can never be eliminated. Through presidential order or parliament bill a new force should be recruited. They should be reserved to arrest terrorists. They should be always patrolling in all villages, towns and cities. They should be provided modern equipments to arrest the saboteurs. We should organize special branch of intelligence wholly solely reserved to do surveillance of the terrorists. Then we should form special anti-terrorist courts only dealing with these cases. The cases should be conducted in camera. Their decision should be final. There should be no delay in decision. Justice delayed is justice denied. With these new radical and revolutionary measures terrorism can be eliminated. Watery snakes are like fish. In my opinion majority of religious scholars and clerics are very moderate and they are like watery snakes. Such people are lovable and can be great asset to preach tolerance and coexistence. They must be projected and assisted to work for harmony and peace. I do not call them snakes; they are the best creation of God. As they are poisonless they must be cared and caressed.

THE ISLAMIC CONCEPT OF FOOD

Islam permits only the kind of food and drinks that are healthful for the body and mind of humans. The things that are injurious for mankind are strictly prohibited in Islam. The Quran, of course, has its dietary restrictions. It has its clear and complete schedule. The Quran in Sura Maida(the Table Spread) announces:

" Forbidden to you(for food) are: dead meat, blood, the flesh of swine, and on which the name of other than Allah has been invoked; that which has been killed by strangling, or by violent blow, or by a headlong fall, or by being gored to death; that which has been partly eaten by a wild animal; unless you are able to slaughter it(in due form); that which is sacrificed on stone(altar); (forbidden) also is the division(of meat) by raffling with arrows; that is in piety. The 115th verse of Sura "The Bee" also mentions the forbidden foods. In Sura the Cattle in verse 121, the Quran also says: "Eat not of (meats on which God's name has not been pronounced". So far as the lawful food is concerned the Quran in Sura Maida says: "They ask you what is lawful to them (as food). Say "Lawful to you are (all) good and pure things; and what you have taught your trained hunting animals (to catch) in the manner directed to you by Allah: eat what they catch for you, but pronounce the name of Allah over it; and fear Allah, for Allah is swift in taking account".(5:4). The first verse of Sura The Table Spread mentions about the lawful food as such: "Lawful unto you (for food) are all four-footed animals with the exception named: but animals of chase are forbidden while you are in the sacred precincts or in pilgrim garb." (5:1). The Sura Maida also announces: "This day (all) good and pure things are made lawful to you. The food of the people of the book is lawful to you and yours is lawful to them." (5:5). It is quite clear that the things good and pure have been made lawful and the things bad and impure have been made unlawful. We cannot alter or introduce any innovation as in Sura Maida the Quran says: "O you who believe; don't make unlawful the good things which Allah has made lawful for you, but commit no excess; for Allah does not love those given to excess." (5:87). But the Quran also discusses the exceptional case that emerge in the form of necessity or compulsion. The general rules cannot be changed. They are permanent rules. Exceptions under necessity are permitted. The Quran in Sura the Heifer says: "But, if one is forced by necessity, without willful disobedience nor transgressing due limits, then he is guiltless (2:173). Islam is a natural religion and in exceptions grants permission to ease human life.

It is the bounden duty of Muslims scholars and clerics to decide the matters in the light of "Ijtahad"(Fact-finding intellectual process). The law about exceptions is also mentioned in the

Sura The Cattle: "why should you not eat of (meats) on which Allah's name has been pronounced, when He has explained to you in detail what is forbidden to you-except under compulsion of necessity" (6:119) I am mostly asked by the Muslims living in America, England and other western countries about "Halal" meat. "Halal" means lawful and "Haram" means unlawful. From the Quran it is clear that the prohibited meat is one the name of God was not invoked at the time of slaughtering. Second; all four footed animals are lawful with exceptions named. The Jews slaughter like Muslims but don't invoke the name of God thrice as Muslims do. Since non-Muslims slaughter mechanically in bulk and the name of God is not invoked on the slaughtered animals what the Muslims should do? Majority of the Muslim clerics in the wake of traditionalism opine that the Muslims must not eat such a meat on whom the name of God was not invoked and is not slaughter according to Muslims ritual. But we find a Hadith of the holy prophet of Islam telling us if Halal meat is not available' under necessity or compulsion what should be done. Once the prophet was asked: "Some desert people bring us meat, but we do not know whether the name of God was mentioned over it or not". The Prophet replied, "mention the name of God over it and eat" (Al-Muwatta, 24.1; Bukhari 3.273). It shows that under unavoidable circumstances in non-Muslim countries a Muslim can eat meat but he will have to invoke the name of God thrice on it before eating it. In my opinion the Muslims must avoid eating meat which is unlawful if they can do it. But the Quran and Hadith permit them to eat even unlawful meat under exceptional circumstances. It shows that Islam is an easy religion providing genuine and necessary facilities to its believers. The Bible about meat say: "for it seemed good the Holy Ghost, to us, to lay upon you no greater burden then these necessary things: That you abstain from meats offered to idols, and from blood, and from things strangled, and from fornication: fro which if you keep yourselves, you shell to well"(Acts 15:28-29). The Torah in this regard announces: "A- What you can eat: all animals with parted hoofs, which are cloven footed, and which chew the cud; marine animals which have finis and scales, every flying creeping thing that goes on all four feet (such as locusts, beetles, grasshoppers) B: What you can not eat (a) Animals which chew the cud, but their hoofs are not divided; Camel,

Coney, Hare; (b) Animals with divided hoofs which are cloven footed, but which do not chew that cud: Swine; (c) Marine animals which have no fins and scales; (d) Birds: eagle, ossifrage, osprey; vulture and kite; raven, owl, might hawk, cuckoo; (e) owls, cormorant, swan, pelican, gier eagle, stork, heron, lapwing, but; (f) Fowls that creep; (g) other flying creeping things having four feet (except hose permitted above); (h) Animals which go on paws; (i) creeping things such as mouse, tortoise, ferret, chameleon, lizard, snail, mole: (j) Animals which die natural death, even among those which are permissible to eat. C: Containers: These can become unclean by contact with the prohibited animals." We find that the Old Testament is the basic divine source of lawful and unlawful foods. The net result of the dissertation is that the foods which are poisonous and injurious for the mind and body of human have been prohibited in religion and we must stick to the divine laws for our bodily and spiritual growth.

THE ISLAMIC CONCEPT OF VEIL

Two verses of the Holy Quran succinctly and candidly deal with the basic concept of veil in Islam. First; in Sura An-Nur (The light) the Quran says: "And tell the believing women to lower their gazes and be modest, and to display of their adornments only that which is apparent, and to draw their veils over their bosoms."(24:31)

In this verse it is clearly mentioned that sex parts must not be exposed and must be covered. "Adornment which is apparent" alludes to the common body parts between male and female sexes. The face, hands and feet are common parts and are exposed without any indecency or immodesty. Second; The other verse of the Holy Quran is in Sura Al-Ahzab (The confederates). The Quran says: "O; Prophet! Tell thy wives and thy daughters and the women of the believers to draw their cloaks close round them (when they go outside). That will be better, that so they may be recognized and not molested". (33:59). The ancient Arab history reveals the fact that the immodest and immoral ladies used to expose their bodies and walk in market without veil. They were purchasable commodities. They did not wear hijab or scarf. They were improperly dressed. The corrupt people could easily decipher and unravel about their character or profession. They were prostitutes. Hence the Quran announced that pious ladies must be properly and modestly dressed so that when they go out of their houses people should recognize them as domestic chaste, pure and pious ladies and they should not be teased or chased. From these two above-mentioned Quranic verses it is clear that God ordains to cover the bodies and strictly rejects and condemns nudity and obscenity.

Now the question arises as to what is the concept of veil in Islam. Different jurists and interpreters have differently interpreted the above-mentioned Quranic verses about veil. Here I would like to cite from two illustrious contemporary scholars. Maulana Moududi of Pakistan in his Urdu book entitled "Pardah" (The veil) considers the covering of body obligatory for a Muslim woman. In his book entitled "Towards understanding Islam" on page 150 he writes: "Nor should a woman expose any part of her body except her face and hands to anyone other than her husband." Ustad Murtaza Motaheri Shaheed of Iran in his Persian book entitled "Hijab" (The veil) does not consider the covering of face obligatory. But both scholars of eminence believe that a Muslim lady must wear "scarf" and cover her head for identity and sobriety. They also in detail discuss that covering of sexual parts was obligatory in ancient Greek and Roman culture and was religiously obligatory in the society of the Jews and the Christians as well. They have given examples that only immodest and indecent ladies used to expose their bodies. To date the ladies who expose their bodies in the name of modernity and progressive civilization represent the ladies of ancient times who were considered the ladies of market having no value and culture. The history is repeating itself. In the name of freedom we are exploiting and insulting the women folk. The woman has been turned into a purchasable commodity. It is happy omen that the Muslim society believes in the covering of the womenfolk but it is divided in its concept and practice as mentioned earlier. The Muslim world is divided in to three groups. First; those who claim to be modern wear European dress. They do not care about the Quranic injunctions. They pay lip service to Islam. We can find some Muslim ladies wearing skirts or mini skirts in some Muslim countries like Turkey, Lebanon, Egypt and the Middle East. Second; there is an extreme known as retrogressive ladies. These ladies cover their bodies from top to toe. It is known as 'Burqa'. It is a kind of veil with eyeholes to it, covering the whole body from head to foot. You cannot see the face, hands or feet of the women. It is rampant in Saudi Arabia and in some other states. Third; we find some moderates who do not believe in extremism and give the moderate interpretation of religion. These ladies neither wear western dress nor Saudi dress. They cover their bodies but do not cover the face, hands and feet. Some of them wear scarf and some do not. They do not make "scarf" an issue. They are more concerned about sex parts and the matter of their covering. Majority of them believe that scarf is the part of Islamic dress while some others do not consider scarf the part of Islamic dress, as there are no clear Quranic injunctions about headscarf in the Quran. But the Muslim history testifies this fact that wives of the holy Prophet (P.B.U.H) used to cover the head with a sheet or scarf. Hence such ladies consider scarf an Islamic obligation. Such ladies are mostly found in India, Pakistan, Bangladesh, Iraq, Iran, Libya, Malaysia and Indonesia. During the performance of pilgrimage the Muslim ladies cover the head with a scarf but do not cover the face, hands and feet. It seems the pilgrimage gives women respect, place, position and status on the bases of knowledge, character, dignity and modesty. Islam does not make womenfolk as sex commodities or play things in the hands of commercialism. The female body is used for selling everything from cosmetics to clothing. The woman has been made a marketable commodity in the name of so called freedom. We must resist. We must give natural honor to women through Islamic teachings.

In the end it is necessary to mention that the prohibition of scarf in schools or offices by the French government is discriminatory. It is against human rights. The French officials say that hijab is a religious symbol and must be prohibited. But the crux of the matter is that if some ladies are free to wear miniskirts or reveal their bodies how the other ladies can be asked not to cover their bodies. If the Jews can wear the Star of David or Yamaka (A skull cap worn by the Jews) and the Christians can wear the cross, then why only the Muslim women are asked not to wear scarf. It is a discriminatory law and exhibits prejudice against Muslims. Let us respect the religious symbols and right of all believers and be tolerant to maintain a culture respecting Inter Faith dialogue and religious co-existence.

THE ISLAMIC VIEW ON WAR

Islam preaches peace and condemns war. There is a general impression that Islam is a militant religion and it was spread by sword. Islamic concept of Jihad is always misrepresented. Eminent British philosopher Bertrand Russell was also of the opinion that Islam is a militant creed. The question arises why such views cropped in the minds of people? There is not a shred of doubt in it that some of the Muslim rulers in the greed of expansionist designs exceeded the Islamic limits. They were aggressors, tyrants and despots. In the name of Islam they raided the peaceful countries and in the monarchic zeal they trampled the human rights under their feet. Their acts should not be regarded as Islamic acts. Islam and Muslims are altogether two different things. Not only the Muslims are to be blamed. The human history is drenched and weltered with human blood. The blood baths in the name of territory or religion are the specks on the brow of history. The way the Mongols ransacked and persecuted the innocent people it is unprecedented in human history. In the book "Prisoners of War" in the story of the Mongols the writer depicts the horrible picture of their invasions. The Mongols were known for brutality, brigandage and bloodshed. Genghis Khan looted, plundered and pillaged mercilessly. The Mongols killed seventy thousand persons in Khorasan and thirty thousand people in Bukhara, Samarqand and Nishapur. The men, women and children were brutally massacred. Stepping into the foot steps of Genghis Khan, Hulogu also mercilessly killed hundreds of thousands Muslims in Baghdad. The crusades between the Christians and the Muslims also brought untold miseries to humans. Those were ancient days. We condemn savagery and curse war. But what our modern and cultured people have done with human race? America dropped atom bombs on Nagasaki and Hiroshima and killed nearly about three hundred thousands people in the space of few hours. The World War I and the World War II split the blood of million humans. The British trampled the human rights under jackboots in India, Iraq, Egypt and Sudan. Imam Muhammad Shirazi in his book entitled "War, Peace and Non-violence- In Islamic Perspective" writes: "In Sudan, the British soldiers would cut off the heads of those killed and send them to London to be made into ashtrays out of hatred for the Muslims". In Libya, the Italians killed half the populace, which in those days reached a million. Like wise French in Algeria killed a million Muslims out of nine million people. The Russians killed five million Muslims in various ways in Tajikistan, Turkmenistan and Afghanistan. The Pakistani Muslim Army massacred hundreds of thousand Muslims of their own part East Pakistan in 1971. Instead of solving the differences politically, military was used and blood was spilt. In retaliation East Pakistan emerged in the shape of present Bangladesh. Today India is mercilessly killing the Kashmiries in Kashmir. The Palestine seeks just and peaceful settlement as soon as possible. Whether they are Muslims or non-Muslims bloodshed is not accepted. It must be condemned and stopped. Man is the best creation of God. Man must be loved, respected, protected and promoted. Let us see what Islam says about the war and horrors of war. In Sura "The Heifer" the Quran says: "O ye who have faith, enter in to peace all of you, and do not follow the footsteps of Satan" – (2:208). Islam calls to peace and abhors war. Jihad is the last resort in Islam, because the Quran time and again invites to dialogue. To date we realize the importance of Interfaith dialogue but the Quran fourteen hundred years ago had invited the people of the Book to come to peace full terms through dialogue. About peace Allah Almighty says: "And if they incline to peace then incline to peace and put your trust in Allah."(8:61). Islam emphasizes on the need of peace and avoids war. If war is thrust upon Muslims, then they are asked to defend themselves. Islam does not permit transgression and aggression in any case. In Sura Mumtahana (The woman to be Examined) the Quran says: "Allah does not forbid you, with regards to those who do not fight you for (your) faith nor drive you out of your homes, from dealing kindly and justly with them: for Allah loves those who are just – Allah only forbids you, with regard to those who fight you for (your) Faith, and drive you out of your homes and support (others) in driving you out, from turning to them (for friendship and protection). It is such as turn to them (in those circumstances), that do wrong." (60:8-9) These verses clearly show that when the Muslims are mistreated and attacked then they must resist and defend themselves. Against aggressors the Quran is very sensitive and specific. Not only about the non-Muslim, even about the Muslim aggressor in Sura Al-Hujurat (The inner Apartment) the Quran says: "If two parties among the Believers fall into a quarrel, you make peace between them: but if one of them transgresses beyond bounds against the other then you (all) fight against the one that transgresses until it complies with the command of Allah: but if it complies, then make peace between them with justice, and be fair: for Allah loves those who are fair (and just)." (49:9) The Quran severely condemns injustice, cruelty and bloodshed. The Quranic warfare values are mentioned in the Suras the Spoils of war; the Repentance; the Inner Apartments; the Gathering; the Spider and the Holding.

A narration in related by Hazrat Ali, Hazrat Jafar Sadiq, Hazrat Jabir bin Yazid, Hazrat Ibn Abbas and Hazrat Abn Said al-Khudri that the Holy Prophet (PBUH) did not permit the people who wanted to join Jihad without the permission of their parents. The women, the children, the slaves, the handicapped; the diseased and the insane are exempted from participating in Jihad. Besides the women, the children, the wounded, the monks, the elderly lot and neutral people can neither be imprisoned nor killed during Jihad. In Sura "The Heifer" it is written that during the sacred months i.e. during the months of Rajab; Dhul-Qaedah: Dhul-Hijjah and Muharram the Muslims are ordained to cease fire. But if they are attacked in these months then they can defend themselves. Syed Ali Ibn Tawous in his book "Kash al –Yaqeen" notes the tradition of the Holy Prophet (PBUH) that Islamic war can not be initiated with out a just cause and without a just Muslim ruler. In the book entitled "Daimal-Islam" it is related that the Holy Prophet (PBUH) on the day of the battle of Badr released some prisoners of the clan of Abdal-Muttalib on the plea that they were forced to fight against their wills. The Holy Prophet (PBUH) said: "He who kills a man from the people of the Dhimma (non-Muslims under the protection of Islamic state) will be forbidden paradise the perfume of which can be smelled at a distance of twelve traveling." If any Jew or Christian is killed in a Muslim state on religious differences it is a great sin and must be forcibly abandoned. On different occasions the Prophet said; "the emissary is not to be killed. Trees are not to be felled. The animals are not to be slaughtered. The houses are not to be razed and the supply of water is not to be cut off". Islamic views on war teach us that Islam promotes peace and discourages war and bloodshed.

Some religious extremists preach the younger generation to kill the people of other faiths and issue them the tickets to enter the heaven. No body is permitted to kill anyone on religious differences. The Quran in Sura "The Woman" declares: "and as far he who kills a believer deliberately, his reward will be Hell." (4:93). It is related from Jafar ibn Muhammad, from his father, from Hazrat Ali who said: "The Messenger of Allah said: 'There is a valley in Hell named 'Sair' which if opened the fires will roar from it. Allah has prepared it for the murderers'". How the bloodshed is cursed the following saying of the Prophet of Islam in a sufficient to prove that: "the first thing that Allah will look at on the Day of Resurrection will be blood." At a place the Holy Prophet has said: "He who aids and abets in the killing of a believer has taken himself out of Islam." It does not mean that the blood of non-Muslims is not sacred in Islam. About the non-believers the Prophet of Islam time and again said that their blood, life, property and honor is as sacred as of the Muslims. The motto; message; mission; and mantra of Islam is universal peace. In Sura "The Heifer" the Quran says: "Enter in to a state of peace one and all." (2:208). Jesus Christ says, "you have been told to love thy friends, but this is not what is important, for even the tithe collectors love their friends. I say to you love thine enemies." If today the world acts upon this beautiful message of Jesus there will be no war and no blood letting. Hazrat Ali in Nehj Al Balagha says: "People are of two types: either your brother in religion or your equal in creation". The equal in creation means that the non-believers have equal rights as humans in an Islamic State. Violence is extremely condemned in Islam. To resolve the issues through peaceful means and dialogues is the spirit of Islam. Islam is anti-War and Pro-Peace. Hence it can be said that Islamic view on war is that there should be no war at all.

THE MESSAGE OF THE HOLY BOOKS

Hazrat Abu Darr Ghafari narrates, once I asked from the Holy Prophet (PBUH): "How many books God revealed to the Prophets"? He responded: "one hundred and four books. Fifty scripts to sheeth; thirty to Idris; ten to Abraham and ten to Moses were revealed. Besides four books were reveald: The Torah, The Bible, The Psalm and The Quran." Harzat Abu Darr Ghaffari says I again enquired from the Holy Prophet(PBUH): "What was in the scripts revealed to Prophet Abraham"? The Holy Prophet (PBUH) answered: "They all consists of proverbs." I asked: "What was in the scripts revealed to Prophet Moses?" He answered: "They carried admonitions." If we study the revealed scriptures we find that these books give divine message of the worship of God and service of humankind. The message is one. With the passé of time the changes had been introduced but they are not about fundamentals or basics. In Islamic terminology we say the Dean (Religion) is one but the Shariahs (The laws) have been changing- Besides, the interpretation of laws has created discords and differences. The dresses and their styles have been altering with the passage of time but the body wearing the dresses is the same old one. This is the reason the necessity of "Ijtehad" i.e.; the use of analogical and analytical interpretation of religious matters has been much emphasized in Islam. But it is very tragic that the hard liners of all religions made non issues as issues and divided humankind in to sects and factions. The publishers of a book entitled "Mankind's search for God" writes: "During the thousand of years of mankind's history, man's search for God has led down many pathways. The result has been the enormous diversity of religious expression found world wide – from the endless variety of Hinduism to the monotheism of Judaism, Islam and Christendom and to the oriental philosophies of Shinto, Taoism, Buddhism, and Confucianism. In other vast regions, mankind has turned to animism, magic spiritism, and shamisism. Has this search for God been successful?". These lines make it clear that thre are so many path ways and people pave on different pavements of faith. Whether these are Abrahmic religions or other non-revealed religions or isms we must fear it in mind that religion is spiritualism not spiritism. All these pat ways lead to one destination and that destination is God.

Let us briefly comment on the basic message of revealed books. For forty years the verses of the Torah had been revealing to Prophet Moses. Ten commandments revealed to Moses are the basic laws for all humankind. In Exodus under the caption of "Laws of Justice and Mercy" it is written: "Do not spread false reports. Do not help a wicked man by being a malicious witness." (23:1) Then the Torah in Exodus announces: "Do not deny justice to your poor people in their law suits. Have nothing to do with a false charge and do not put an innocent or honest person to death, for I will not acquit the guilty." (23:6-7) "Do not accept bribe" and "do not oppress and alien" are also the commandments of the Torah. The Psalm of David also preaches human values and human rights. The very first Psalm condemns the wicked and the sinner and praises the righteous. In Psalm 86 David praying to God says: "Hear, O Lord, and answer me, for I am poor and needy." In the Psalm of David we find intense love for Lord and quest for mental peace, spiritual purity and people's safety. The message of the proverbs of Solomon in the Torah is replete with wisdom and spirituality. The wicked, the sinners and the oppressors are condemned. A few lines from proverb II are quoted to judge the real message of God. "The Lord abhors dishonest scales, but accurate with wisdom and spirituality. The wicked, the sinners and the oppressors are condemned. A few lines from proverb II are quoted to judge the real message of God: "The Lord abhors dishonest scales, but accurate weights are his delight.

THE NAMES OF ALLAH IN THE QURAN

Allah is "Ism-e-Zaati" (Personal Name) of God. Besides there are ninety nine "Asma-e-Hasana" (Attributive or Adjective or beautiful) names of Allah mentioned in the Quran. The Muslim Sufis, scholars and sages have said that Allah is Ism-e-Azam (the Greatest Name). When we say Allah-o-Akbar it also means no body is great except Allah. "Allah – the Greatest" is a philosophy. It is not only an announcement or a slogan. It teaches us a lesson. It tells us that we should not bow before any worldly power. We should only prostrate before God. This is a commitment to serve and praise Allah. It negates the concept of tyranny, idolatry, monarchy and adulatory. No one is equal to Allah. No one is his partner. He is neither begotten nor begets. Allah, God or "Raam" are his names. Different people in different languages call His name. The last words uttered by Jesus Christ on altar according to the Bible were "Eli, Eli, Lama Sabachthani;" my God, my God, why has thou forsaken me". (Mathew27:46)

The attributive names of Allah also depict the positive values and qualities ascribed to Allah. Though there are ninety nine beautiful names of God in the Quran, only eight attributes are regarded as "safaat-e-Thabutayya" (the Existential Attributes). They are: Qadeem (The eternal); Qadir (The Omnipotent); Alim (The omniscient); Haiy (The Living); Murid (The Willing); Mudrik (The Comprehending); Mutakalin (The Conversational) and Sadiq (The Truthful). On the contrary there are also eight attributes which cannot be ascribed to God. They are : Shirkat (Partnership); Tarkeeb (mixture); Makan (space); Hallol (Incarnation); Mahal-eHawadith (Gradational); Marey (visible); Ihtiaj (Need); and Sanawiyyat (Duality). Now let us briefly define these above mentioned existential and non-existential attributes of God. Eternal means that God was not created. He is first even to first cause or creation. He is beyond time. He has created time and space. He is omnipotent. It means that He can do what so ever He wants. His power is beyond question. Whether it is through natural laws or miracle He can do what ever He desires. Omniscient means he is aware of everything. He knows about our future. He is All-knowing. Haiy means he is alive. Death can never touch or reach him. He did not come out of nonentity. He was present when nothing was present. He wills and things are done. It is his power of decision. Whether it is Khalq (creation) or Amr (Immediate creation) he has the power over every object. He is Mudrik. It means He is conscious of all objects whether apparent or hidden. Nothing is hidden from him. He is Mutakalim. It means he can talk to anyone through angels or objects. He spoke to Moses through a tree on the mount of Sanai. He is Sadiq. It means he speaks truth. God is all truth. His message is truth. We must believe in above eight existential attributes of Allah. Then there are eight attributes which cannot be ascribed to Allah. Earlier mentioned those qualities do not suit the image of God. They negate the positive concept of God. When we say there can be no "sharik" of Allah it means God is one and we believe in His Oneness. Tawhid is the antonym of "Shirkat". God cannot be ascribed to Tarkeeb. God is not made of different elements, cells or atoms. Makan means God cannot be limited to any place or space. Halool means God does not enter in to anyone's body. The concept of incarnation is un-Islamic. God is not gradational or the outcome of any evolutionary process like other creatures. A baby is born, then it becomes adolescent; then young; then old and then dies. Stages are for creation not for creator. God is invisible. He cannot be seen with naked eyes. Marey means if we see God with naked eyes then He becomes our imaginative creation. Our eyes can not encompass his vision. The seventh point is of Ihtiaaj. It means we are needy but God is not needy. He is free from need. And the last point is about Duality. God is one, neither two nor more than two. The universe is one and the creator of the universe is also one. These eight existential and non-existential attributes cover the basic concept of God. There are other general attributes of God which are mentioned in the Quran besides the above cited. Let us mention a few of them in the light of the Quran. The Quran in Sura The Heights says; "The most beautiful names belong to Allah: so call on Him by them; but shun such men as use profanity in His names; for what they do, they will soon be requited."(7:180). In Sura the Israelities the Quran about Allah says that He is Samih and Baseer. The words are: "verity, He is the All-Hearing, the All-Seeing(17:1). In Sura The Heifer the Quran says: God is (Waseh) All- Pervading and (Aleem) All knowing." (2:115). Allah is Al-Mujib. The Quran in sura Hud says: "For my God is (always) near, (ready) responder."- God is Khabir (well-acquainted). The Quran says: "For Allah is well aware of all that you do." (3:153). God is Best of Judges (6:57) – God is bestower of Forms and colors (59:24) God is Al-Hasib (The Reckoner).(4:6). The Quran time and again mentions that God is Nourisher; God is sustainer and God is Just. About Allah and his attributes Hazrat Ali in Nehjul Balagha says: "you should not imagine Allah to be a magnified model of yourself. Your attributes should not be attributed to Him. Neither try to understand His attributes on your standard nor believe them to be on the same level with yours." It means we do not possess permanent attributes. They are temporary. Suppose one man can be very intelligent today but tomorrow he can go mad. One can have sight today but tomorrow he can be blind. One is young and energetic today but in old age he becomes feeble, frail and frivolous. But God possess eternal attributes. What is He today He will be the same forever? In a saying of the Holy Prophet (PBUH) we have been asked: "create godly qualities." It means God is just we should be just. God is mercy we should be merciful. God is truth we should speak truth and so on. Mawlana Rumi writes that when blacksmith puts a piece of iron in blazing coals to mould the iron, its color is black and it is cold. But when it absorbs the heat of firebrands it becomes red and hot. Now it can burn us. Basically it is iron but it has absorbed the attributes of fire. Now it can act like fire. Similarly when the Sufis and saints get the color of God as mentioned in the Quran they attain spiritual and miraculous powers. They do not become God but God gives them divine attributes which is the height of human spiritual sublimity.

THE QURAN SPEAKS ABOUT THE QURAN

The etymological meaning of the Quran is to read. It is a book which is like a fathomless and boundless sea. One has to dive in to it to fetch the pearls of wisdom. The very first verse revealed to the Holy Prophet Muhammad (PBUH) in the cave of Hira was: "Read! In the name of your Lord who created." (96:1) By Quran we mean the verses revealed to the prophet of Islam. It is the word of God. It is the Greatest and the Ever-current miracle of the Holy Prophet Muhammad (PBUH) the last Apostle of God. It was revealed on the Night of Qadr (2:185; 44-3; 97:1). About the authenticity of the Quran the disbelievers used to create doubts in the minds of the people. They used to make hue and cry about it. The Quran says: "And those who disbelieve say: listen ye not to this Quran and make noise therein" – But about the Quranic truth and genuineness the Quran in the chapter The Heifer declares: "This is the Book, there is no doubt in it (being the word of God). (It is) a guidance for the pious ones" (2:2). In Sura Al-Imran once again Allah regards the Quran as the Book of Guidance. The Quran says: "Here is a plain statement to men, a guidance and instruction to those who fear Allah." The people who are not pious and chaste and who do not fear Allah are incapable of enjoying the fresh and sweet fruit of this spiritual tree. They are misguided because of their stale souls and dullness of minds. About them in Sura The Heifer the Quran says; "Allah has set a seal on their hearts and on their hearing, and on their eyes is a veil; great is the penalty they (incur)" – (2:7). At another place the Quran says that many people get astray and many receive guidance from the Quran. The Quran clarifies that only the wicked and unchaste ones go astray. Such immoral debauches have no clean heart and mind to sip the pure water from the Eternal spring of Sagacity. The Quran is a Book of Wisdom for wise people. In Sura Yunus it says: "These are the verses of the Book of Wisdom" (10:1). There is a full chapter in the Quran entitled Luqman (The wise). Luqman was a physician, philosopher and saint. The ascription and dedication of a full chapter to his name shows immense reverence for the man of wisdom in the sight of God. This Sura starts with these words: "These are verses of the Wise Book, a guide and a mercy to the doers of Good."(20:2-3). The miracle of the Quran is that it gives eloquent and elegant message in a few words. Its preciseness and conciseness makes it marvelous. It has 114 chapters and 6666 verses. But according to the punctuation ascribed to the Holy Prophet by the Majmou-ul-Byan the number of the Quranic verses is 6263. The different schools of the reciters-Kufi, Hijazi, Macci, Madani, Egyptian and Syrian differ in this regard. It carries injunctions, parables, admonitions, exhortations, advices, stories and tenets. The Holy Quran at different places makes different claims about the nature of the Quran. Briefly they are as such. The Quran is the revelation of Allah. In Sura Fussilat the Quran says: "Falsehood cannot reach it from before it or behind it. It is revelation from one who is All-wise, praiseworthy." (41:42). Then in Sura Abraham the Quran announces: "A Book which we have revealed to you in order that you might lead mankind out of the depths of darkness in to light." (14:1). In Suras, The Poets: The Crowds; The Sure Reality: The Adoration: The Pilgrimage and The Israelites, the Quran announces it to be the revelation and word of God. The infidels who challenged its truth and authenticity the Quran in Sura Yunus are likewise mentioned; "Thus is the word of your Lord proved true against those who rebel: verily they will not believe." Then in the same Sura they are challenged in these words: "This Quran is not such as can be produced by other than Allah; on the contrary it is a confirmation of (revelation) that went before it, and a fuller explanation of the Book – wherein there is no doubt from the Lord of the worlds – or do they say, he forged it? Say: Bring then a Sura Like it, and call (to your aid) anyone you can, besides Allah, if it be you speaks the truth" (10:37-38). It has been brought by the arch angel Gabriel. In Sura The Poets, the Quran says: "verily this is a revelation from the Lord of the worlds. With it came down the spirit of Faith and Truth. To your heart and mind, that you may admonish in the perspicuous Arabic tongue" (26:192-195). The following verses also mention about Arabic language (12:2; 12:37; 41:3). The reason being the people directly addressed is to understand its message and act on it. The Quran is a guide and warning for all human beings. In Sura, The Sure Reality the Quran announces: "It is a reminder for the heedful." (69:48). The Quran says that only the men of thinking pay heed to its verses. In Suras, The Cattle; The Abraham; The Saad; The TaHa; The Al-Imran: The Light; and The One Wrapped Up, The Quran says that it is the Book of Admonition and warning. It is mentioned in the previous scriptures. In Sura, The Poets the Quran says: "It (The Quran) is certainly in the scriptures of the previous peoples." There can be no omission and commission in the Quran. It is free from "Tahreef". Allah has promised to preserve it. The Quran in Sura, The Rocky Tract says: "It is WE who have sent down the reminder (The Quran) and WE will preserve it "(15:9). Then in Sura The Inevitable Event Allah says: "That this is indeed a Quran most honorable in a Book Well-guarded, which none can touch but those who are clean; A revelation from the Lord of the worlds" (56:77-80). The Holy Quran is the fundamental reference of source and guidance for judgments. No Un-Quranic verdict, decree or decision can be accepted by the Muslims. The Quran in Sura The Table Spread says; "Do they then seek the judgment of the Time of Ignorance? Who could be better at giving judgment than Allah for people with certainty?" (5:50).

In Suras, The Mary; The Cattle; The Pilgrimage and The light, it is said that our verses are clear and explicit. In Sura, The Time the Quran says; "It is we who have sent the Quran down to you little by little" (76:23). The Quran is a light of Allah to show the right and straight path to humankind. In Suras, The Battle Array; The Table Spread: The Consultation and The Mutual Loss and Gain the Quran has been regarded as Light from Allah. The Quran is a criterion between right and wrong. It guides to the Right path. It is a healing for the believers. It is a book of Balance and Justice. Hence we see how the Quran speaks of the Quran. The Quran was compiled during the life time of the Holy Prophet. He had set its order. The Quran was recorded in writing at least by the following persons on the instructions of the Holy Prophet; Harzat Ali bin Abi Talib; Abdullah Bin Masood; Maaz bin Jabal and Obai Bin Kaab. During the life time of the Holy Prophet (PBUH) it was duly collected and had been given the form to be called a complete Book. As it had seven to ten recitations Harzat Usman gave instruction to Zaid bin Thabit to prepare its final copy on one recitation. The other copies he ordered to destroy or burn. Since then there is only one Quran in the whole Muslim world and all sects of Muslims recite the same Quran. There are no two or three Qurans. The Quran which Hazrat Ali had complied and collected on the guidance and instruction of the Holy Prophet was also the same Quran with the correct punctuation, pronunciation and recitation. During the period of caliphate Hazrat Ali people recited the same Quran, collected by Zaid bin Sabit.

Hajjaj Bin Yusuf, a cruel and tyrant Muslim ruler ordered for the punctuation of the Quran for easy and correct reading and understanding of the Quran for the non-Arabs. But for non-Arabic speaking people still it is a problem. They do not recite the Quran with translation in their mother tongues and do not follow it. They should recite the Quran with translation. On the other hand most of the Arabs recite it but do not ponder over its meaning and do not learn any lesson from the Quran. They are oblivious of message. For all such people the Quran in Sura The Criterion says; "Then the messenger will say; O my Lord! Truly my people took this Quran for just foolish nonsense." Let Allah grant us grace and wisdom to recite the Quran with understanding and act upon its glorious message. In the words of Dr. Allama Iqbal "I make open what is hidden in my heart. The Quran is not only a Book, it is more than that." What is more than that? Let us ask the Quran about this mystery. In Sura Hashr (The Gathering) the Quran says; "Had we sent down this Quran on a mountain, verily, you would have seen it humble itself and leave asunder for fear of Allah. Such are similitude which we propound to men that they may reflect." (59:21) The Quran claims that it can cleave the earth and move the mountains. It is a book of Law, wisdom, system, code and miracles. It is a final revelation carrying the basic message of earlier prophets. It is a master piece of immense literary, intellectual and spiritual value. The Quran provides bases for universal values and is a complete code of life.

While concluding a few citations from the writings for some non-Muslim scholars about the Quran may seem befitting. Thomas Carlyle says: Sincerity, in all sense, seems to me the merit of the Quran." J.C. Wilson opines: "The Quran is the most esteemed and most powerful religious Book in the world." Harry Gaylord Dorman states: "It is a literal revelation of God, dictated to Mohammad by Gabriel, perfect in every letter." Hence the Quran aptly announce: "we have revealed for you (O Men) a Book which is a message for you: Will you not then understand." (21:10)

THE WORLDS OF CREATION AND COMMAND

There are two worlds; the world of creation and the world of command. The world of creation belongs to the material world which is created stage by stage. When we sow wheat it takes time to grow. A tree does not give fruit overnight. A baby is born in nine months, not in a day. It is called the law of Nature. Nature functions according to natural laws. The fire burns. The water flows downwards. The chunk of wood floats on the surface of water. The stone sinks in the water. This material universe is very scientifically woven. It is neither accidental nor haphazardly constituted.

Aldous Huxley at a place had written that this universe is accidental and is not the creation of God. To support his plea he further writes that if a monkey learns how to type and he starts pressing the keys of the typewriter haphazardly and one day we see that a sonnet of William Shakespeare has been typed it will be a wonderful accident. Similarly, the universe came into existence by an accident. We can only laugh at Huxley's argument on the blind creation of the universe. Darwin also believed in the blind force of matter. In his book entitled "The Origin of Species" he has propounded his theory of Evolution. He has also rejected the notion of God's creation of the universe. On the other hand the father of modern physics whose book entitled "Out of My Later Years" is a compendium of wisdom writes: "The universe is too organized to be the result of an accident." An American scholar Carl Sagan who died in 1995 writes that the uniformity of elements is amazing. If you want to prepare Apple Pie from beginning you will have to re-create the whole universe. The Quran tells us about the creation as a serious and designed plan of Allah. It is not a joke. It is not a game. It is not a mirage. It is a scientific and organized world. It has purpose. It has mission. Man is the master of the material and natural forces. Man has to worship God; not the material forces. You are not permitted to worship idols. You are not supposed to prostrate before snakes, fire, rivers or the Sun or Starts. You are the best creation of God. About the creation of this material universe the Quran in Sura "The Heights" says: "Your Guardian – Lord is Allah, Who created the heavens and the earth in six days, and is firmly established on the Throne (of Authority): He draws the night as a veil over the day, each seeking the other in rapid succession. He created the sun, the moon, and the starts, (all) governed by laws under His command. Is it not His to create and to govern? Blessed be Allah, the Cherisher and Sustainer of the worlds."(7:54). The Torah also in the book of Genesis discusses the beginning of the universe and regards it the creation of God. The Torah says: "in the beginning God created the heavens and the earth. Now the earth was formless and empty, darkness was over the surface of the deep, and the spirit of God was hovering over the waters." Science believes that the universe is created out of water. The Quran in Sura "The light" says: "And Allah has created every animal from water; of them there are some creep on their bellies; some that walk on two legs; and some that walk on four. Allah created what He wills; for verily Allah has power over all things" (24:45). Some of the thinkers who even believe in God seem to be under the influence of material laws. The Law of Returns or the Law of Requital seems to influence their minds. The proverb: "As you sow, so shall you reap" is true. It is a law of nature. Maulana Rumi also at a place writes: "wheat grows out of wheat and barley grows out of barley." This is, of course, the law of nature which is in practice and usually is unchangeable. Under the impact of this law some Muslim thinkers such as Sir Syed Ahmed Khan and Ghulam

Ahmed Pervaiz have denied the existence of miracles. Miracles belong to the world of command. The other world is the world of command or the world of "Amr"- according to the Quranic terminology. In Sura Al-Imran the Quran about the miraculous birth of Mary says: "She said: "O my Lord! How shall I have a son when no man has touched me? "He said: "Even so; Allah creates what He wills: when He has decreed a plan, He but says to it, 'Be', and it is." (3:47) The Bible about the birth of Jesus Christ says: "This is how the birth of Jesus Christ came about. His mother Mary was pledged to be married to Joseph, but before they came together, she was found to be with child through the Holy Spirit" (Matthew 1:18). In Sura Yasin the Quran says: "verily, when He intends a thing, His command is, 'Be', and it is." (36:82). In Torah in the chapter Exodus we read the miracles of Moses. We see water oozing from the Rock. On Mount Sinai and in the Desert of Sinai we see various miracles. In the Bible we read the miracles of Jesus Christ. In the Quran we read about the miracles of Abraham, Moses and Jesus. These are not allegories. These are not false stories. Some people say that these are allegorical events not the actual events. Such people are at fault. The belief in natural laws is truth as they are governed by Nature and the laws of creation. But the belief in miracles is also true because super natural laws are also there and they are governed by the laws of command. This is not only a material world. Matter and spirit exists side by side. The supremacy of spirit over matter is the proof of the existence of God. We should believe in both forces; the material forces and the spiritual forces.

THE IMPACT OF RELIGION

Human history is drenched with bloody events in the name of religion. The negative use of religion has brought immense miseries to humankind. In my opinion, religion has both a positive and a negative impact on human life, The positive impact is our learning that God is the center of our lives and that only God is worthy of our worship. When we believe in one God, we believe in the oneness of humankind. In Sura "The Heifer" the Quran says: "Mankind was (at one time) one single nation". (2:213). Our belief in noble human values and human rights is the result of the positive aspect of religion. The spirit of all religions is one and the same. This is the reason that Quran in Sura "The Heifer" announces: "Those who believe (in the Quran), and those who follow the Jewish (scriptures), and the Christian and the Sabians, and who believes in Allah and the last day, and work righteousness, shall have their reward with their lord: on them shall be no fear, nor shall they grieve." (2:62). Actually we find such great saints and mystics in all religions. They believe in God and in man. Mostly these saints love all humans irrespective of their class, creed, country and color. These people are the real followers of God who heed the message of His messengers. They are known as Sufis, mystics, saints and gnostics. They do not harm even an ant or sparrow. They do not condone oppression, bloodshed, dictatorship, extremism and terrorism. They espouse love, mercy, virtue, forgiveness, freedom, fraternity, compassion, equality, justice, virtue and peace

The God of Moses was a universal God. There is no doubt in it that in the Quran the Jews with piety have been praised much. In Sura "The Table Spread" the Quran says: "It was we who revealed the Law (to Moses): therein was guidance and light. By its standard have we judged the Jews, by the prophets who bowed to Allah's will, by the rabbis and the Doctors of Law." (5:44). Islam has a universal approach. It does not believe in a racial, tribal or geographical God. It lays down scientific and spiritual universal laws. The Quran praises the noble and pious Jews and Christians. In Sura "Al-e-Imran" the Quran announces: "They are not all the same. There is a community among the people of the Book who are upright. They recite Allah's signs throughout the night, and they prostrate. They believe in Allah and the Last Day, and enjoin the right and forbid the wrong, and compete in doing good. They are among the righteous. And whatever good they do, never will be removed from them. Allah knows those who guard against evil (3:113-115). In the verse 75 and verse 199 of Sura "Al-e_Imran such pious Jews and Christians are praised as well. The verse 69 of the chapter "The Table spread" gives glad tidings of redemption to noble Jews, Christians and sabeans like the verse 62 of Sura "The Heifer. But there are also some verses which condemn the deeds of some Jews given to hypocrisy and usury. For such ill deeds some specific persons have been cursed. The Quran in Sura 'The Women" says: "That they took usury, though they were forbidden, and that they devoured men's substance wrongfully; we have pre-pared for those among them who reject faith a grievous punish-ment." (4:161).

About Christians the Quran has very sympathetic approach. The noble and righteous priests have been lauded. The Quran only differs with the Christian concept of God as a Trinity. The Quran teaches that God is One. But time and again the Quran invites the people of Book to enter into a decent dialogue. To-day, the need for interfaith dialogue is more critical than ever. The Quran in Sura Al-e-Imran says: "Say" People of the book! Come to a proposition which is the same for us and you- that we should worship none but Allah and not associate any partners with Him and not take one another as lords beside Allah."(3:64). The great Muslim historian Mohammad ibn Jarir Tabari writes that the prophet made a peace treaty with the Jews of Medina. He also hosted the Christians of Najran and dialogued with them in a decent and friendly manner. Islam extends the hand of peace and co-existence to all faiths. Of course; there are some verses in the Quran which criticize the behavior and beliefs of some Jews and Christians. These verses exhibit some political and ideo-logical differences with the people of the time of Prophet Mohammad. These are historical differences. Islam does not believe in enmity and bloodshed. Now the believers of all faiths must unite in the name of God and must show tolerance and moderation. When we behave illogically, immodestly, indecently and irrationally, we demonstrate the negative impact of religion.

The job of religion is to offer sound advice to live as God requires us to live. It is not the job of religion to punish. Some people would paint religion as something troublesome and bur-densome. Eminent Muslim scholar Sheikh Fadhal Al-Sahlani, while sermonizing on the Sura Wal-Asr, states: "The Prophet (PBUH) has said: Religion is Advice. This means that a reli-gious society has to practice this advice if it wants to develop along the Righteous path" – Advice is positive, but imposing that advice upon others is negative.

In the beginning I had mentioned that the negative impact of religion has destroyed humanity. Extremists of all religions have brought untold misery to humankind. Those who use the sacred teachings of religion to dominate and control others for their own political ends have let down all of humanity. It is because of people like this that philosophers like Nietzsche, Hegel, Karl Marx and Bertrand Russell became atheists, agnostics and skeptics. Religious extremists have ignored the spirit of religion. They lay more emphasis on rituals. They will ask you to offer prayers and fast but they will never tell you the real purpose of these religious rituals. Narrow interpretation of religion to make any tribe or people appear superior constitutes a negative impact of religion.

The positive impact of religion is the creation of humanitarian values. Some modern thinkers emphasize a need for international religion. John Reeves in his book entitled "Politics in Future" writes: "International order for all mankind is the time's foremost need." Robert Murray also in his book entitled "The Individual and the State" writes; "we need a religion that can transcend nationalism and make the world one nation." But the question arises as to which religion could provide us with the basis for such universal values? The Quran claims to be a universal religion. What do honest Western thinkers say about this? Arnold Toynbee in his book "The World and the West" writes: "Only Islam can transcend the boundaries of nationalism." About Islamic dynamic and progressive universal system Eric Fromm, in his book "The Sane Society," writes: "No tangible forces, no intangible powers, can stop Islam from becoming the universal faith. This is because only Islam can march along with the evolution of human civilization."

My study of religion and philosophy has made me a staunch believer in human values and human rights. When you negate Man from religion then that is the religion of Satan, not of God. It was Satan who deceived Adam. Adam represented man. In these critical times we have a dire need to promote true respect of universal human rights and the spiritual values which every religion teaches. Any rhetoric which claims that God is the defender or property of a single people mocks the true meaning of religion. Either we reject religion or we accept it. If we accept it, then we must love and serve our fellow man as God loves us. We must promote the positive aspect of religion and abandon all lesser use of it.

TWO VIEWS ABOUT THE PROPHET OF ISLAM

On February 29, 2004, a Hindu named Jai Hariom emailed me a letter entitled "Non-Muslims to observe 33rd anniversary of Bangladesh Holocaust". In this letter Jai Hariom has presented one view about the Prophet of Islam. On June 16th 2004, an eminent Sikh writer and scholar Surjeet Singh Lanba visited me and kindly presented me his latest Urdu book titled "Quran-e-Natiq", which means the speaking Quran. In this book he has presented another view about the Prophet of Islam. Let me present the views of both non- non-Muslims.

Jai Hariom writes, "33 years ago the Muslim soldiers of Pakistan killed 3 Million Bengalis, almost all Hindus. Another 10 million Hindus were driven out of Bangladesh. The percentage of Hindus in Bangladesh dropped from 33% to less than 15% now. The holocaust was not the latest holocaust engineered by Muslims. The first was the murder of Jews by Muhammad when he killed 3000 male Jews, perhaps half the male Jewish population of Arabia, sold their widows and children in the slavery and expelled the rest from Arabia. He had successfully carried out the first human holocaust in recorded history". This statement needs analysis. Pakistan has been divided into West Pakistan and East Pakistan. In the province of Sindh, in West Pakistan, some Hindus live, even today. In the past 56 years since the inception of Pakistan we have never heard of any ethnic cleansing, crisis or clash. The temples of Hindus are protected along with their properties, lives and honor. In East Pakistan, it was India who engineered treason and rebellion through Hindus inhabiting East Pakistan. They distributed ammunition and money to youth to incite them to take arms against their own Muslim army. When their conspiracy succeeded, turned East Pakistan into Bangladesh. India violated international law and attacked Pakistan, penetrating its borders. With this illegal act, India succeeded in fracturing Pakistan. The Indian premier Ms. Indira Gandhi boastingly declared: "Two Nation Theory has drowned in the Bay of Bengal."

Personally, I have never supported the military action of General Yehya Khan in East Pakistan. This issue should have been politically resolved as Fazlul Qadir Chaudhry and Moulavi

Farid had desired. However, it must be said that Indian infiltration left no choice for the Pakistan army but to crush the rebellion by force. Here, I would ask Mr. Jai Hariom whether what India did in East Pakistan can be justified by any standard, rule, norm or law. I would further ask how he would exonerate what the Hindus have been doing in Kashmir for the last 55 years to the innocent, armless and docile Kashmiri Muslims. And how would he justify what did the Indian Hindus did to the Sikhs by demolishing the Golden Temple and mercilessly killing them. What about the actions of the Indian Hindus against the Muslims of Gujrat? Is that not a matter of shame? Let me make it clear that I am not blaming Hinduism. I am just pointing out what some Indian Hindus have done. Recently they demolished the Babri Mosque.

In my opinion, the character of the followers of any religion should not be ascribed or attributed to the religions themselves. Relative to Mr. Hariom's assertion that the Prophet Mohammed (PBUH) killed Jews, it would seem that he is ignorant of Muslim history. The number of Jews killed, as recorded in authentic history books such as Tabari and Ibn-e-Hisham, was seven hundred; not three thousand. When the Holy Prophet of Islam migrated from Macca to Madina, he made a social contract with local Jews and extended his hand of friendship to them. There was a provision of the truce which related to mutual support when attacked by alien clans. When Muslims were attacked by Maccan pagans and the war of Badr broke out, the Jews did not support the Muslims, as they had agreed to do. Afterwards the Jews further breached the treaty by supporting the Maccan pagans against the Muslims. The Prophet of Islam asked them about this matter. They nominated a man to decide the punishment. Their nominee gave the verdict of Capital punishment to the Jews who had supported the enemies of Islam and participated in conspiracy. This is far from the allegation of murder levied by Mr. Hariom.

These tragic events have far more to do with politics and power struggles than with the inner Love and Wisdom at the core of true religion. In his lengthy letter Mr. Jai Hariom concluded: "The Islam-fascist movement believes in supremacy and was launched in the seventh century by Muhammad. Muhammad was the model for Hitler and Mussolini who were admirers of his successful ethnic cleansing of Jews from Arabia". Jai Hariom has presented Muhammad as a fascist and killer. Apparently he is unaware of the unimpeachable nobility of the character of the Prophet of Islam. To balance the assertions of Mr. Hariom, here are some passages from the book of Surjeet Singh Lanba, a Sikh scholar, in his Urdu book "Quran-e-Natiq," On page 135 he writes: "As a conqueror of Macca the first order which Prophet Muhammad issued was general amnesty. He said; the one who disarms himself willingly is safe. The one who closes his door is safe. The one who takes refuge in Kaaba is safe. The one who even takes refuge at the house of Abu Suffyan (the deadliest enemy of Islam) is also safe"- On page 172. Mr. Lanba writes about the humane and noble character of the Holy Prophet of Islam: "Muhammad's heart was free from enmity, vengeance, obstinacy and cruelty. Truthfulness, honesty and kindness were his traits. He was a humble man". Then on page 187 he writes: "Once a delegate of Christians from Najran called on Prophet Muhammad. He made them stay in Holy Mosque of Medina. At evening, when Christians desired to offer religious service, the Prophet permitted them". Then Mr. Lanba writes: "A dead Jew was being carried to the graveyard for burial, when the Holy Prophet saw the funeral procession and bier he stood up to show respect for the dead. When told that the deceased was not a Muslim but a Jew, he said: The funeral may be of a Muslim or a non-Muslim we must get up to show respect". Then on page193, Mr. Lanba poses some basic questions: who established the practice of God-worship instead of Idol-worship? Who ended superstitions and drew humankind out of the cave of ignorance? Who taught human kind to master the Universe instead of worshipping it? Who showed us the path of democracy and freedom in a monarchic and tribal society? Who laid down the foundations of realism and scientific varieties instead of abstractions and speculations? Who introduced justice and equality in the face of injustice? These views of Mr. Lanba may stir the soul and mind of Mr. Jai Hariom to restudy Islam in the light of neutrality and rationality. The behavior of followers of any religion does not represent their religion. Prophet Muhammad was not a fascist but a challenge to fascists.

WHERE LIES THE SOLUTION?

In my previous article, "Clash of Civilizations," published in *Muslims Weekly* New York on September 22, 2004 I disagreed with Professor Samuel Huntington of Harvard University and inferred that we should strive for conformity, co-operation, co-existence and congruence between different faiths instead of menacing the younger generation with projections of ongoing clashes The other day I received an email from an American reader named Carollane White. She very wisely and aptly commented on my views. It is worth quoting.

She writes,
"Dear Professor Jafri,
   I have just read your most interesting column. As an American, may I echo the hope that there will indeed by no "clash of civilations.
   However, (Isn't there always a however?) I am not, at this moment feeling as optimistic as you apparently are. The cultural differences are great, and at times I have felt cast aside by friends I have made in your part of the world simply because I am an American. Of course, to be fair, I have a great passion for world politics and I might have just driven them away with my desire to discuss said politics - a lot.
   I'm afraid until Palestine/Israel is settled the dislike, even hatred for Americans will continue to grow. I have encountered the attitude that America and Israel are the "same." Then there is the belief that Americans single out Muslims, especially at airports. For myself, I have trouble understanding that. As a Catholic, I would hope I would accept that if Catholics alone had participated in 9/11, I would be watched a bit more carefully and try to be patient. However, I do understand the feelings of Muslims in this regard. I would not like to keep hearing "Catholic extremists" all the time.
   For my part, living in America, I never hear anything negative said about Islam or Muslims in general. Muslims do well economically in America. If they were being attacked on the streets of the US, wouldn't the media be full of that? Having said this, would you agree that in parts of Pakistan, I, as a blond, blue eyed American, would likely not be safe on the in some

parts of your country? I mean no harshness in this statement. I think Pakistan is quite wonderful. What I want to say is, may this tolerance and acceptance of Muslims and Islam continue in my country, no matter what the future brings.

I could wish for a miracle and see the Palestine/Israel conflict settled. I know the feeling is America is not doing enough. My question is, can America do everything?

The world, for the most part, remains silent in the face of such cruelty. We do not speak out against the monsters that blow up Iraqis, children and citizens of other countries and even behead some of them. We point fingers at each other. We say we must look at the "root causes" first. It seems, at times, we have all lost the ability to even regognize evil.

Sincerely,
Carollane White
Gray, Maine, USA

P.S. One thing that is really impossible to understand. Why are the crimes of America so great and those of Mr. Hussein hardly mentioned? Perhaps your part of the world just didn't know? Are we about to start pointing fingers again? I merely asked.

No sincere and sane person would disagree with Carollane White. It is a self explanatory and well intentioned statement. But a few points could do with elaboration. In the first paragraph Carollane White expresses regret at losing two friends from the Middle East simply because she is an American and Christian. The question arises whether the Muslim world is solely anti-American or whether they are also anti German and anti-British. It is a serious question which begs an answer, for two reasons. First, America claims; "Liberty and Justice for all." The Muslims therefore expect America to be neutral and non-partisan in resolving world issues. It should not support dictators and military rulers. If America attacked Iraq for the purpose of liberating the oppressed Iraqis from the yoke of a tyrant like Saddam, then why America is supporting the callous emperors of Saudi Arabia and other Middle Eastern monarchies? This is an obvious dual standard. Secondly; America strongly supports Israel against Palestine instead of accelerating efforts to resolve this longstanding, crucial issue. No sane Muslim advocates genocide of the Israelis, who are human beings with social, political and human rights. By the same token, Palestinians are also human beings with these same rights who should be protected. If we succeed in providing justice to both concerned parties there will be no disturbance in the Middle East.

In the second paragraph Carollane White is correct in her words about some extremists. She alludes to the tragedy of 9/11. There is no disagreement on this point. No sane person would justify this tragic act. The bloodshed of innocent civilians cannot be justified. But I agree with Carollane White that only a few extremists and not all Muslims were involved in this act. Handful extremists have put all Muslims in trouble who live in America and in the West. The majority of the Muslims are against terrorism. We should not mistreat or disgrace them. The Indian Hindus have nothing to do with 9/11 episode. Yet the former Defense Minister of India was mishandled in a New York Airport. On his return to India he issued a press statement that in future he would never like to visit America because of this mistreatment. This action on the part of Americans infuriated the Hindus. Perhaps this was the reason that, as reported in the Indian newspapers, a few days ago an American tourist woman was searched and undressed in an Indian airport. The Indians acted on the proverb: "Tit for Tat." It was actually a reaction of Indian security staff. Similarly a Pakistani prominent political leader and member of parliament Imran Khan in his recent visit to America on Houston Airport was detained for three hours. He said he was mishandled. On his return to Pakistan he fostered a hostile attitude towards America and appealed people to oppose American policies at all levels. Such things create hatred and hostility against America. In the name of security no one should be harassed, intimidated and insulted. There are better ways of to seize and search. The Americans are much loved for their friendly attitude and fine manners. They should protect this glorious heritage while making random enquiries.

The third paragraph of the email is full of truth and good intentions. Generally the Americans are broad minded, liberal and democratic. The racists and extremists are found in every class and country. In Pakistan a handful extremists have not only killed a few local Pakistani Christians but have killed so many Muslims belonging to other sects as well. It is all because of ignorance, poverty and prejudice. We will have to crusade against such social and human evils. We will have to educate the world for peaceful coexistence and tolerance. To resolve all these problems Carolline White is right when she writes "Settlement of Palestine/Israel is the key". But she seems to be pessimist when she writes "Problem is this seems absolutely impossible." Here I humbly submit that when there is a will, there is a way. The rulers, the politicians and clerics have failed to resolve this issue. Let the human rights activists, scholars and reformers come forward to resolve such issues. They must play their part. It may be difficult but it is not impossible.

In the end it seems necessary to mention that some religious hardliners deem it their religious duty to persecute the followers of other religions. Recently in an article of published in the Daily Jang of Pakistan pleads that we should not recognize Israel as the Quran ordains us not to befriend with Jews and Christians. He has quoted from Sura Al-Maada and Al-Nisa not to be friendly with the above mentioned communities. Then he has quoted some battles and skirmishes which occurred between the Jews and the Muslims, like the Battle of Khaibar. These are, of course, historical bitter realities. But it does not mean that the Quran has ordained us to permanently keep on fighting with the Jews or the Christians. Why we forget that when the Holy Prophet of Islam migrated from Mecca to Medina he desired friendship and peace with the Jews of Medina. The Medina Treaty is an example of his step towards peace and mutual respect. When the Jews of Medina breached that sacred pact and started conspiring with the infidels and idolaters of Mecca against Muslims then the Prophet announced his plan of battle against the Jews. The Quran has on many occasions praised the peace loving and noble Jews and Christians. Only the mischief mongers had been cursed. In Sura The Heifer in verse 62 and in Sura Al-Aaraf in verse 159 the Quran praises the noble Jews and gives them glad tidings of happiness in hereafter. The universal message of Islam is a boon and blessing for all humankind. The historical bitter past should not motivate us for bloodshed. We should seek the positive and healthy human aspects. Let once again the Jews and Muslims honestly make a treaty like the Treaty of Medina and honor it. No one should breach it or dishonor it.